MEN OF VALOUR

MEN OF VALOUR

New Zealand and the Battle for Crete

RON PALENSKI

Hodder Moa

Front cover photo: Men of the Division on the march. These men were from C Company of the 20th Battalion but they could have been from any company of any battalion. They were marching in the North African desert, but they could have been anywhere, these Kiwi men of war, "the most resilient and practised fighter of the Anglo-Saxon armies," as they were described. *Alexander Turnbull Library DA-03717-F*

National Library of New Zealand Cataloguing-in-Publication Data
Palenski, Ron.
Men of valour : New Zealand and the battle for Crete / Ron Palenski.
Includes bibliographical references.
ISBN 978-1-86971-305-8
1. Freyberg, Bernard Cyril Freyberg, Baron, 1889-1963—
Military leadership. 2. World War, 1939-1945—Campaigns—
Greece—Crete. 3. World War, 1939-1945—New Zealand.
4. Crete (Greece)—History—Occupation, 1941-1945. I. Title.
940.5421959—dc 23

A Hodder Moa Book
Published in 2013 by Hachette New Zealand Ltd
4 Whetu Place, Mairangi Bay
Auckland, New Zealand
www.hachette.co.nz

Designed and produced by Hachette New Zealand Ltd

Printed by Griffin Press, Australia

'In the New Zealander you have qualities of heart and mind that place him high among men. It is to resolute courage in our junior officers and men that this Division owes its fighting record.'

— Bernard Freyberg

Contents

Preface

Crete holds, or should hold, a special place in the national memory of New Zealand for a number of reasons: although British, Australian and Greek troops were also involved, it was very much a New Zealand fight and the man in overall charge was Bernard Freyberg, who regarded himself as a New Zealander. Greece in the month before had been the first time in action in the Second World War for the whole of the New Zealand Division, and the Greek fighting withdrawal was very much a prelude to the fighting on Crete. So the fight for the island became a bit like the fight for the peninsula on Gallipoli a quarter of a century before: New Zealanders were heavily committed, it was a tactical and strategic loss and the New Zealanders, with the others, had to withdraw. But Crete was also a costly victory for the Germans, and such was the ferocity of the defence of the island that the Germans never again attempted a similar airborne assault. Crete became a source of pride and a rallying call for New Zealanders for the rest of the war: it was where the steel was tempered, where the baptism of fire had been withstood. And so appreciated were the New Zealanders that there remains a special bond still between one island in the Aegean and a collection of small islands on the other side of the world. New Zealanders who travel today to Crete, or even Greece generally, invariably are still met with smiles of gratitude and wonder even though the fighting was two generations ago.

When Warren Adler, Editorial Director of Hachette New Zealand in Auckland, suggested I write about the events of May 1941, I got the 'Yes!' out as quickly as I could. Oh, I knew of most of the books written about the battle from the 1940s and for the next 70 years, and I could guess that very little could have escaped the various authors, some of them eminent. But it was a story so particularly New Zealand, and so related to New Zealand's place in history, that I did not want to resist it. It remains a compelling story and deserves to be told and retold; each succeeding generation needs to know what happened there. Crete was more uniquely a New Zealand battle than any other in either of the world wars. Reading and digesting the stories of Crete, I was struck that the type of New Zealander then — male New Zealander by force of circumstances — was a disappearing species. This was the New Zealander whose speech was unaffected by television and Americanisms, whose concept of duty was simple and generally unquestioned; men were described, I believe accurately, as laconic — which I supposed could be translated to 'laid-back' in today's vernacular — of being compassionate and of an independent enough spirit to question orders when they felt they needed questioning.

I was fortunate to be able to listen to recordings of some of the participants, especially Geoffrey Cox, Win Ryan and Robin Miller, and was struck by how different they sounded to New Zealanders today; there was an English influence to their speech that has all but disappeared today (although Cox of course lived more of his life as an expatriate in England than he did in his homeland).

Not for the first time, I was pleasantly surprised at the amount of praise that went the way of the New Zealand soldiers. When I mentioned this in an earlier book, I was asked whether it was a bit one-sided, and had I just noted the good bits out of some nationalistic pride. I answered no then, as I would again. The encomiums came mostly not from New Zealanders but from others, and they were all the more valuable because of that. I make no apology for repeating some of them; it is the only way a new generation will learn how highly regarded the fighting men of an earlier generation were.

The research for this book involved the always helpful and knowledgeable staffs at the Hocken Collections in Dunedin, the Alexander Turnbull Library in Wellington and Archives New Zealand, also in Wellington and just a convenient block from the ATL. I was also grateful for the assistance provided by Sarah Johnston of the Sound Archives, by Lee Richards of ARCRE in Britain who copied some essential material from the United Kingdom National Archives, and the ready cooperation of Shane Doolan at the Waihao Forks pub. A friend, Peter Sinclair, had had the good fortune to go to Crete and traipse over the wearied miles where men fought, and he and I had many conversations about the battle and its participants. In Wellington, Max Lambert as ever was helpful with suggestions and quick with responses to my queries. Warren and the staff at Hachette were enthusiastic supporters as usual. I am also grateful to Allan Kynaston for his expertise with the map. My wife Kathy was supportive as always and vigilant as my first reader.

Ron Palenski
Dunedin
January 2013

Some words of explanation

Anyone who has visited Crete or just read about it knows that there are different ways of spelling in English the island's place names. Canea, for example, as soldiers knew it, is also Chania, Hania or even Xania. For the sake of consistency, spelling used here follows the style of the volumes in the *Official History of New Zealand in the Second World War*. The names that recur most are Canea, Galatas, Heraklion, Maleme, Retimo and Sfakia.

The 2nd New Zealand Expeditionary Force was the name for the whole force in the Middle East, North Africa and Italy (the 1st NZEF was from the First World War). The 2nd New Zealand Division, more commonly just 'the Division' or 'the Div', was the fighting arm of the 2nd NZEF and Bernard Freyberg was in command of both throughout the war, except for occasions such as Crete and Cassino when he had command of other forces as well. He then handed command of the division to subordinates. 'The Div' was essentially a citizen army, raised from volunteers on the outbreak of war in September 1939. (Conscription was introduced in June 1940.)

Following the British system, the Division was organised in three brigades, 4th, 5th and 6th, each comprising three infantry battalions plus artillery, engineers, machine-gunners and other support troops. New Zealand had 11 battalions — 18th, 19th and 20th (4th Brigade); 21st, 22nd and 23rd (5th Brigade); 24th, 25th and 26th (6th Brigade), plus the 28th (Maori) Battalion and the 27th (Machine Gun) Battalion. The first two battalions in each brigade were drawn from the North Island and the third from the South. The 28th was drawn from throughout the country but reflected the distribution of the Maori population. Each battalion at full strength was up to 800 men, although the whole complement was rarely committed at any given moment. Each battalion was divided into four infantry companies and they in turn were divided into three platoons. Efforts were made for company and platoon strengths to represent geographical areas and, in the case of the 28th Battalion, to represent iwi.

Prologue

When can their glory fade?
O the wild charge they made!
All the world wonder'd
Honour the charge they made!
— Alfred, Lord Tennyson, 'The Charge of the Light Brigade'

The noise was deafening but even above it could be heard the bellow of the pipe-smoking Rangiora lawyer: 'Stand for New Zealand! Stand every man who is a soldier!' A bit melodramatic perhaps, but men don't critique their cries from the heart. The lawyer was Howard Kippenberger, brigade commander on Crete and reckoned later to be one of the finest, if not the finest, soldiers produced by New Zealand. He was 'Kip' to his fellow officers and 'Kip' to his troops (if not to his face). He was Kip to be followed.

Kippenberger's cry was entirely in keeping with cries that rent the early evening air when a few New Zealanders and a few odds and sods from other forces charged up the hill to take on a vastly bigger and better equipped German force. The intention was to retake the whitewashed stone village of Galatas because it was feared some men of the New Zealand Division could be isolated in its desperate defence. But there was another reason behind the charge at Galatas, and charge was what it was. The New Zealanders were sick of being pushed around, they were tired of losing, they'd had enough of withdrawing. They'd been unceremoniously jackbooted out of Greece and now within four days they had lost effective control of Crete. Amateur soldiers most of them, town boys and country boys thrust into uniform: barbers and lawyers, labourers and university students, farmers and truck drivers, clerks and grocers, schoolteachers and accountants. Now they were fighting not just for their lives, but for the honour and prestige of their country and for all those real and some abstract causes for which the Second World War was fought. But perhaps most of all they were fighting for themselves and for their mates. There's a time to withdraw and a time to fight and, if the fates demand it, a time to die. This was the time.

This was not what would be called a well-organised, coordinated military force. It was cobbled together in a time of great danger and stress. There were some frontline soldiers, but there were also cooks, bandsmen, members of the Kiwi Concert Party. There was an officer's batman who was a jockey in peacetime and who was waiting court martial for insubordination. He volunteered to take part in the charge. So too did a gangly lance-corporal: 'Is it okay, sir? The bastards got my brother today.'

A 20-year-old English lieutenant with the 3rd King's Own Hussars, Roy Farran, a career soldier, provided the armoured support with two old tanks. Farran took one of them up the road to have a look and clanked back to Kippenberger with the news: 'The place is stiff with Jerries.' Asked if he'd go back up the road again, he looked hurt that the question was even put and said: 'Certainly.' But before he could he needed replacements for two of his men who were wounded. There was no lack of volunteers. Farran reckoned 300 offered themselves; perhaps imprecise as to number, but indicative as to mood. Farran gave them quick instructions about the handling of a tank and its guns. One of the volunteers, Ben Ferry, later noted:

> This one-pipper bloke was a man of action, he gave us many words of instruction and a few of encouragement, finishing up in a truly English manner — 'Of course you know you seldom come out of one of these things alive.' Well, that suited me all right — it seemed a pretty hopeless fight with all these planes knocking about and a couple of my bosom friends had been knocked.

Ferry reckoned he was up to it anyway. After all, he'd been a corporal in the Vickers gun platoon at New Plymouth Boys' High School seven years before so 'reckoned I knew as much about 'em as anybody'.

One of the company commanders under Kippenberger was Mark Harvey, a Palmerston North salesman in normal life. 'It's going to be a bloody show but we've just got to succeed,' he told his men.

Sandy Thomas, at the beginning of a glittering military career, was in charge of a platoon and described how the tanks revved their motors then passed through the ranks, Farran waving as he went by. 'This was our signal to attack,' Thomas wrote.

> Someone blew a whistle. Orders barked along the line. I found myself shouting to my men and we were away, 200 men in line advancing steadily and grimly.
>
> And then it happened. I don't know who started it … but as the tanks disappeared as a cloud of dust and smoke into the first building of the village the whole line seemed to break spontaneously into the most blood curdling of shouts and battle cries.

It could be heard above the roaring and clanking inside the tanks. Ferry related later: 'The howling and shouting of the infantry sounded like the baying of dogs from inside the tank. As it rose and fell it made my flesh creep.'

Kippenberger's cry of a few minutes earlier was made commonplace by the cries of others. Stanzas of school hakas and school songs were bellowed as men ran for all they were worth, firing from the hip at the startled Germans in the distance. 'Kia kaha! Ake! Ake! Ake!' split the Cretan air. So too 'Ka Mate! Ka Mate!' Someone remembered hearing 'Hook, forwards, hook!' being maniacally screamed out. It was learnt later that came from the mouth of Lieutenant Rex King, a footballer of renown who played against the British team of 1930 and captained the Kiwis league team in England in 1939 before the war brought an end to the tour. He went home with his fellow players, immediately enlisted, and returned to England, there to play some rugby for the NZEF before joining the division in Greece. Now here he was, a leader of men once again, in determined pursuit of a different goal-line.

Prologue

King and Thomas had tossed a coin to determine who would lead the mad dash. It wasn't recorded who won, but both went hell for leather anyway.

Surviving men of the 18th Battalion, exhausted beyond reason after fighting that nearly wiped the battalion out, joined in. They were tired to death, filthy with dirt and sweat and blood. But as the battalion's *Official History* noted: 'In those few minutes caution and reason went to the winds. Men did crazy, desperately heroic deeds that they couldn't remember later.'

Robin Miller, the 2nd NZEF war correspondent who had started his soldier's life as a signaller, watched the attack and likened the noise to that of a crowd at a particularly close Ranfurly Shield match.

At the moment of supreme endeavour, one of the tanks clattered back down the road as fast as its driver could make it. 'Let me through — get out of the road,' the commander in the turret shouted. 'For Christ's sake, run for it. The place is stiff with the bastards.'

Thomas, only 22, recognised a moment of crisis when he saw one. The frenzied figure continued to shout and was, thought Thomas, beyond all reason. But Thomas wasn't. He approached the aperture through which he could see the driver. He thrust his pistol into the slit and to within inches of the driver's forehead. 'Turn around and advance or by heaven, I'll shoot.'

The Cockney driver was not as panicked as his commander above him. 'I'm game, sir, there's no need for that. I'll do anything I'm ordered. It's the bastard above who needs the pistol.'

The driver slowly turned the tank to renew its assault. The commander, still shouting and cursing, leapt to the ground. Thomas thought his weakness could infect his own men. Thomas raised his gun again, intending to shoot the man. His duty was clear. But he could not bring himself to pull the trigger. Someone else could, though. A shot rang out, the man fell, and a private soldier turned away, returning his rifle to his side. No one spoke. The crisis was past.

Perhaps characteristic of such a frenzied, close-order attack, there was confusion about how many tanks there were. Farran, Kippenberger and a gunner who was later one of the official historians, Walter ('Spud') Murphy, all thought there were just the two. But Ferry and the other New Zealand volunteer, Charlie Lewis, swore there were three. As the tanks waddled up the road in the twilight, Lewis was adamant there were two in front of him. His tank was caught a glancing blow by what he thought was a shot from an artillery piece firing for all it was worth from somewhere near the centre of Galatas. The ratchet of the turret jammed.

'I was a bit of a fool,' Lewis told the *RSA Review*. 'As the slit restricted visibility, I stood up on my seat. I got splinters in the forehead; my eyes were cut about a bit. I thought it was time to duck.' He ducked but in doing so sent the speaking tube flying which meant he had lost control of the tank. He bawled out to the driver, but there was too much other noise. Eventually, they got up to the square and, luckily for them, the artillery piece had been withdrawn. 'Hell had broken loose down the street,' Lewis said. 'The infantry was on the job. Our chaps were going through the houses with Tommy guns, rifles and bayonets.'

Colonel John Gray, another peacetime lawyer, later wrote in a letter home: 'I shall never forget the deep throated wild beast noise of the yelling, charging men as the 23rd [Battalion] swept up the road. There was a hell of a battle in the village.'

Among the charging men was Clive Hulme, among the bravest of the brave. The Germans had a prepared machine-gun post in a school and were picking off New Zealanders almost as they pleased. Hulme attacked the school on his own, chucking grenades through the windows and sending the surviving Germans into a hasty retreat. The next morning, Hulme learnt his brother 'Blondie' (Harold) had been killed so went in search of more Germans with a renewed hatred. Hulme later was given a Victoria Cross for that and other valorous deeds.

A Danish-born cook fighting for New Zealand found himself in the bearhug of a big German. The cook was held with one arm while the German fished for his knife with the other. Two New Zealanders burst into the room, saw what was going on, and speared the German with their bayonets. One private, a tractor driver at home, skirted round the backs of some buildings so he could get in behind German machine-guns. He charged into the enemy, firing his Bren gun from his hip. There were so many men, so many battles, so many stories. 'It is a case of an eye for an eye, a tooth for a tooth,' a German message captured later said.

Kippenberger himself, prevented from running with his men because of a sprained ankle, recorded 'the most startling clamour, audible all over the field. Scores of automatics and rifles being fired at once, the crunch of grenades, screams and yells — the uproar swelled and sank, swelled again to a terrifying crescendo.'

Celebrated author and editor Dan Davin in the *Official History* volume called the charge at Galatas 'one of the fiercest engagements fought by any New Zealand troops during the whole war'.

In the face of the yelling, shooting New Zealand mob, the Germans ran. They were beaten out. But it was a temporary victory, a consolation success for a force outnumbered and outgunned. The town could not be held and the New Zealanders knew it; they were withdrawn the next day. Temporary success it may have been, but it achieved its purpose and it burrowed its way into the hearts and minds of New Zealanders. Galatas became the word to make the New Zealand soldier lift his head a little more, stiffen his back and lengthen his stride.

The Germans knew they were beaten. 'There is thunder and lightning in every corner and cranny,' the captured German report read, 'and the flashes of grenades flicker like a fire … our machine guns fall silent, one after the other … The crews are nearly all wounded or dead … with a heavy heart our lieutenant decided to evacuate the village.'

'I was really pleased,' Kippenberger wrote. 'It gave Jerry a terrible jar and completely checked him for the night. By everything I could see or find out, it was exactly at the right time and place.'

It was the last fight for a while for Sandy Thomas, shot and hit by grenade shrapnel; he was captured and taken to hospital in Greece. (Eventually, he escaped and rejoined the division. He told his tale in one of the war classics, *Dare to be Free*.)

It was the last fight of the war for Rex King, whose gallantry that night earned him the Military Cross. Shot through both legs, he was taken to hospital and then to a prisoner of war camp in Germany, where he spent the rest of the war. His battalion commander at the time, Lieutenant-Colonel Doug Leckie, wrote to King's wife: 'By his fearlessness — he did not know the word fear — bravery, initiative and leadership he saved us many casualties and endeared himself to us all.' (Like Thomas, King too turned to writing but while he was a prisoner. A master's graduate from Canterbury, his forte was academic essays, and one he wrote about industrial design won a Royal Society of the Arts prize in 1943.)

As the battle wound down, the voice of the English lieutenant, Roy Farran, could be heard: 'Good show New Zealand, jolly good show. Come on New Zealand!'

Introduction

'The gallant defenders of Crete … are putting up a brilliant defence in one of the most difficult forms of fighting which it is possible to conceive and in one of the most vital struggles of this war.'
— Historian and First World War soldier Cyril Falls

For a short, sharp and angry time in the Second World War, anxious eyes of the world gazed upon Crete, a rectangular shaped island in the eastern Mediterranean whose strategic position had made it the plaything of the powerful over centuries. Now it was caught up in war again. It was May of 1941 and the war had been going badly for the Allies; in fact, nothing much on land had gone right. Britain and its Allies had just been bundled out of Greece and the fight moved on to Crete. Successes for the Allies — which at this stage essentially meant Britain and its Empire — had been few. There had been the Battle of Britain in the summer of 1940 when Allied air authority prevented a likely German invasion attempt; and the Royal Navy was ahead on points. The fear of an invasion of Britain remained, however, and there were worries that Crete was a practice run for airborne landing of troops.

Benito Mussolini, so keen to show the world he was a military genius, sent Italian forces into Greece, and they made such a hash of it they were tossed out again and had to be rescued by the Germans. Britain went to the aid of Greece and, as it was a time of 'where she goes we go', New Zealand troops went there as well. But they too were soon tossed out. It was a one-sided affair; hardly a fight at all.

The New Zealand Division was among those who made a fighting withdrawal from Greece and the bulk of it was evacuated to the Greek island of Crete. The original intention was for Crete to be just a staging post and rallying point for the division on its way back to Egypt, but politicians had other ideas. The division's commander, Bernard ('Tiny') Freyberg, was put in charge of the overall defence of Crete on the recommendation of his old friend Winston Churchill and told: Hold it at all costs. Churchill was desperate for success against the Germans for all sorts of reasons. Crete was just one of several balls Churchill had in the air.

The fight for Crete became Tiny's fight. It was gallant, but it was a lost cause. In truth, it could never have been a winning cause. The defenders, many of whom arrived on Crete from Greece with just the clothes they stood up in, had few of the tools with which to do the job. They were not just New Zealanders. There were Brits and Australians and Greeks as well as various other nationalities, some parts of organised units, some not. Many of them were not even frontline infantrymen — cooks, bandsmen, entertainers, technicians; all at some stage had a rifle or a grenade thrust into their hands and told to get stuck in. Some eagerly joined in a bayonet charge even though they had no bayonets. One soldier waved a walking stick; women joined in one charge brandishing bread knives and meat cleavers.

The defenders had no heavy artillery, they had very few anti-aircraft weapons, they had no air cover, they could dig trenches only with their tin helmets, round cigarette tins became cups … they had little of anything. Yet they had to withstand the mightiest airborne invasion the world had yet seen. The year before in France British and French troops had been mown down by a blitzkrieg on land. This time, the blitzkrieg was from the air.

Wearily, warily, both sides fought almost to a standstill. It was a German victory but at such a cost that it was the end of airborne assaults; Germany never again attempted such an assault from the air. New Zealanders, the Australians, the British, got away thanks to the Royal Navy or on boats they begged, borrowed or stole; many never got away at all, destined to forage and fare as best they could in the Cretan countryside or be taken prisoner.

A year on from Dunkirk, where the Germans drove the British out of France, New Zealand troops had had their own Dunkirk. Beaten and bedraggled, they made their way back to Egypt; they'd fought for the first time as a division and twice been beaten. For the first time, they had fought as New Zealanders under the overall command of a New Zealander (well, technically an Englishman but almost a New Zealander). This was a Kiwi-led action, and it was a disaster.

A quarter of a century before, the fathers of the sons had fought not far away at Gallipoli. It too was a strategic gesture and a gallant defeat; there too they slipped away in the night; now it had happened again.

Inquiries followed and have continued for years: was Freyberg at fault? Did he make mistakes that allowed the Germans to make key advances? Were his subordinates, schooled in the tactics of the First World War, incompetent? Were some just too old? Did some of Freyberg's officers do the dirty on him? Was he betrayed to his closest supporters, New Zealand Prime Minister Peter Fraser and British Prime Minister Winston Churchill? And what did Freyberg really know in advance of German intentions and what could he have done differently?

Or was the whole affair just a matter of an unequal battle of man against machines, what one of the participants, Geoffrey Cox, called Frankensteinian in its nature? There were two battles, Cox thought. The first was man against man. 'That was the battle that we won.' The second was man against machines. 'That was the battle that we lost.'

Churchill was dismayed the island had been lost and he thought he'd been let down by his old mate, the man he later called the Salamander of the Empire after a lizard-like creature that was reputed to have been able to live through fire. (Freyberg was so touched that when he was ennobled he had a salamander incorporated in his coat of arms.)

Peter Fraser after Greece and Crete wondered whether Freyberg was the right man to lead the 2nd New Zealand Expeditionary Force. He was concerned that Freyberg led the division to Greece without properly consulting the government and even though he did not think the move a wise one. Fraser was so upset he raised the question of a replacement for Freyberg with both Freyberg's old boss, Archibald Wavell, the Middle East commander at the time of Crete, and his new one, Claude Auchinleck. Wavell, who had been shunted off to India by Churchill, told Fraser that if New Zealand didn't want Freyberg, he'd certainly find a job for him in India. Auchinleck told Fraser it would be a great mistake to change.

Freyberg stayed.

There are questions to which there have been various answers, most of them offered honestly; there are questions to which there can be no answers. Some answers died with the men who had them; Freyberg himself died in 1963 — finally succumbing to a rupture of one of his many war wounds — without being able to tell his side of the story. It has been held against him that he knew full well the enemy's intentions because Poles had cracked the German codes and passed on their knowledge to Britain; it is true that Freyberg benefited from the Ultra intercepts, deciphered at the now-famous Bletchley Park in Buckinghamshire, a fast 60-kilometre motorbike ride from Downing Street. But knowing when and where a better equipped enemy was coming was one thing; doing something about it quite another. The secrecy attached to the breaking of the German codes was so sensitive that it was not made public until 1974. Even now, the actual wording of some messages remains locked away in the National Archives in London, restricted still. Some were read and instantly burnt.

Like the British after Dunkirk, the New Zealanders rose again. Freyberg led the division through North Africa and Italy, adding to their battle laurels as they went and striking fear and respect into the hearts of enemies. For all their successes, though, there remained a belief that the best, most effective fighting by the Kiwis had been amid the olive groves, dry riverbeds and rocky hills of Crete.

For all the wondering, for all the accusations, for all the imponderable 'ifs' which follow any military campaign, one thing at least seems not to be in dispute. Dan Davin, an intelligence officer with the division and who wrote the *Official History* volume of the battle, put his typing fingers clearly on it: 'One thing at least can be said roundly, in a field where little is certain. Soldiers never fought better than they fought on Crete; and not least among them the soldiers of the New Zealand Division.'

Ironically, Crete was left behind in the war, occupied by Germans, but the fighting had gone elsewhere and no one (other than the Cretans) wanted it any more. It was often remarked that those who conquered Crete did so at the peak of their powers, that everything afterwards for them was downhill. So it was for the Germans. Within a few weeks of the victory on Crete, Hitler sent his forces east against his erstwhile friend, the Soviet Union. As with Napoleon more than a century before him, the masses of Russia and the cruel winter proved too much. If the fighting on Crete delayed the start of the Russian invasion, and if that delay meant Hitler's forces fought deeper into the Russian winter than intended, that alone was worthwhile. Napoleon had a Pyrrhic victory — the win you have at such great cost it's really a loss — at Borodino in 1812 before the final humiliation and withdrawal from Moscow; Crete may have been New Zealand's Dunkirk, it was also Hitler's Borodino.

As the days rolled by

1940

28 October: Italy attacked Greece, but a Greek counter-attack forced the Italians into Albania.

1941

6 April: Germany took over where Italy left off and sent forces into Greece as well as Yugoslavia. An Allied force, including the New Zealand Division, the 6th Australian Division and the British 1st Armoured Brigade, were sent to stop them.

17 April: Britain authorised withdrawal from Greece of Allied troops as Germans penetrated defensive lines.

24–25 April: Allied troops evacuated from Greece; most New Zealand troops sent to Crete. On 25 April, Hitler agreed to Operation Merkur, the airborne invasion of Crete.

27 April: Athens taken over by German troops.

28–29 April: The commander of the New Zealand Division, Major-General Bernard Freyberg, and other senior officers left Greece with the last troops for Suda Bay, Crete.

30 April: At Winston Churchill's urging, Freyberg was put in command of all Allied forces on Crete, known as Creforce. Edward Puttick, the brigadier in charge of the 4th Brigade, was given command of the NZ Division.

1 May: German aircraft began bombing and strafing Crete.

15 May: The Prime Minister, Peter Fraser, arrived in Egypt on his way to Britain. He met troops evacuated from Greece and remained to meet those from Crete.

20 May: German parachutists and glider-borne troops began their assault on Crete and, despite heavy losses, gained control of Maleme aerodrome. The Germans failed with their other objectives.

21 May: Royal Navy ships destroyed a German troop convoy heading for Crete. Mortar and machine-gun fire and air attacks forced 22nd Battalion to leave its dominant position at Maleme. The first German aircraft, a Junkers 52, landed at Maleme.

22 May: A New Zealand counter-attack by 20th and 28th Battalions failed to regain Maleme. The Royal Air Force withdrew the last of its personnel.

23 May: New Zealand troops under Lieutenant Win Ryan of Auckland took charge of the Greek royal party, including King George II, and began escorting it to the south coast for embarkation for Egypt. The entourage and the New Zealand escort got away on a destroyer, HMS *Decoy*.

23–24 May: New Zealanders abandoned Maleme and fell back to new defensive positions. The naval commander-in-chief, Admiral Sir Andrew Cunningham, said the scale of air attacks was such that his ships could not continue to operate in daylight. One of the British destroyers sunk by German Stukas was HMS *Kelly*, commanded by Lord Mountbatten, second cousin of the heir to the British throne, Princess Elizabeth, and uncle of the man she later married, the Greek-born Prince Philip of Greece and Denmark.

25 May: Galatas was taken by the Germans but, fearing the bulk of the division risked being isolated, New Zealanders — mainly 23rd Battalion — counter-attacked successfully with small arms and bayonets. They left the newly won positions the next morning. The RAF mounted one of its few attacks on Maleme and destroyed 24 Ju-52s.

26 May: Troops began a general withdrawal from positions west of Canea towards Suda.

Peter Fraser escaped uninjured when his car rolled four times on the road between Alexandria and Cairo; his private secretary, Cecil Jeffery, and the commander of the NZEF base in Cairo, Brigadier Norris Falla, were both seriously hurt. The head of the Prime Minister's Department, Carl Berendsen, escaped unhurt. Two British Government officials also in the car were admitted to hospital with various injuries.

27 May: The complete evacuation of the island was ordered. A new defensive line was formed at a position called 42nd Street, from which New Zealanders and Australians inflicted heavy casualties with a bayonet charge. It was estimated 300 Germans were killed and about 40 from the joint Allied force. The delay caused was held to have gained time for the Allies to be evacuated. Nearly a thousand British Commandos, 'Layforce', were landed by the navy in two groups to act as rearguard. Wavell told Churchill Crete was no longer tenable.

28–29 May: The Heraklion garrison was abandoned, all troops being taken off by the navy. Efforts to get the evacuation order to Australian troops at Retimo failed.

30 May: Organised resistance ended and Freyberg was ordered to Egypt by flying boat. Australians left at Retimo surrendered or dispersed.

31 May: The navy lost several ships in the final stages of the evacuation; about 5000 soldiers were left stranded on Crete. Altogether, about 17,000 men were taken from Crete to Egypt. Between 20 May and 1 June, nine Royal Navy ships were sunk and eight damaged. Total New Zealand casualties were 671 killed, 967 wounded, 2180 captured (including 488 wounded); total 3818 from a strength of 7702. Nearly 300 New Zealanders eventually made their own way off Crete back to Egypt.

1 June: The senior British officer remaining, General Eric Weston of the Royal Marines, was flown out by flying boat; the last soldiers were evacuated.

1

Island in the sun

'Men of various nations now looked to Crete.'
— Herodotus, *The History*

Herodotus, that wily old Greek teller of tales, reckoned everyone at some stage wanted Crete. He was known as 'the father of history' but also as the 'father of lies' because in his wanderings around his limited world he just wrote down and repeated what he was told. Fact got mixed up with mythology and fable with fantasy, but his tales are remembered because no one else bothered to write anything or, if they did, it got lost over the centuries. The translated words of Herodotus are with us still.

Mind you, he didn't know the half of it. Herodotus lived from 484 BC until 425, or so it has been estimated, and Crete had an awful lot of living to do after that. Crete is the fifth largest island in the Mediterranean and sits strategically, sometimes ill at ease, between three continents — Europe to the north, Asia to the east and Africa to the south. The covetous eyes have gazed mostly from the north and east.

Some of those eyes weren't real. One set belonged to Theseus, prince of Athens, and he had himself sailed to Crete so he could slaughter the Minotaur, the monster with the belly of a man and the head of a bull. (And a New Zealand artist showed in 1941 the fable had not been entirely forgotten.) Theseus followed a silken thread that led him out of the labyrinth, which had been built by Daedalus. He was the chap who made wings for his son, Icarus, and off they flew. How the Allies would have loved to have been able to imitate Icarus in 1941. Crete was the birthplace of the mightiest of them all, Zeus, the father of the gods.

But never mind the mythology, Crete has had enough trouble from real people. Settled originally apparently around 7000 BC by tribes from the north, it became the home of the Minoan civilisation that became a progenitor of European culture. At its heart was the city and palace of Knossos, excavation of which began early in the twentieth century by an English archaeologist, Sir Arthur Evans. He called the Bronze Age period in which Knossos was built the 'Minoan civilisation' after Minos, a legendary king of Crete.

The Minoans had an advanced culture that was borrowed and adapted throughout the Mediterranean; it fell not because of the predatory tendencies of people but because of the unseeing ruthlessness of nature: earthquakes apparently caused it to fall. After that, every group of people who fancied their chances, it seems, had a crack at invading and occupying Crete. Two ancient tribes of the Hellenes, the Dorians and the Achaeans, each carried their barbarian ways across the water until each was driven off by the next invader. Given its maritime crossroads position, it's hardly surprising that Crete became a haven and base for pirates. Philip of Macedonia tried to move in, there was infighting among the Cretans themselves and finally — well, not finally as it turned out — the Romans said enough was enough and they moved in to settle down the eastern end of the Mediterranean and put Crete under the control of the Byzantine part of their empire.

The Saracens were the next to come calling and they were there for nearly 200 years before once more the Cretans came under the Byzantium emperor. But just as they got rid of one lot of religious zealots, along came another. This time it was the Christians, calling in at Crete which was something of a way station to and from the Crusades. The island was claimed by an Italian noble, the Marquis of Montferrat, and he had an eye for a profit and sold it to the Venetians. This upset another trading city state, Genoa, which tried to take it but ultimately failed. The merchants of Venice were in for the long haul because once they'd got rid of the Genoese they divided Crete into fiefdoms, tossed out the Greek Orthodox hierarchy, forced the Cretans into serfdom and installed Roman Catholic bishops.

If the Germans in 1941 had read their history books, they would have known that taking and holding Crete was no light touch: it has been estimated that for the 450 years the Venetians ran the place, the local population revolted 25 times to try to regain their liberty and ownership. Eventually, the Turks invaded and sent the Venetians packing, and if the Cretans thought this was liberation, they were sadly mistaken. The Turks hung around until the end of the nineteenth century, proving to be every bit as unpopular and domineering as the Venetians before them. And, as with the Venetians, the Cretans continued to try every trick they knew to get rid of the Turks. They showed that the Cretan does not know when or how to quit.

One revolt from 1866 to 1869 made European countries take notice and, for some of them at least, to question their alignment with the Ottoman Empire. Everyone then tried to befriend the Turks because it was seen as a way of stopping the Russians from heading south. This geopolitical manoeuvring and back-scratching was called 'the Great Game'. Some liberal voices were raised in protest and their cries were helped by the recent introduction of the telegraph, which allowed word to spread more quickly than by horseback. The revolt, which cost thousands of lives, may have been the beginning of the end for the Turks.

Thirty years later, a massacre of Christians by Turks at Canea stirred Greece, which had gained its own independence in 1831, into action. A small Greek army landed and Crete was declared Greek territory, but the Turks wouldn't have any of it and promptly declared war. The Greeks were beaten and Britain, France, Italy and Russia teamed up to organise a workable peace.

Britain was not then on Greece's side. It offered its support to the Ottoman Empire as a southern bulwark against Russian aspirations for Constantinople (Istanbul) and access to the warm-water ports of the Mediterranean. A young army officer, Winston Churchill, did not agree with his government. Britain was doing a very wicked thing in firing on the Cretan insurgents and blockading Greece so it could not aid them, he wrote to his mother. 'I look on this question from the point of view of right & wrong: Lord Salisbury [the prime minister] from that of profit and loss.' Salisbury, he continued, 'does not care a row of buttons for the sufferings of those who are oppressed by that [Ottoman] Empire'. In this he seems to have remained consistent. Churchill by 1915 was in the forefront of advocacy of a military campaign — at Gallipoli — against the Ottoman Empire and a quarter of a century later sent troops to the aid of Greece and of Crete.

The Turks finally went too far on 25 August 1898 when a mob of them killed hundreds of Cretans at Heraklion as well as the British consul and 17 British soldiers. Britain and its mates, known as the Great Powers, ordered the Turks to leave and at the end of the year, Prince George of Greece arrived as high commissioner. Even then, there was still work to do. Eleftherios Venizelos, a Cretan who later became Greek prime minister, haggled with the prince over the future of Crete but eventually, in 1912, Crete was formally united with the Greek mainland.

Centuries of foreign incursions, domination and subjugation were now behind the Cretans. But were they? To the list of Dorians, Romans, Saracens and all the others could now be added the Germans.

It was again Crete's strategic position that thrust it in the front line of yet another battle. The development of shipping, from sail to steam, and navigation had increased enormously and lent added importance to Crete because of its geographical position and the fact it had a natural deepwater anchorage at Suda Bay. Churchill talked of it becoming 'a second Scapa' (after Scapa Flow in the Orkneys off the north of Scotland where the Royal Navy made use of its anchorage).

Crete became doubly important, however, because of another element that its attackers and defenders over the centuries had never had to consider: air power. The rapid development of military aircraft since the First World War had greatly added to Crete's significance. If it were in Allied hands, not only could it be used as a base for the British fleet (which had dominance in the Mediterranean), but used also as a base for air attacks on Axis positions to the north and bombing raids on the oilfields in Romania on which Hitler relied. But if Crete were in Axis hands, it could be used as a stepping stone for invasions of other islands, particularly Malta to the west and Cyprus to the east, and for bombing raids on Egypt, the Suez Canal or on British positions in Palestine and Syria.

This was plain to planners from both sides in the early months of the war when other priorities held sway. The British knew well Crete's strategic importance and gained the approval of the Greek Government to base troops and aircraft there and to supposedly stiffen the island's defences. It was also Britain's intention to fully develop Suda Bay as a naval base.

There seemed to have been two views on Germany's reason for regarding Crete so highly. One was to use it as a base for other attacks on the Allies by air and by sea, but the other, it was learnt only later, was for it to provide a southern armed curtain for Hitler's costliest gamble of the war, the invasion of the Soviet Union. That ultimately terminal toss of the strategic coin began three weeks after the battle for Crete over the last 13 days of May 1941. Some argue that the fierceness of the defence of Crete forced Hitler to delay the start of his drive to the east, Operation Barbarossa, and thus the Germans lost crucial summer weeks. Others say that if the Soviet invasion had indeed been delayed by what was happening on Crete, it was of minimal significance. Still another view of Germany extending its Balkan footprint to Crete was that it provided an ideal location for the commander of German airborne forces, Kurt Student, to test his theories of invasion from above. It was Student and his political boss, Hermann Goering, who persuaded Hitler to give it a go.

Britain's road to Crete may have been paved with good intentions, but the fact was it was just a backwater in an evolving war until it found itself thrust to the centre of the action. Defence works planned for the island had not happened, commanders were swapped around so much it was a wonder anything was done, Suda Bay was a great natural harbour but it had little infrastructure, and the island's aerodromes were barely operational and, even more crucially, lacked substantial defence.

If the Cretans of the past, and their myriad persecutors, could talk, they would have spoken of the topography of the island as being the most significant factor for both defenders and attackers. The island is about 250 kilometres from east to west and about 60 from north to south. A spine of mountain ranges, with three main groups of mountains, separates the north from the south; on the southern side of the mountains the coast is especially rugged and in 1941 was reached by just a couple of winding roads which were practically tracks. Most activity on the island was concentrated on the northern side, about 100 kilometres south of the most southerly point of Greece. The nearest land to the south was the North African desert coast, about 300 kilometres away. The aerodromes, the towns, the defensive positions — all were in the north. There was, in effect, one road, which ran east–west, and there were only a couple of limited narrow-gauge railway lines. Communication between one point and another was slow and haphazard; under the frenzied, confused conditions of a full-scale attack, they were unreliable and at times non-existent.

Another thing that Cretans might have said was that it seemed a truism that a people who conquered Crete were at the peak of their powers, at their zenith. Never again would they be so powerful as they were at the time they mastered the island and its stoic people. That was as true of the Germans as it was of the Romans, the Saracens and every other invading force that set foot on Crete.

2

An island in waiting

'The only subject on the agenda was the defence of Crete ... there
was not very much to discuss.'
— Bernard Freyberg

Around the time in late 1940 that British troops were first deposited on Crete, a Cambridge academic noticed a leading article in *The Times* that talked of the value of Crete and of air bases there. Dr Ernest Barker just happened at the time to be translating a passage from Aristotle, as one did, and he thought it so apposite he decided to share it with other readers of the newspaper. His translation went:

> The island of Crete seems to be intended by nature and to be well situated for the mastery of Greece. It lies close to the Aegean Sea as a whole, around which nearly all the Greeks are settled; at the western end it is not far distant from the Peloponnese; at the other it is close to the part of Asia around Cape Crio and Rhodes. That was why Minos gained the mastery of the sea ... and finally invaded Sicily.

Modern strategists could not help but agree with old Ari. Even before Italy attacked Greece, that embarrassing show of might-have-been by Mussolini which led to the German invasion, Crete was being talked about as a prize worth having. An Italian correspondent of a Belgrade newspaper wrote in September 1940 that the focus of operations in the eastern Mediterranean was Crete. The value of the island as a naval base for Britain was apparent, and when British troops landed there in November 1940, Italian ships were effectively cut off from the Aegean Sea and the British could blockade the Italian bases in the Dodecanese islands.

Cretans were ecstatic when the first British troops arrived, according to *The Times*. After initial hesitation while the identity of the new arrivals was determined, 'a terrific welcome has been given to our expeditionary force by the Greeks,' said a *Times* correspondent in Cairo. 'Shepherds, shopkeepers and fishermen in the island poured down to the waterfront, cheering madly as the troops came off the British warships,' he wrote. 'Presents of nuts, fruits and wine pressed from the local vineyards are being sent to them by grateful Greek farmers.'

A few days later, the commander-in-chief in the Middle East, Lieutenant-General Archibald Wavell, arrived to have a look, having been told by his political masters that the island had to be defended. He, like the troops, was greeted with enthusiasm and staff with him were astounded to see old pictures of Lord Byron — that gifted and sybaritic advocate of Greek independence in the nineteenth century — and the First World War British prime minister David Lloyd George adorning the walls of a restaurant, presumably to show how pro-British they were, even though the Greeks in the previous war were ambivalent. The intention in 1940 was to protect Crete from a landing by Italian forces.

But things changed. As conditions on the Greek mainland worsened, the Cretan Division was dispatched to bolster the front, leaving just three Greek battalions on Crete. Wavell thought he needed at least a division for the defence of the naval and air base on Crete in the event of Greece being overrun. Various discussions took place about what forces should be on the island and how they should be dispersed but, as a later inquiry showed, no actual defence plan was ever drawn up.

As the situation in Greece worsened, Crete seemed to have slipped some minds. For a period of six months, the island's forces had five different commanding officers, some of them with conflicting briefs and some no doubt wondering what they'd done wrong to be posted to such a backwater, scenically idyllic as it was. There was a marked lack of clarity about what precisely their forces were supposed to be defending — Suda Bay and the aerodromes, other key areas, or the whole island? By the end of March, when the end result in Greece was plain, 45-year-old Brigadier Brian Chappel took over what was still just a garrison. He had some handy entries on his CV, including receiving a Distinguished Service Order for his role in organising the evacuation of British Somaliland in 1940. He admitted when he arrived on Crete to being at a bit of a loss to understand precisely what it was he was supposed to defend.

It became clearer towards the end of April, when the Allied withdrawal from Greece was all but over, and General Eric Weston of the Royal Marines arrived with instructions from Wavell to write a report. He told the later inquiry he understood he had to contend with two sets of circumstances: The first was the conditions applying at the time when his main role was the security of the fleet base, and the second if 'a serious attack' on Crete became imminent. Weston acknowledged that if that happened, his role would be to defend the whole of the island.

In working out what he would need to do and what he would need to do it with, he reckoned on a German seaborne invasion with support from fighter and bomber aircraft along with, perhaps, parachutists. He said he would need at least two infantry brigades as well as the Greek battalions and would need Royal Air Force support, especially fighters and bombers based on the island. To this end, he said new aerodromes would need to be built.

He'd no sooner finished his last sentence than the decision was made to evacuate Greece. His unwanted guests were on their way and hardly any preparations had been made.

Francis de Guingand, later a knighted general and 'Freddie' to his friends, was on the Middle East planning staff in early 1941 and remembered that planning for the proper defence of Crete was a task too far. 'Being told to defend a very large island like Crete,' he wrote, '... is not an attractive proposition ... it is easier to say these things than to do them, particularly as the time available was so short.'

De Guingand, who made his military name as Bernard Montgomery's right-hand man, expressed sorrow at the outcome:

> But remembering the small margin between failure and success, as well as what was achieved in a last-minute endeavour to put the defences of Crete in order, I have a feeling that we might have defeated this first Axis attempt at capture. It seemed so sad that such magnificent troops were not given a better chance.

One of the recurring themes of reviews of the Battle for Crete has been the scarcity of Allied air cover. When the evacuation from Greece began, the only available aircraft on Crete were a Fleet Air Arm fighter squadron based at Maleme for the defence of the anchorage in Suda Bay, and RAF 230 Squadron had flying boats in the bay. Aerodromes on the island were supposed to have been gradually improved and upgraded since the original occupation in November, nearly six months before, but a lack of urgency, a lack of trucks and skilled workers, and other priorities meant not much had happened. Maleme, Retimo and Heraklion airfields were operational, Weston found, but hardly a thing had been done about developing more. A rudimentary radar station, aimed at anticipating attacks on ships in the bay, had also been installed. Pens for the protection of aircraft were constructed only after 17 April and the arrival of a new (and more senior) air officer, Group Captain George Beamish. His predecessor had been a flight lieutenant, who could hardly have been on equal speaking terms with Weston or other senior army men. He could hardly have matched the physical presence either of Beamish, who was a hulking forward in the 1930 Great Britain rugby team that toured New Zealand.

It was said of Beamish that during the tour his party trick was to bend pennies out of shape between the thumb and forefinger of one hand. There could have been some interesting conversations about test matches past: Beamish was there; Jack Griffiths, All Black from 1934 to 1936, was aide-de-camp to Freyberg; the 20th Battalion commander was Jim Burrows, an

All Black in South Africa in 1928; Bill Carson, a double All Black, was an artillery officer; and a company commander in the 1st Battalion, the Welch Regiment, was John Ford, a tall and fast wing who had one test for Wales against England in 1939. A blow to the kidneys ended that match for him and the war ended his career. And there was Rex King, a fine rugby player before he switched to league and captained the Kiwis on their tour of England in 1939, the tour ended by the war. Beamish made the acquaintance of Griffiths before either of them got to Crete. In early April in Cairo, Griffiths had captained the Wellington Battalion team that beat a Welsh regimental side 11–9. Beamish was the referee.

Beamish found a site for a second aerodrome about eight kilometres south of Maleme, but it was not developed because its presence would merely have been an additional burden for defenders.

Although the RAF was conspicuous by its overall absence, the operations it could mount stood out all the more. Gordon Cunningham, an officer with the 23rd Battalion, recalled a lone Hurricane on the Sunday before the invasion climbing into the air to take on the latest German sortie. He recalled:

> During a raid in the middle of the afternoon, a lone Hurricane (the only serviceable aircraft on the drome) took off but before it could reach sufficient altitude to be able to manoeuvre, it was swooped upon by about seven enemy fighters. They roared over our heads just above tree level and the Hurricane met its fate not far away from the battalion area. Of all the gallant deeds in Crete, none were more meritorious than the action of the pilot of this Hurricane.

(It's possible the gallant pilot was an Australian, Flight Lieutenant Charles Fry, of the RAF's 112 Squadron. He was reported to have accounted for eight Messerschmitt fighter aircraft before his aircraft was hit and he had to bale out. He was struck by his aircraft's tailplane as he did so and although he landed safely, he was so badly injured he could not be evacuated and he spent the rest of the war in a prison camp. Fry's final flight, however, was on the preceding Friday, not the Sunday. On the 18th that Cunningham mentioned, two Hurricanes and two Gladiators were airborne and when they returned to their base at Retimo, they were directed to evacuate to Egypt. One of the pilots was 'Jerry' Westenra of Dunsandel, later a squadron leader and winner of the Distinguished Flying Cross.)

Crete was never ready for the reception of fighting soldiers told to defend the island at all costs. That was not entirely, or even necessarily, the fault of the British troops who had been there since November nor that of the passing parade of commanders they had. Hindsight compels the view that much more should have been done. But, at the time, the concentration of minds, men and material was on fighting in and for Greece; Wavell had had to scrape the bottom of his Middle East barrel to find enough troops for Greece, the Western Desert and the defence of Egypt as well as an uprising and general unrest in both Syria and Iraq.

The naval commander-in-chief, Admiral Sir Andrew Cunningham, who was reckoned to have been one of the outstanding tactical commanders of the war, put his ships at risk time and again until he could risk them no more because there was not an endless supply of either them or the men who sailed in them.

And even if more resources had been available, an attack of the scale and intensity of that mounted by the Germans was never contemplated. Most of the talk, at least until April, was not of a German attack on Crete at all, but one from the Italians.

It was, then, an island in the sun with few defences when the evacuees from Greece began to arrive. To troops who had been shot at and bombed for the previous three or four hectic retreating weeks, Crete was an island paradise. They could lie in the sun, swim in the sea, get some decent clothes, have a good meal, have a shave, get acquainted with the local wine, women and song. Well, they could do some of those things, but not too often and not for too long.

When their boss, Bernard Freyberg, arrived on 29 April, he soon learned Crete was no paradise. He thought it was going to be just a stopping point on the way back to Egypt; a bit of reorganisation, getting units back together again, a proper counting of heads, then on the ships and back to Maadi for some decent desert training. Some New Zealand troops were already on their way. These included the division's 6th Brigade under Harold Barrowclough and, to Freyberg's horror, his divisional staff and headquarters. They had been on navy ships in Suda Bay throughout the day on the 29th and, when dusk fell, the ships sailed. Freyberg was due to leave by flying boat for Egypt at dawn the following day, the 30th. But his orders were changed overnight and when he woke, thinking he would be dressing for a flight to Egypt, he was told he had to be at a conference with the commander-in-chief at Canea.

The overall commander in Greece, Henry ('Jumbo') Wilson was already on Crete and he was joined the following day by Wavell. The meeting was called for 11.30 in the morning of 30 April at a small villa between Maleme and Canea. Freyberg went with his senior staff officer, Keith Stewart. All the senior men from the services were there as well as the British ambassador to Greece, Sir Michael Palairet, at 58 one of the British Foreign Office's most experienced diplomats.

As Freyberg noted, Wavell 'looked drawn and tired and more weary than any of us'. As well he might. He was in charge of several campaigns over a vast area at the same time and did not have enough tools with which to do his various jobs. Churchill later admitted that it was only after he had sacked Wavell in the wake of Crete that he realised how 'overloaded and under-sustained' Wavell's organisation was. Wavell at the time of the conference was five days shy of his 58th birthday.

Freyberg wrote that Wavell and Wilson had a heart-to-heart in a corner of the room, then Wavell called Freyberg over. He told him how well the New Zealand Division performed in Greece and said he did not think any other division could have carried out the withdrawals as well.

'His next words came as a complete surprise,' Freyberg wrote. 'He said he wanted me to take command of the forces in Crete and went on to say that he considered Crete would be attacked in the next few days.'

Freyberg demurred, saying he needed to get to Egypt to train and re-equip the division. But Wavell told him it was his duty to accept, and Freyberg knew there was no choice. The conference then got under way. 'The only subject on the agenda was the defence of Crete … There was not very much to discuss. We were told that Crete would be held.' This much was recorded in Dan Davin's *Official History* volume and various other books about Crete.

What was not written until much later was that Wavell and Freyberg had another conversation which Freyberg's son Paul said took place in the villa's garden. It was then that Wavell, according to an unpublished report by the younger Freyberg, told the new OC Crete about the highly secret source revealing German intentions. Wavell told Freyberg he would be the recipient of deciphered intercepts of German messages known as Ultra. Paul Freyberg recorded:

> Wavell gave Freyberg two specific orders in relation to Ultra. The first was that under no circumstances whatsoever was he to mention to anyone else on Crete the nature and purpose of Ultra. The second was that he was not to make any changes in the deployment of the Allied forces on Crete as a result of what he had learned from Ultra, without Wavell's prior approval. This meeting between Wavell and Freyberg on 30 April was the only one that they had until after the Battle for Crete was over.

The idea that Freyberg should take command on Crete came from Winston Churchill, though others may have suggested it anyway. The only real choice, if Wilson was out of the equation, was between Freyberg and the Royal Marines general, Eric Weston. Churchill had known Freyberg since the early days of the First World War when Churchill was First Lord of the Admiralty and Freyberg a freshly arrived volunteer from New Zealand via the United States and Mexico. Freyberg joined Churchill's brainchild, the Royal Naval Division, and the two evidently got along famously, so famously that when they were together in a country house in England in the 1920s Churchill asked him to show him his wounds. Freyberg stripped off and Churchill counted 27 separate scars and gashes. They had a bit of a falling out after Crete when Churchill was misinformed, but relations were later repaired and Churchill wrote in his account of the war: 'Freyberg is so made that he will fight for King and country with an unconquerable heart anywhere he is ordered, and with whatever forces he is given by superior authorities and he imparts his own invincible firmness of mind to all around him.'

Only those close to Freyberg during the war and afterwards could have known what an intolerable burden the knowledge of Ultra was. At no stage could he defend or justify himself because the knowledge of Ultra was made public only in 1974, some 11 years after his death. But even in his lifetime Freyberg must have wanted to tell someone. The senior administrative officer who ran the 2nd NZEF, Bill Stevens, was a friend and companion of Freyberg's throughout the war. He told the story that Freyberg on several occasions would put an arm around him or beckon him outside and ask: 'Can you keep a secret?' The assurance delivered, Freyberg would then tell him about some pending action or movement that was supposed to be secret. Within hours, Stevens would discover that Freyberg had done the same with several other senior officers, each of whom believed that he alone was privy to the 'secret'. But for all such childlike bursting to tell, Ultra remained a secret.

In 1948, when Freyberg was governor-general, he wrote to the British Government and emphasised that he left Wavell in no doubt at the 30 April conference about his doubts whether the island could be held. Wavell told him there were not sufficient ships to evacuate the island. They couldn't run; they had to fight. 'I was quite certain we could make a fight of it,' Freyberg said in his letter, 'but I felt the responsibility that rested upon my shoulders, especially with regard to the fact that the New Zealand forces had very nearly been lost in Greece and they were now once again in grave danger of being surrounded and captured.'

Churchill and the military chiefs in Britain wanted Crete to be held at all costs, for strategic and political reasons, and the military men in the field had to obey. They knew they were being asked to achieve the improbable: Wavell could have thrown words back at Churchill — never in the field of human conflict has so much been asked of so few.

As Freyberg told the Brits seven years after the battle: 'No soldier looking at the full picture, bearing in mind the scale of attack envisaged, could consider holding Crete with less than an army corps of three complete infantry divisions, plus a mobile striking force.' Freyberg knew well that he had much, much less than that at his command.

He soon enough learnt that the Germans intended to begin their invasion on 17 May, giving him less than three weeks in which to organise as much of a proper defence as he could and to have brought from Egypt the material and machines he would need. The fact the start date was later delayed by three days hardly made any difference. The forces at Freyberg's command were insufficient and ill-equipped. He also lacked a headquarters staff. By the time he was appointed overall commander, the navy ships carrying the 6th Brigade and Freyberg's headquarters had already arrived in Alexandria. 'For all these mistakes,' he later wrote, 'we were to pay a high price.'

To provide some context and to perhaps better understand the desperate need Churchill and the British people had for some sort of success, Britain at the time was in the midst of the Blitz, the daily bombing raids by the Luftwaffe. While Freyberg and his troops planned what to do on Crete, London on 10 May was heavily bombed and the House of Commons destroyed. Liverpool and other ports came under their heaviest attacks. Yet, in the midst of all this, Churchill still exhorted Wavell to greater efforts. As one of Wavell's biographers, John Connell, wrote: 'Churchill's strategic ideas may have been amateurish, his judgment on people and events often mercurial, and his attitude toward senior commanders ambivalent, but his courage and his zest in a dark time were matchless.'

For the soldiers who arrived from Greece and who were now charged with hanging on to Crete at all costs, the darkness became more impenetrable. They wondered how on earth they were going to do it. Alexander ('Acky') Falconer, who commanded the 23rd Battalion and was briefly in charge of a brigade, recorded in his diary how tools which were in short supply on Crete were needlessly left in Greece.

'Troops were ordered by some embarkation officers to dump picks and shovels on the beach, and some other valuable equipment was unnecessarily lost in this way,' he wrote. And when they arrived at Suda Bay on Anzac Day:

Port officers again caused confusion and unnecessary loss by ordering
the dumping of weapons in a shed on the wharf, despite the protest of
the Bde Cmd [brigade command]. Most NZ units refused to obey these
unwarranted orders and carried their weapons with them, but some
were lost in this way and not recovered.

One New Zealand sergeant wrote that when boarding the ship in Greece, he
and his platoon had been told to have both arms free to climb the rope ladders
to the deck. 'Some heavier gear such as mortars had been dumped from the
landing craft. We were told to throw them away and to get up the ladders.'

Among the equipment either in short supply or in some cases totally
absent was entrenching tools, essential for the digging of slit trenches which
were needed during air attacks. Slit trenches were essentially as they sounded,
just indentations in the earth sufficiently deep and wide to protect a man's
body from the enemy's attention from the air. There were no trenches of the
First World War type, in which men could walk around at full height. Without
spades or shovels, men improvised and used the rims of their tin helmets or
their bayonets to scratch away at the ground.

It wasn't just weapons of war men lacked. There was also a shortage of
basic cooking and eating implements. Gordon Cunningham, a Central Otago
stock agent until he enlisted, said disused petrol tins salvaged from Maleme
aerodrome were washed out — in a once-over-lightly manner — and used for
cooking and carrying water. He didn't need to say that food and water would
have had a petrol taste to it for days. Any stray tins which could be found
were used for eating and drinking — the army supplied meat and vegetables
(mixed and known to the troops as M&V), bully beef and powdered milk
in tins and once emptied these were reused for eating and drinking. Round
cigarette tins which held five Three Castles cigarettes were used as mugs, but
only after the cigarettes were lovingly cared for and smoked — cigarettes and
tobacco were among the shortages felt most keenly by the men.

Food was also in short supply because of the vastly increased numbers of
mouths to feed and the dependence by Crete on importing much of its food

from the mainland, a source now lost. The navy did its best with night supply runs, but some of the soldiers took matters into their own hands. There was also a shortage of firewood, and one soldier reported that while he was out looking for wood, he was attacked by a sheep. Naturally enough, he had to defend himself and in so doing killed the sheep. As evidence for his story, he carried it back to camp where the cooks relieved him of his burden. His platoon dined well for a few days.

A report about supplies by 18th Battalion was typical:

The shipping difficulties … meant that food was short — for most of the time, units were on half rations, which, said an 18 Battalion man, seemed like quarter rations. Luckily it was a good time of year for living off the country. Eggs and oranges were abundant, and potatoes, beans and tomatoes grew in small patches among the vines.

Ships also brought in picks and shovels, clothing, ammunition and enough blankets so that most men had one each. Some trucks were landed and more promised, but they never arrived. The supplies shipped in 'unloaded at Suda in the face of daily air raids were a drop in the bucket compared with the shortages', William Dawson noted in the 18th's *Official History* volume.

The evacuation from Greece was so chaotic in parts that there were many men on Crete not attached to specific units or who had otherwise lost contact with their colleagues. These were not necessarily New Zealanders, although some were. Aside from New Zealanders, Brits, Australians and Greeks, seemingly leaderless Palestinians and Cypriots also wandered around. Since there was no fighting but plenty of work, some of these men took advantage of the bars and taverns in the Cretan villages. The local wine was an acquired taste and, it seems, a taste quickly acquired. This became a problem.

As Falconer noted in his diary during the second week: 'Troops settling down slowly but still too much AWL [absence without leave] and drunkenness, with some unpleasant offences against civilians.'

One incident was more than just unpleasant. A New Zealand soldier, well

Left: A signed, official portrait of Bernard Freyberg when he was governor-general.

Below: The war memorial at Galatas.

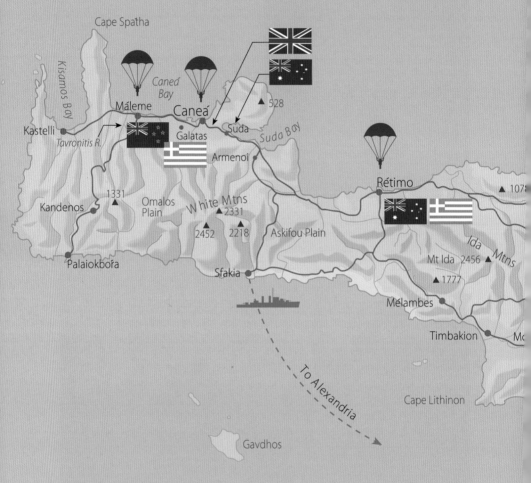

SEA OF CRETE

Cape Spatha

Kisamos Bay

Máleme

Canea Bay

Caneá

528

Suda

Suda Bay

Kastelli

Tavronitis R.

Galatas

Armenoi

Rétimo

▲ 107...

1331

Kandenos

Omalos Plain

White Mtns ▲ 2331

Askifou Plain

Ida Mtns

▲ 2452   ▲ 2218

Mt Ida 2456 ▲

Palaiokbora

Sfakia

▲ 1777

Mélambes

To Alexandria

Timbakion

Mo...

Cape Lithinon

Gavdhos

LEGEND

New Zealand Division

Australian troops

British troops

Greek troops

German parachute and airborne landings 20 May 1941

Commonwealth forces evacuation route

Main road

Dia

To Alexandria

Heraklion

Kastéllion

760

Neápolis

Gulf of Merabellau

Nikolaos

Sitia

Dhikti
2148
Mtns
2141

1237 Sitia Range

819

Pirgos
terousia

Ierápetra

MEDITERRANEAN SEA

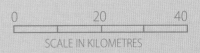

A dressing station at Maleme; Germans on the right.

Paratroopers over Galatas.

Germans landing on and near the hospital in one of the more controversial aspects of the invasion.

A reminder of war 60 years later.

Gliders landed in this dry riverbed, thinking the surface would be smooth. It wasn't.

Peter McIntyre's painting of the barge with its blanket sail that made it to Egypt.

Peter McIntyre's 'The alert at dawn, 27th Machine Gun Battalion in Greece'.

Ted's unfinished bottle with its poppies in a glass case in the Waihao Forks pub.

A painting of Clive Hulme by John Cameron Duncan.

Peter McIntyre's portrait of Charles Upham.

James Hargest pictured in 1939.

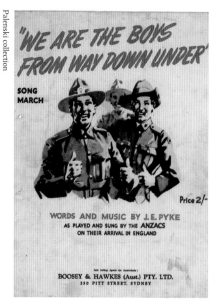

Sheet music for 'Tiny' Pyke's best-known song.

The jacket of the first edition of Sandy Thomas's book, *Dare to be Free*. This was the copy of the book Thomas gave to 23rd Battalion historian Angus Ross.

acquired, demonstrated in a bar how brave he had been in Greece. He waved his rifle around and fired shots through the ceiling. Unfortunately, a young woman in the room above was seriously wounded. The brave soldier was carted off to prison. The woman survived. Geoffrey Cox, journalist turned soldier, happened to be duty officer at the time. It was his field dressing that was applied to the woman's wound and on his authority the young soldier was imprisoned. As Cox recalled:

> He went off next day to the punishment squad to be worked hard and drilled hard until the attack came — in which the squad fought magnificently. [This may have been the punishment squad under the command of Clive Hulme when the attack came].
>
> Against a background in which the highly planned killing of thousands was about to erupt this wounding … of a civilian seemed all the more poignant and unnecessary.

The availability of cheap and potent wine — potent especially to young men from the Antipodes for whom beer was almost the only alcohol they'd so far known — also became a problem with the Australians. One of the units at Retimo contained this passage in its war diary: 'The local wine meant a lot of activity at orderly rooms. If the powers that be will treat the troops as children, they will continue to behave as such.' Like the New Zealanders, the Australians noted sorrowfully the lack of tobacco.

For all the threats which all knew and the incessant speculation about when the threats would turn into reality, the soldiers were having a high old time. As the Auckland weekly newspaper, the *Observer*, put it:

> It was during that glorious three weeks' rest cure spent on the beaches about Canea, when the blue skies, the brilliant sunshine, the crystal-clear, incredibly blue waters of the Ionian Sea, the luscious oranges, the good cheap wine and the pretty, gracious girls of Crete combined to present life most attractively to the war-shattered Anzacs.

One particular trade had flourished in the last few days and a provost sergeant's report noted there were now 37 brothels in Canea, 'most of them owner-driven'.

An affinity developed during this period between soldier and civilian which, even when the participants were dead, has continued and strengthened over the years. The name 'New Zealand' continues to mean a great deal to the people of Crete and bring tears to eyes. Visitors today are astounded and gratified when, once their nationality is known, they are greeted and treated as the warmest of friends.

Ian Stewart, who was medical officer to the 1st Welch Battalion in 1941 and later wrote one of the enduring books about the battle, remarked on this spirit of kinship. To the soldiers' surprise, he wrote, they were caught up in admiration 'for this staunch Mediterranean race of which they had known nothing. Here was a feeling for freedom to match their own, backed by a courage and resolve ...'

The men learnt a few words of Greek — 'nero' for water became the most important — and Cretans a few words of English and, in some cases, Maori. In the households where there were just women and young children, troops took up the heavy chores in return for simple meals and just the pleasure of civilised living. Some of the Cretan women took up washing soldiers' clothes. Stewart wrote of a radio blaring out in Galatas with a popular mocking song about Mussolini. At its climax, the old men (the young ones were in Greece), the women and children made a throat-slitting gesture and, in time, the soldiers learnt to follow suit.

Brian Bassett, a Christchurch lawyer at home, was intelligence officer with the 23rd Battalion and recorded in the first week of May: 'Conditions very pleasant in this peaceful waiting existence — parties bathe in the Mediterranean and bask in the sunshine; the area is fertile with vineyards, cornfields and vegetable patches, and orange vendors ply a steady trade.'

It was partly to keep soldiers occupied in harmless pursuits that Freyberg, for all the demands pressing on his time, sent word to Cairo for the recently formed Kiwi Concert Party to be sent. Freyberg had arranged for its formation the year before and had seen at first-hand how professional a troupe it was, so professional that British soldiers at one performance in Cairo thought infantryman Wally Prictor, dressed in ballgown and blonde wig and singing soprano, was really a woman. The truth was revealed only when the wig came off. Freyberg was first on his feet to applaud and the fooled 'Tommies' had to follow suit.

The Kiwis, as they were known, were all trained soldiers, seconded to the concert party from their units. They were founded, organised and led by choirmaster and organist Tom Kirk-Burnnand of Christchurch, who wrote what became their signature tune, 'The Kiwis on Parade'. Someone at Maadi camp decided that not only should the concert party go to Crete, but so too should the 4th Brigade band. So off they went in a Dutch passenger ship, appropriately the *Nieuw Zeeland*, and on arrival they were told that for military purposes they were attached to the 20th Battalion as extra platoons. Until they were needed for those military purposes, they could entertain.

Kirk-Burnnand's successor as leader of the Kiwis, Terry Vaughan, recalled that open-air troop concentrations were naturally enough banned because they would have been like a magnet to German aircraft. So Kirk-Burnnand found a derelict theatre, the Olympia, on the outskirts of Canea, and there they began their Cretan season. Word spread around the island and the Kiwis performed to packed houses and even Freyberg found time to call in. He promised that next time he would bring the King of Greece, who was under New Zealand protection on the island. Vaughan wrote that he had visions of renaming the troupe the Royal Kiwis Concert Party but, before he could, the king left and the Germans arrived.

The Kiwis' last performance was on 19 May, the day before the invasion. Like all the other soldiers on the island, they had other things to do. And, like the others, they eventually had to evacuate, making the long arduous trip across the mountains to Sfakia and the welcoming — and welcome — arms of the Royal Navy. But the concert party instruments had to be left behind in Canea. Four of the concert party stayed as well to become prisoners of the Germans. Kirk-Burnnand's hearing was so badly damaged by the bombing on Crete that he eventually had to be invalided home. (The concert party soon re-equipped with help from home and performed for the rest of the war in North Africa and Italy and for another nine years after it on tour in New Zealand and Australia.)

Among the party's repertoire was the song march 'We Are the Boys from Way Down Under':

> We are the boys from way down under,
> Marching to victory,
> Shoulder to shoulder, we shall stand,
> And fight for the right to be free.

Its composer, J. E. Pyke, known as 'Tiny' or 'The Piker', was, coincidentally, a member of the brigade band that accompanied the concert party to Crete. He was in the thick of the fighting when the Germans invaded and, with the other bandsmen, joined the long trek across the mountains to Sfakia. Unlike the others, though, Pyke also toted a euphonium he was determined not to leave to the Germans. It wasn't just one of the biggest of instruments; it was also in its bulky leather case. Pyke also carried his rifle and other military gear.

The *Observer* newspaper heard of Pyke's feat a couple of months later:

> Words are inadequate to describe just what it takes to turn in such an effort in such circumstances. Most men were stripped down to their weapons and some were in such bad shape that they had foregone even these stamps of the soldier and the man. Tiny, the colossus, performed the feat. The navy holds the heartfelt thanks of all Kiwis. They're the last word in coolness, efficiency and kindness, but they crushed old Tiny that night when they didn't have any room for his euphonium.

Artist Peter McIntyre began the war as a gunner in the London-raised 34th Anti-Tank Battery and evidence that his pencil was mightier than the sword came when Freyberg made him the 2nd NZEF official artist. McIntyre was disgusted that he had not been allowed to go to Greece, making the reasonable complaint that a war artist could hardly paint the war if he was not allowed to see it. He was delighted therefore when he was told to pack his kit and get to Crete at the same time as the concert party and the band.

Another idea of Freyberg's for the welfare and knowledge of the troops was their own newspaper. Freyberg was concerned about the number of rumours that flew round the island and he thought an official newspaper could dispel the worst of them. Reception of the BBC was patchy and, according to Dan Davin, 'Civilian sets found it easier to get German stations and the circumstances were ideal for Lord Haw-Haw's sardonic malice.' Lord Haw-Haw was the name given by British newspapers to propaganda broadcasts in English from Berlin by several broadcasters, but most notably William Joyce, an Englishman who was executed in London in 1946. Joyce, in his educated English, called Crete in one broadcast 'the island of doomed men' and said there was 'a German bomb for every olive tree and a bullet for every blade of grass'. (Joyce borrowed the 'island of doomed men' line from the title of a popular film of 1940. Starring Peter Lorre, it was about a forced labour camp on a fictional Pacific island.)

In a business that rightly prides itself on producing a paper every day despite sometimes extraordinary odds, the story of the *Crete News* is one of the most remarkable.

If ever a newspaper was published in conditions which on the face of it were impossible, this was it. The man who accomplished it, or at least led the accomplishment, was Geoffrey Cox. He'd been a Rhodes Scholar and left Oxford to go into journalism, in which he worked for the national dailies *News Chronicle* and *Daily Express* at the Spanish Civil War and further north in Europe as events raced toward the Second World War. When it began, he enlisted in the army, anxious to be a soldier rather than a journalist. But his fame went with his name. Ideally, he wanted to be a platoon leader, but within a few days of arriving in Crete he was commandeered by Brigadier Jim Hargest as his intelligence officer. But Hargest was outbid by Freyberg, who put the word out he wanted to see Cox just as the young lieutenant was packing for his new role.

Cox was met by Jasper Blunt, a colonel who had been military attaché in Athens and was now (temporarily, as it turned out) Freyberg's intelligence overseer and liaison with the Greek royal party. Cox was ushered into the general's presence and recalled the orders as being brief and clear: 'I want a newspaper to be produced for the troops that looks like the newspapers the men read at home.' And he wanted it quickly.

Cox must have found the orders daunting. He'd been a journalist for about five years but just as a reporter; he didn't say so, but it's unlikely he had had anything to do with the production of a newspaper. All he had had to do was write the stories and others would do the rest. Now Cox was 'the others'. The story was all around him and, he knew, coming towards him any day now. But the question was how to get it set in type and get it printed. He was introduced to a Greek journalist, Georges Zamaryas, who introduced him to the owner of the local paper, who agreed to print the *Crete News*. Accommodation was provided by Ian Pirie, who had been based at the British embassy in Athens and who was thought to be a part of the shadowy spy world. Pirie's villa was renamed Fernleaf House. The biggest lack was English type — when it came to newspapers, it was all Greek to the people of Crete. Fortuitously, Zamaryas found a couple of boxes of French type on a boat that had just arrived from Athens. It had apparently been destined for a propaganda paper planned for Athens by the Vichy government. The aid of Prince Peter of Greece, liaison between the Greek forces and Freyberg's headquarters, was enlisted next. He commandeered a supply of newsprint from somewhere and produced a compositor called Alexei. Another compositor, Nikko, was borrowed from the printer, as were Nikko's two daughters, both of them skilled typesetters. None spoke or worked in English. Cox found a couple of journalists, Arch Membery and Barry Michael, and a printer, Alex Taylor, from among the New Zealanders. Others joined after a couple of days, and Cox also happened upon a wood carver, who fashioned the masthead block bearing the words *Crete News*.

When dissing — sorting out — the type, Cox realised the French language had no 'w' except in foreign names well known in French such as Waterloo or Walloon. So he used a lower case 'm' — the Greek letter Omega — upside down. Another delay occurred when Zamaryas, the Greek journalist, refused to take directions from the printer because he was Cretan. Cox, with infinite patience that was remarkable in the circumstances, explained that it was he who was giving the orders, not the printer or anyone else.

In the preparation of the paper, Nikko and his daughters set the type and read the proofs with the aid of a torch; since none could speak or write English, it was a laborious task. The first edition was eventually printed on the old treadle press and copy No. 1 was delivered to Freyberg at force headquarters. Cox and his two journalists used the BBC as their main news source, although after 20 May Crete was the news. The fourth issue was being prepared while Canea was being bombed; the town was on fire and the paper shed had been hit, but the composing room had been moved to a cave. Somehow, 600 copies of the final edition were published before the print shop was flattened by a bomb. The papers were on a truck and it too was destroyed; Dan Davin said he believed only two copies of the fourth edition survived.

One of the New Zealanders 'working' for Cox later painted a pen portrait of Fernleaf House and Cox reproduced it in his book, *A Tale of Two Battles*:

> Inside Fernleaf House: Two women servants in the kitchen, on their knees praying. A Greek, wearing a tin hat, sprinting smartly out the back door to the slit trench in the garden, where at least one of the English officers was already established. Out on the big front veranda, 'the majaw' pot shotting at the planes to the accompaniment of his own running commentary: 'Bai jove, this is much better than duck — Ha, I made that blighter turn — Great satisfaction that — Rathaw — Better than duck much …' Behind the Majaw the butler (or maybe steward), a big splendidly handsome figure of a man, waiting impassively to pass the tea or the ammunition, as might be required.

Cox wrote that the major's comments were sometimes more pungent and, with a Heinkel circling overhead, he once turned to him and said: 'God damn that fellow Chamberlain.'

Wavell, Freyberg and others may well have been thinking something similar about Neville Chamberlain's successor, Churchill. It was at his behest that an insufficient number of soldiers, without proper equipment, were waiting to engage a highly trained elite who had all the equipment they needed. Freyberg's early views on whether he could hold Crete were questioned, if not criticised, by Alan Clark, the historian-politician-polemicist, in his 1962 book, *The Fall of Crete*. Clark, the son of Kenneth Clark, the noted art historian, was well used to discommoding senior military men. It was he who had written the year before *The Donkeys: a History of the BEF in 1915*, which echoed the saying that the British troops on the Western Front in the First World War had been 'lions led by donkeys'. It was a generalised, savage attack on the competence of senior British military men and struck a chord with a British public that was increasingly inculcated in its views of history by popular culture rather than by serious reading and research. Clark's 'Donkeys' led to the play 'Oh What a Lovely War' and the film of the same name, and it inspired the view of the war projected in the British TV comedy series *Blackadder Goes Forth*. Needless to say, it was a superficial, trivialised view of events that was deeply resented by the military establishment.

Clark wondered how Freyberg could one day tell Wavell and anyone else who listened that he did not have enough troops or material to hold Crete, but then on another tell his old mate Churchill not to worry, she'll be right. Clark made much of Freyberg's seeming contradiction. On 1 May, Freyberg had cabled Wavell: 'Forces at my disposal are totally inadequate to meet attack envisaged.' On the same night, he sent a cable to Peter Fraser in Wellington:

… Crete can only be held with full support from Navy and Air Force. There is no evidence of naval forces capable of guaranteeing us against seaborne invasion and air force in island consists of 6 Hurricanes and 17 obsolete aircraft. Would strongly represent to your government grave situation in which bulk of NZ Division is placed and recommend you bring pressure to bear on highest plane in London to either supply us with sufficient means to defend island or to review Crete must be held.

It was this message that prompted Fraser to get from Wellington to Cairo as quickly as he could (which in 1941 was not quick at all). Freyberg said later he was outspoken with Wavell because arrangements in Greece had been so bad that there could not afford to be any more misunderstandings. 'I wanted him to know clearly how bad the situation in Crete was.'

Clark, however, couldn't reconcile those comments with a cable from Freyberg to Churchill four days later. Clark quoted it as saying: 'Cannot understand nervousness; am not in the last anxious about airborne attack; have made my dispositions and feel can cope adequately with the troops at my disposal.' But Clark, politician that he became, told only part of the story. The rest of Freyberg's message, which Churchill republished in the third volume of his history of the war, went: 'Combination of seaborne and airborne attack is different. If that comes before I can get the guns and transport here the situation will be difficult ... When we get our equipment and transport, and with a few extra fighter aircraft, it should be possible to hold Crete ...'

When Clark wrote his book, Freyberg was in residence at Windsor Castle but was not consulted about what he did or did not say. Freyberg's son Paul said his father was upset by Clark's account and described it as inaccurate and unfair. But even if Clark had gone to the source, he could not have learnt at that stage about the nature of the secret information that was passed on to Freyberg. Knowledge of the Ultra intercepts, which added a whole new chapter to the intrigue that was Crete, was not made public until 1974, 12 years after Clark's book and 11 years after Freyberg's death. Neither could Clark have known the text of Freyberg's correspondence with the British Government and with Churchill (other than that in Churchill's book). They remained secret until 1980.

As invasion time approached, and as the Germans stepped up their daily bombing and strafing runs, as well as continual and almost unchallenged reconnaissance flights, Freyberg became increasingly concerned about the chances of holding the island. That much was evident. But he also had to appear to his troops to be confident and keep their morale up. 'The men had to be told the urgency of the situation in a way that would prepare them for the battle which was now about to burst upon them,' he wrote. 'At the same time it was important to say nothing which would reveal to them my grave doubts as to our ability to hold Crete.'

'It'll be tough but we can do it' would have been a more encouraging message to his troops than to say: 'This is hopeless, I don't know why we're even bothering.' Freyberg was no Henry V on the eve of Agincourt (Shakespeare's version at least), who talked about a happy band of brothers and how 'gentlemen in England now a-bed shall think themselves accursed they were not here'.

But he knew well the gravity and the significance of what was about to unfold.

3

From peace to war

For what avail the plough or sail,

Or land or life, if freedom fail?

— Ralph Waldo Emerson, in 'Boston', quoted by

New Zealand acting prime minister Peter Fraser

in a speech on the BBC, November 1939

It has been well recorded that during the 1930s, when politicians' minds were preoccupied with overcoming the effects of the Great Depression and when economic considerations were uppermost, Britain's military strength fell away. People such as Winston Churchill argued for rearmament, knowing that was precisely what the First World War enemy, Germany, was doing. But Churchill at the time was in the political background. A future American president, John F. Kennedy, was so intrigued by the British defence somnambulance of the 1930s that he wrote a book about it. He called it *While England Slept*.

No one accused New Zealand of sleeping, not even dozing. But there were concerns that the country was not fully awake to the prospects of the war that some could see coming. Others looked the other way. The Labour Government of Michael Joseph Savage, first elected in 1935 and retained in 1938, devoted itself to getting the economy right. The government went further than any since the reforming Liberal administration of the 1890s, creating what came to be known as the cradle to the grave welfare state, trying to ensure that everyone could lead a safe, dignified life. No one wanted a return to what a historian, Tony Simpson, called 'the sugarbag years', the years of hand-to-mouth feeding and hand-me-down clothing. Or worse.

Savage had been an opponent of conscription during the First World War and some members of his government had spent time in jail for their pacifist views, but he was alive to the menace of a re-emergent militant Germany. Some of the conservative newspapers in New Zealand (and in those days most were) criticised Savage after he had been to Britain for King George VI's coronation in 1937 and questioned Britain's appeasement policy towards Germany. He also wondered aloud about the value of Britain's naval base in Singapore in case Japan extended its aggression beyond China. For these views, Savage was accused of disloyalty towards Britain and of an 'embarrassing and deplorable display of Empire disunity'.

The Australian-born Savage was keenly aware of what could be coming. When the British prime minister, Neville Chamberlain, met Adolf Hitler in Munich in 1938 and returned happily to London waving a bit of paper and declaring 'peace in our time', Savage was not impressed. He refused to join the Australian and Canadian governments in congratulating Chamberlain for taming the tyrant. Savage's former parliamentary colleague and high commissioner in London, Bill Jordan, told him that Britain and France were more opposed to the spread of communism and socialism than they were with opposing fascism, whether Hitler's version or that of his Latin lackey, Benito Mussolini.

But for all Savage's awareness of the military threat and the pending dislocation of a fragile peaceful world (the old League of Nations, the predecessor of the United Nations, was practically impotent), he and his government were accused by senior New Zealand army officers of not doing enough. The officers were all in one way or another linked with the National Party (founded in 1936), but while that may have made their action understandable, it didn't make it any better. It certainly didn't make it right. Army officers neither then nor now were supposed to publicly criticise the government they were sworn to serve. They could, and probably still do, mumble into their beers and gins in the officers' mess about how politicians didn't understand the armed forces or their needs, but such moans had to be kept private.

In May 1938, though, four senior colonels in New Zealand's tiny army sent to newspapers what they called a 'manifesto' disputing a contention by the Defence Minister, Fred Jones, and the chief of the general staff — the head of the army — Major-General John Duigan (Sir John from 1940), that New Zealand land forces were in a state of efficient readiness for combat.

The colonels, knowing full well their comments were in breach of army regulations and traditions, reckoned that the government had reduced the territorial force to a point that it was not good enough to defend the country. They argued that training was poor, numbers were low and that the physical condition of recruits was not good enough. They blamed not just the Labour Government then just ending its first term, but a succession of governments.

The four were not non-entities. They were Colonel Charles Spragg, a farmer who commanded a Rifle Brigade battalion in the First World War and later commanded New Zealand Mounted Rifles; Colonel Neil Macky, who won a Military Cross when a captain in the Rifle Brigade in the First World War; Colonel Alan Wilder, who was a Hawke's Bay farmer and had an MC and a Distinguished Service Order; and Colonel Reg Gambrill, like Macky a lawyer. Gambrill, who plied his trade in Gisborne, was said to be a close friend of Sir Andrew ('Guy') Russell, New Zealand's most distinguished and most senior soldier in the First World War.

The colonels played the martyr card when they said in their manifesto: 'We would like the people of New Zealand to realise the gravity of the situation is such that we feel all personal consideration must be put aside if we are to carry out our duty to our country as citizen soldiers.'

In other words, they were prepared to fall on their (ceremonial) swords for the good of the country. The 'colonels' revolt', as it became known, was news to an astounded general public, but Jones, Duigan and other senior army men had known for months that the quartet of colonels was unhappy. They had been writing to Jones and Duigan for months, putting their points of view and arguing what the government should be doing. One of their arguments was against the voluntary system of recruiting, saying it was inefficient. Jones replied that conscription was contrary to government policy and, in any case, was not in force anywhere in the Empire.

Gambrill wrote back with the benefit of his experience: 'The sight — witnessed by me on Gallipoli in 1915 — of half-trained troops (from the English Midlands) of undoubted bravery, being slaughtered in an endeavour to do that which trained troops would have found unnecessary.'

Colonel Edward Puttick — who later commanded the New Zealand Division on Crete — was adjutant and quartermaster-general and he wrote to each of the colonels asking for confirmation that it was indeed they who had written the 'manifesto'. Indeed it was, they replied. At the end of June 1938, 15 months before the Second World War began, Puttick told each of them they had been posted to the retired list — in civilian terms, they had been sacked. They thought they would be court-martialled. They were told they could retain and use their rank and could wear their uniforms on certain prescribed occasions. When they sought a meeting with the governor-general — as the King's representative, their commander-in-chief — they found that wasn't one of the prescribed occasions. They showed up at Government House in civvies and got a dressing down from the vice-regal personage, Viscount Galway, a Life Guard in 1914–18 and a career soldier.

As Hitler's intentions in Europe became clearer and as Chamberlain's hopes for peace became increasingly distant, Savage and Jones acted and implemented much of what the colonels had sought. The quartet seemed vindicated, and as the *New Zealand Herald* noted in an editorial: 'A government that is failing to discharge its primary responsibility to organise national security should not be allowed to gag those best qualified to judge the position and inform the public.'

The fact remained, though, that the colonels went about their protest in the wrong way and in a manner that no government, whether left or right wing, could tolerate. The odium in which they were held on high eased and, eventually, two of them were fully reinstated. Spragg died a month after the war began, his condition said to have been exacerbated by the strain of the controversy. Gambrill, Macky and Wilder were put back on the reserve list of officers and, in due course, Macky and Wilder received overseas commands. Gambrill was refused active command and saw the war through as a Home Guard group director.

Only rarely have serving officers publicly questioned decisions of the government of the day. Keith Stewart, a key member of Bernard Freyberg's headquarters during the war, was later a major-general and chief of the general staff. He disagreed with his prime minister, Sidney Holland, about the dispatch of troops to Korea in 1950. When Stewart retired in 1952, he was not knighted, as was customary, and had to wait for that royal accolade until there was another Labour government, in 1958. There have been more recent celebrated cases, such as David Lange deriding senior military men who raised concerns as 'geriatric generals', and more recently some retired defence chiefs published their own green paper on defence.

The colonels were proved by events to be right; for their successors of the 1980s and 1990s, it was just a matter of opinion. It is not possible to know what impact New Zealand's state of readiness for war had on the events of 1941 when the whole division went into intense action for the first time. If more territorials had been able to be trained in the late 1930s, if a more rigorous recruiting policy, while stopping short of conscription, had been implemented, if more modern equipment had been bought, if more officers had been sent off for more training in Australia or Britain, would anything have been different? It's impossible to know. The view of the quasi-official *Oxford Companion to New Zealand Military History* was that the country was not as ready for war in 1939 as it had been in 1914.

When the war began in 1939 and when the call for recruits went out and men drifted into military camps up and down the country, New Zealand was in effect starting from scratch. Those first men went away in January 1940 as the First Echelon to Egypt. The Second Echelon was going to go there as well, but the threat of invasion of Britain saw them diverted and they stayed on duty in Kent until the threat was in abeyance (if not gone altogether). The Third Echelon meanwhile had gone, like the First, direct to Egypt. The 2nd NZEF's officer commanding, Bernard Freyberg, could reasonably have expected that once his three echelons had joined together in the North African desert, he and his senior men could start shaping them into a compact fighting division. But to Freyberg's dismay and anger, that couldn't happen.

What Freyberg found, and what he later reported to Prime Minister Peter Fraser, was that the British Army command regarded the New Zealand Division as just another unit of its own troops, to do with as it wished. The New Zealanders were treated, in effect, as colonials, as hirelings for the mother country, not much different from their status in the First World War. Freyberg himself, for all his stature as both a general in the British Army and a winner of the Victoria Cross and just about every other gallantry award imaginable, was either not consulted about the deployment of his troops or simply told where they were going and what they would be doing when they got there. This understandably annoyed Freyberg. He had been in New Zealand in early 1941 and when he returned to Egypt he found that his division, which he had left under the care and command of Puttick, was scattered hither and yon. Freyberg told Puttick that it wasn't good enough, and Puttick complained that it wasn't his fault and, in any case, the units that had gone were only on loan. Freyberg also complained to two of his superiors, Richard O'Connor, commander of the Western Desert forces, and Archibald Wavell, commander-in-chief, Middle East. 'Dick' and 'Archie' replied in friendly fashion, using Freyberg's first name rather than rank or the English public school habit of just surname, and said they perfectly understood his concerns. Understanding was one thing, rectifying an unsatisfactory situation was quite another.

Freyberg was more explicit in 1953 when he made his maiden speech as Lord Freyberg in the House of Lords. Friction between the British and New Zealand commands in the first 30 months of the war 'did harm to our war effort,' he said. It was harmed in two ways: the division could not be trained as a division while elements of it were scattered all over North Africa and its headquarters staff was twiddling its collective thumbs in Cairo; and Freyberg's resentment at the way he and the division were treated created a gulf between him and senior British officers and engendered a layer of mistrust.

Freyberg related how Middle East headquarters had a conference at which he was not present and decided to split the New Zealand division into six. Bits were to go under Australian, Indian and British command. Under this arrangement, Freyberg and his headquarters were to remain in Cairo. He told the Lords:

'There was an angry exchange of letters and from that moment our relationship deteriorated … that period in the Middle East was unpleasant and things were said and done that cannot be too quickly forgotten. Naturally, I kept the New Zealand Government in touch with all I was doing and they agreed entirely that the New Zealand forces should be kept together.'

Another factor in Freyberg's frustration was that he was a major-general on the British Army List; there were other generals senior to him and each would have known his particular pecking order on the List. Red tabs on the lapels don't stop pettiness.

Freyberg had more than a cooling of relations with British officers to be concerned about. It was evident from the outset, when he first went to New Zealand after his appointment in London on 22 November 1939, that some of the army hierarchy resented his sudden and, they thought, unwarranted elevation. It is necessary to look at such a situation through 1939 eyes and not far back from a position when subsequent events, attitudes and changing circumstances compelled a different view. Freyberg was not a New Zealander and had never served with New Zealand forces in the field. He was known, in 1939, by military people who kept an eye on such things as a man who had been brought to New Zealand at a young age, who made a name for himself as a swimmer, had been a weekend soldier and in 1914 took himself off to North America and Mexico (where what he did exactly remains something of a mystery). When the First World War began, he made his way to London and quickly established himself as a military man of outstanding merit and bravery. He first distinguished himself on the eve of the Gallipoli landings by swimming ashore in an attempt to lure the Turks away from the real landing places. He won the Victoria Cross in 1916 and apparently became the youngest general in the British Army in 1917. He finished the war as one of the most decorated Allied soldiers. His circle of friends included prime ministers past and future and the playwright J. M. Barrie; standing for parliament and twice trying to swim the English Channel kept his name in the newspapers.

By the late 1930s, he had heart problems and his army career was all but over. He was in charge of a training area when Fraser went to London in search of a commander for the 2nd NZEF. The chief of the British general staff, Sir Edmund Ironside (Lord Ironside from 1944), told Fraser he could have the pick of Britain's generals and mentioned that Freyberg was to be given a division. It turned out later that Ironside rather gilded the lily. Freyberg was one of several who may have been given a division. In any case, Fraser liked what he saw and Freyberg, in a sense, came home and embarked on the second half of his career that endeared him to most New Zealanders.

But not to all. Bill Stevens, an English-born career army officer, went to London with Fraser as 'military adviser' and was suitably impressed with Freyberg, especially when his appointment was confirmed and he 'took me by the shoulders and well-nigh danced me round in his delight'. The euphoria of dancing with the star did not last. Stevens returned to New Zealand to find he had been made assistant adjutant and quartermaster-general (AA&QMG) — a military mouthful that translates adequately enough as chief administrator — in the new force. He also learnt that Freyberg's appointment had not been welcomed by everyone.

'In New Zealand I speedily found out that Freyberg's appointment was not looked on entirely favourably by the more senior regular and territorial officers, some few of whom might have had hopes of getting the position themselves. It was in fact looked on as a slight to true New Zealanders …'

The mood of the senior men was not improved when Freyberg, in New Zealand over the 1939–40 New Year, evidently thought some of them too old and insisted on appointing younger battalion commanders. 'We were all shaken over this action,' Stevens wrote, 'which seemed to us to be going too far and too fast in the solution of a problem.'

The man who may have felt most aggrieved by being gazumped from afar was Duigan, the chief of the general staff. He saw Freyberg come in over him and effectively, if not in fact, become New Zealand's most senior soldier and one with a direct pipeline to the prime minister (Fraser was acting prime minister when Michael Joseph Savage was ill and took over when Savage died in March 1940). Freyberg also ensured appointments for two of the errant colonels whom Duigan had sacked. It may have been a consolation prize for Duigan, then, when he was knighted in July 1940; he retired the following year.

Paul Freyberg corroborated Stevens's view in the 1991 biography of his father. 'Although Freyberg had reservations about several of these officers, he kept his thoughts to himself,' the younger Freyberg wrote. 'His principal concern was that some of them were too old; and although they had gallant First World War records their military experience had been in the slow-moving conditions of the trenches.'

Paul Freyberg thought Brigadier James Hargest provided the most difficult case for his father. There was much to commend Hargest, including his undoubted gallantry, 'but Freyberg was concerned that Hargest had undergone very little military training since the 1914–18 war and lacked modern knowledge, in addition to being middle-aged in military terms'. (Hargest turned 48 in September 1939; Freyberg had turned 50 six months earlier.) The decision about whether to appoint Hargest to command one of the three brigades was taken out of Freyberg's hands: Duigan wrote to him and told him the government had decided Hargest would command the 5th Brigade. Freyberg's reaction to this political interference in a military appointment was not recorded, but it cannot have impressed him.

By the time the division was together as a whole in Egypt preparing for its first fight (Greece, as it turned out), Freyberg therefore had problems at different levels: senior British officers resented him because he wouldn't obey their orders and could get away with it and, moreover, he wouldn't let them play with New Zealand's soldiers; and the 2nd NZEF senior men whom Freyberg had appointed weren't all that thrilled either. Some of them may have thought the top job should have been theirs (but were careful not to say so), some of them didn't like the way Freyberg went about things, and there was a sense that Freyberg was not 'one of us'.

It was hardly the circumstances in which to prepare for battle.

Just to complete the picture of Freyberg, a couple of years later he ran into a legendary Australian journalist, Richard Hughes. Hughes, especially later in his life in Asia, was one of those rare newspapermen who became bigger than the story. An imposing man with a leonine head, persuasive and articulate, he was, as the saying went in Fleet Street, a legend in his own lunchtime. A colleague of author Ian Fleming's, he was the inspiration for the character Dikko Henderson, the Australian security man in Tokyo in Fleming's Bond novel, *You Only Live Twice*. He was also the model for 'Old Craw' in John le Carré's *The Honourable Schoolboy*. Hughes by 1943 was well on his way to his greatness. He had the typically Australian view of British generals and thought Freyberg typical of the breed — stolid, unimaginative, slow of speech and slower of thought who stuck rigidly to what his head had been filled with at staff college and whose strategic instinct was to throw his men at the enemy and see how things panned out. That was Hughes's view until the two met. Hughes cheerfully admitted how wrong he was.

To the colourful Hughes, Freyberg was not Tiny at all. He was 'Bung 'em In' Freyberg. Quite where this nickname came from Hughes didn't say, but he obviously liked it because in one dispatch from Cairo for a collection of Australian papers, after he'd met Freyberg for the first time, he used it half a dozen times. The pair had met at Takrouna in Tunisia in 1943, during the fight for a village at the top of a sheer escarpment that nearly — and some say should have — earned Maori Battalion sergeant Haane Manahi a Victoria Cross. Whatever the merits of Manahi's personal case, and few would doubt his courage, the Maori generally fought with great distinction there, as they did in most places. Hughes came across Freyberg watching the battle through binoculars.

'He is a big man, over 6 feet,' Hughes reported, 'and built like a rugby forward. He has keen eyes which he squints suspiciously, a broad, red, fleshy face, sharp, hard mouth, a big freckled fist and a curious, high-pitched voice.'

Having painted a physical outline, Hughes then joined the dots. Freyberg squeezed himself into his Honey tank, ignored the nearby shell blasts, barked an order and bumped off along the narrow track. 'The parting glimpse of him was the familiar picture which the NZ division had of him throughout the desert war,' Hughes wrote.

> Just as it is literally true that the NZ division led the 8th Army's chase of Rommel from El Alamein to Enfidaville, so is it literally true that Gen Freyberg led the NZ division in that chase. His light tank or his open staff car was always with the vanguard … with Freyberg squinting suspiciously through his glasses, neighing his orders, manoeuvring with cold, bold decision, 'bunging 'em in'.

But that was in the future. In February and March of 1941, British forces under Richard O'Connor stretched west into Libya and could have — and, with hindsight acknowledged by O'Connor, should have — captured Tripoli and forced the Italians out of North Africa. But instead O'Connor did not press home his advantage and the chance was lost. The Italians invaded Greece in October but had been chased back into Albania by the Greeks, and Hitler decided to move. He sent Erwin Rommel and the Afrika Korps to Egypt to take over from the Italians there and march on Cairo, and he sent troops into Yugoslavia and Greece to succeed where Mussolini had failed. The Allies had to react to these changing circumstances and did so to their cost.

Churchill decided Greece had to be assisted, even if such assistance were in name only; he was concerned that Britain should be seen to be doing something for a gallant ally. In order to send troops to Greece, Archibald Wavell had to bring some back from the Western Desert, at precisely the same time the Germans arrived. Among them were Australians and they were joined by the New Zealanders in a short-lived renewal of the fighting Anzac alliance.

If one of Churchill's aims was for the United States, and especially its president, Franklin Roosevelt, to be impressed by all Britain was doing, it worked. Churchill was at this time trying hard to draw more support from the United States or even get it to enter the war, which it did only after the

Japanese attack on Pearl Harbor in December 1941. One of Roosevelt's 'fireside chats' (so called because Americans sat to listen to him on their radios which were typically by fireplaces) was in May 1941. He said:

'Today, the Nazis have taken military possession of the greater part of Europe. In Africa they have occupied Tripoli and Libya and they are threatening Egypt, the Suez Canal and the Near East. But their plans do not stop there for the Indian Ocean is the gateway to the farther east … Hitler's plan of world domination would be near its accomplishment today were it not for two factors: one is the epic resistance of Britain, her colonies and the great dominions, fighting not only to maintain the existence of the island of Britain but also to hold the Near East and Africa …'

(The other factor was China's resistance.)

The results in North Africa were sadly inevitable. By the first week in April, the Germans had pushed so far east they controlled the Libyan province of Cyrenaica and British forces were back to the border of Egypt, having lost (with the exception of Tobruk) all they had gained. Germany invaded Greece on 1 April, and within three weeks the Allied evacuation was ordered. It was disaster piled upon disaster. What the Italians failed to do in nearly six months, the Germans accomplished in a little more than three weeks.

An unnamed New Zealand officer succinctly summed up the Greek campaign: 'When the Greeks and the Yugoslavs collapsed, as was inevitable, we had to get out or be caught, so we got out', he said. 'In spots we had a fairly tough time, but got through, thanks to first-class staff arrangements and the undoubted respect that the Hun had been taught to have of us.'

British high command made the decision to send the division and the Australians to Greece without any reference to Freyberg or the Australian commander, Sir Thomas Blamey. That was in keeping with ordinary procedure, but not in keeping with Freyberg's agreement with the government in Wellington. Fraser had agreed to a request from London that the division be sent to Greece, and when it became apparent that things were going badly Fraser acknowledged it was always 'highly dangerous and speculative'. But to abandon Greece to its fate, Fraser said, 'would be to destroy the moral basis of our cause and invite results greater in their potential damage to us than any failure of the contemplated operation'. This prompted a typically ringing reply from Churchill to the effect that Fraser's comments 'will shine in the history of New Zealand and be admired by future generations of free men in every quarter of the globe'.

Fraser was not happy with Freyberg, though. He wanted to know why Freyberg had told him he supported the Greek operation when in fact he had reservations about it. Freyberg's son Paul quoted his father as telling the prime minister the division was 'fit' for Greece, meaning that it was trained as much as it could be. That did not mean he agreed with the deployment, but he did point out his difficulty in disagreeing with a senior officer. Fraser had thoughts of replacing Freyberg — although with whom was never said — but instead sat down with him and clarified precisely where his duty lay: it lay first and foremost with his men and with his government, regardless of the rank and status of any British officer who might tell him otherwise.

The job of the New Zealanders and others in Greece was to hold the German advance. But first one defensive line had to be abandoned and then another. The weight of German numbers, armour and munitions was just too much. And if that wasn't enough, the hard-pressed Allied defenders, scrambling south quicker than they had moved north, were harassed from the air. By the third week of April, the British commander, Henry ('Jumbo') Wilson, decided the Allies had to get out while they still could. Some of the Allied commanders did not take kindly to being told to run. An Australian brigadier, George Vasey, put his view in earthy Australian: 'Here we bloody well are and here we bloody well stay.' For Vasey, like so many of his soldiers, the next stop was Crete and he distinguished himself there as well.

Puttick was told to destroy the guns under his command so the Germans couldn't use them. He ignored the order and just as well, because they came in handy during the evacuation. Over the last week of April, the New Zealanders retreated to their evacuation points, fighting all the while and adapting to changing circumstances such as when the Germans seized the Corinth isthmus that connected the Greek mainland with the Peloponnese Peninsula. That forced a change of plans for the New Zealand 4th Brigade, which had to make its way to the beaches west of Athens.

The New Zealanders were chased, shot at, bombed and harried almost to the water's edge. They fought to the last; they fought until they could fight no more. Among them was a Southland driver, Jack Hinton, who shouted: 'To hell with this, who'll come with me?' He threw two grenades which left 20 dead, he stormed machine-gun positions with just a bayonet, he smashed his way into a house and bayoneted the startled Germans inside, he kept on with his personal reign of terror until he was shot in the stomach and captured. His courage was rewarded with the Victoria Cross in the most unusual of ways. So many men in Greek and German hospitals mentioned Hinton in letters that the Red Cross told the British Government that it should look into it. It was such a rare step that the King's view was sought and he ordered an investigation, and when it was found the facts matched the stories, the VC was awarded.

The navy, as it was to do a month hence off Crete, took as many soldiers away from Greece as it could. Without the navy's efforts, the story that was Greece would have been unimaginable. New Zealand was faced, as Fraser well knew, with losing its entire division the first time it went into action.

If the words of the unnamed New Zealand officer can be taken to express the feelings of all, there was relief they'd got away from Greece but a determination to square things up with the Germans the next time they met:

> And so here we are at last on the Isle of Crete, all ready for the devils if they should come by parachute. This time the odds will be much more even, and the men are viciously awaiting their chance. We have lots of scores to pay off, and no one could feel anything but confidence with such men as these around.

For all his thoughts, Crete was intended to have been simply a stopover for the New Zealanders on the way back to Egypt. But things changed.

4

'The end of the world'

'It became like an invasion from Mars instead of from Greece.'
— Geoffrey Cox in a radio broadcast

The troops on the ground knew what to expect and when to expect it. But when it came, 'dead on time', as Bernard Freyberg remarked, it still came as a shock. The morning of Tuesday, 20 May, was as brilliantly blue and clear as many another spring day on Crete. Men went to their stand-to positions at dawn as they did every day and as they and military men before them had been trained to do because dawn was supposed to be the ideal time for attack. They stood to their guns, those who had them, and they peered north into the lightening sky. The daily business done with, they went off to other duties or to breakfast.

The German fighters and bombers roared in from the north, spouting and spitting their lethal loads; not aimed, it seemed, at anything in particular, but intended to spread terror and alarm on the ground. It was a daily routine, a softening up process. It was the 'daily hate' as the soldiers called it. But this day it seemed more intense than usual, the shooting more indiscriminate than usual, the terrifying whistling of the dive bombers more piercing than usual. Villagers huddled in their homes and protected themselves as best they could; people in the larger towns such as Canea watched in horror and terror as their livelihoods and society were gradually destroyed around them. The soldiers — New Zealanders, Brits, Australians, Greeks, a few other odds and sods — lay in their slit trenches which afforded reasonable protection from all but a direct hit. Others took advantage of the olive groves where the trees, up to six metres tall, were in leaf and provided good camouflage against prying eyes from the air.

Robin Miller, the signaller who became the only war correspondent on Crete during the battle, had just finished a pre-breakfast swim and stood in a farmhouse doorway as he watched the German show of air dominance. 'Well, it's goodbye breakfast,' he said to himself as he realised that this day was not a normal day. To confirm his thoughts, he watched amazed as a big black glider slipped silently through the air above him and he crept round the farmhouse walls to watch where it landed. No sooner had it done so and disgorged its troops, Miller's attention was captured by a sight that was even more amazing: paratroops tumbling from aircraft, looking for all the world like toy balloons, floating down to earth as the aircraft roared away, their cargo doors still open and flapping in the extreme turbulence.

Geoffrey Cox, a reporter in the first year of the war but by May 1941 serving on Freyberg's staff, also watched. He wrote:

> The roar of planes in the sky, quite apart from the sound of guns or bombs, was like a series of express trains roaring continuously over half a dozen iron bridges. We had known they would try and blitz every blade of grass off the area where their parachutists would land, but we had not expected anything quite as solid as that.

Monty Woodhouse was one of those gifted Oxbridge types who could read Plato in the original Greek and had been with the British military mission in Athens. He'd marked just his 24th birthday the week before and here he was, at Creforce headquarters having breakfast with Freyberg, when he thought his world was coming to an end. He quelled his natural anxiety in the face of Freyberg's nonchalance. 'Here they are, dead on time,' he recalled Freyberg saying. He and others of Freyberg's staff then had to rise with their boss and gaze at the air armada approaching them while every fibre of their being told them to run or dive for cover.

Freyberg was impressed with the German precision with which the invasion was mounted. He wrote later he was enthralled with the magnitude of the operation, but knew too that whatever his troops could do, it was the beginning of an end.

David Hunt, later Sir David and another of the brilliant scholars, was 'something to do with naval intelligence'. He called the invasion from the air 'a sparkling and stirring sight' and said that the senior air officer, George Beamish, who crouched alongside him, stood up in unabashed professional jealousy. 'At least I think that was what he was feeling,' Hunt wrote. 'What he actually said was, "What a remarkable sight — looks like the end of the world".'

Haddon Donald, then a platoon commander with 22nd Battalion (and later its commanding officer) recalled that his platoon's slit trenches were in the form of a V about 1.5 metres deep, one man in each side of the V. He and his runner, Jimmy Christian, were safe in their trench during the 'hate' and, when it eased, Christian went off to get breakfast. While he was away, heavy bombers rained their deadly payload down on the battalion's area, every man thinking every bomb was aimed just at him. 'Finally, my personal bomb landed five feet away on my runner's side of our slit trench and I passed out with concussion,' Donald later wrote. He regained consciousness with Christian shaking a shoulder: 'Wake up boss, there are paratroopers and gliders all around us.'

Two days before, 18 May, was Mother's Day in Germany, but Sepp Roethmaer from Bayreuth was at Tanagra in Greece, just north of Athens, and had no chance to write home. He was a glider pilot and was involved in a series of meetings with others involved in the coming operation. The next day they had the same briefings all over again and that night the troops bunked down at the air base. Reveille on 20 May was at three o'clock and, at 5.25 am, Roethmaer guided his DFS 230 glider with its nine soldiers into the sky. It was a quarter of an hour late because a truck had run into the tow-rope and a replacement had to be fitted.

Roethmaer wrote in his diary: 'I have packed everything into my two rucksacks but I have written no letters. I have the greatest confidence in my return.'

At 8.25, three hours after take-off, he guided his glider to a landing on Crete. 'The landing field was very hilly and strewn with stones and rocks the size of a man. On landing, my glider was badly shattered but my passengers were still able to fight.'

Roethmaer was just a small part of the greatest airborne invasion the world had seen. It would not happen again on such a scale. It was a type of warfare, a type of battle, utterly foreign and new to those who took part in it, to those who were charged to mount it and those who were charged to defend against it.

These momentous days in May were the direct result of the ambition and drive of Kurt Student, a Prussian born in 1890 in the town of Birkholz (now Borow in western Poland). It wasn't he who decided Crete must be captured, but it was he who determined how it would be done. Student had been a pilot during the First World War and between the wars he specialised in airborne assault tactics so that when the world went to war again, Student was in charge of Germany's paratroopers. They first went into action in Norway in 1940 then followed that with stunning successes in the Netherlands and Belgium which were crucial to Germany's sweeping aside of opposition up until the French capitulation.

Student was wounded in the Netherlands but returned to duty in January 1941 in time to lay plans for the invasion of Crete and, he hoped, Cyprus. Student had also been involved in planning an invasion of Britain, which was still an active concern in May 1941, and an airborne assault on Gibraltar. Student took his plans for Crete to Hermann Goering, the Nazi leader responsible for the air war, and he persuaded his boss, Adolf Hitler, to listen. Student saw Hitler on 21 April and four days later — Anzac Day, as it happened — Hitler signed the order giving the go-ahead for the airborne invasion of Crete; 'Operation Merkur' (Mercury) they called it. The planning for it was all done in a bit of a rush: troops had to be sent to take-off points in Greece from all over Europe and Goering had to settle a difference of opinion between various commanders about what targets should take priority. The German attack was spearheaded by fallschirmjäger — paratroopers — of the 7th Flieger Division but they had aerial support from Fliegerkorps VIII, which provided the fighters and bombers, and land support from the 5th Gebirgs Division of about 14,000 men.

In the end, the Germans had about 22,000 troops and four main area targets — the most serviceable aerodrome at Maleme; the island's capital, Canea, and the nearby port of Suda; Retimo, a town and aerodrome, to the immediate east of Canea; and further east again Heraklion, the ancient capital known as Kandia that also had a landing ground. The Germans underestimated the defence they encountered. They didn't realise so many troops had stayed on Crete rather than gone on to Egypt, and they didn't know that the Cretan people would oppose them so violently for so long (if they'd read their history, they would have known). One of the paratroop officers, Friedrich von der Heydte, who ended up a brigadier-general in the new West German army after the war, described the defence of Crete as admirable and the conduct of practically all the Allied forces involved as exemplary.

As a result of the tougher than expected resistance, German actions had to be improvised, just as those of the Allies were at different places. The Germans also had a setback with the death in an aircraft crash of one of their senior commanders, Wilhelm Sussmann, and another, Eugen Meindl, was severely wounded in the first hours of the battle. None of the four objectives was attained during daylight hours on the first day because of the ferocity of the response from the Allies and despite the preponderance of German air power.

Student, back at the Grand Bretagne Hotel in Athens — a sort of Ritz of the Aegean — knew that all would be lost unless one of the aerodromes was taken, and taken soon. As a result, the Germans concentrated all their efforts on Maleme. The fight for control of this primitive landing strip — primitive by later wartime standards — became the most critical battle on the island. Who held Maleme won. And who held Maleme first of all had to get rid of the New Zealand soldiers protecting it, especially those on the high ground overlooking it, Hill 107. As Chunuk Bair was for the New Zealanders at Gallipoli, Maleme was on Crete. It was a battle lost but a battle honour richly won.

The Germans' capture of Maleme on the confusing first night, and the New Zealanders' losing of it, have been the unerring focus of writers and commentators about the battle ever since. What happened on that night, and the precise detail and chronology of what happened, was difficult to establish and now probably cannot be; it made reputations, dented some and destroyed others. Friend turned against friend, colleague against colleague, as the embers of the heat of that battle were raked over, over and over, during the following years.

Even as late as 2012, 71 years after the event, one of the young officers on Crete who was involved in the fighting that first night pointed an accusing finger. Fault, if fault there was; mistakes, if mistakes there were; faltering resolve, if that was the case; all of these things will be examined in a later chapter.

As soon as the German command decided to drop all its eggs into the Maleme basket, its troops elsewhere on the island were told to remain on the defensive and consolidate their positions. Maleme was the vital sector and by the second day, 21 May, the airfield was under the control of and at the disposal of the German troops. The Germans had been given an inch and they took the whole nine yards. To explain simply how such a thing happened cannot tell the whole story. Perhaps the whole story now can never be told.

Freyberg distributed his forces as best he could given what he knew was lacking and given also, thanks to the Ultra intercepts, what he knew — or was told — was coming. He established his Creforce headquarters in a quarry above Canea, and as it turned out he had a panoramic view of the fighting. The New Zealand Division, now under Edward Puttick's command, was deployed around the Maleme-Galatas area in roughly the same region as Creforce headquarters. The 5th Brigade, under James Hargest, comprised the 21st, 22nd, 23rd and 28th Battalions and was responsible for Maleme. The 22nd, comprising men mostly from the southern North Island, was on the perimeter of the airfield, with the 21st and 23rd Battalions further east towards Canea. The Maori Battalion was held in reserve. A crucial factor in Freyberg's disposition of his forces was that he was told to also expect a seaborne invasion, a type of assault much more familiar to the 1941 fighting man than one from the air. What eventuated was not so much an invasion but a fleet of naval vessels and caiques — the traditional Aegean fishing boat — which carried equipment, supplies and reinforcements. It was a backup to the airborne invasion. That became obvious, like most things, after the event. It was not the first and far from the last example of later analysts of the battle having the comfortable luxury of knowledge that neither Freyberg nor his troops could have had.

The fighting on the first day choreographed the rest of the battle. The commander of the Germans' Mountain Division, Generalmajor Julius 'Papa' Ringel, was supposed to have been in charge of the assault in the east of Crete but was held back in Athens when the scale of the resistance on the first day became evident. He was switched to the assault in the west and given control of the Maleme-Canea area. While he reorganised, regrouped and reinforced Germans who had Maleme as their main objective, the invaders in the east fought to maintain their positions.

Equally strong resistance came from the other Allied defence positions. Immediately east of the New Zealanders was the Marines' Mobile Naval Base Defence Organisation — MNBDO, exactly what it sounded like, a moveable naval base, in this case designed to protect Suda Bay — under the command of Freyberg's predecessor as the overall commander, Major General Eric Weston. He had the support of composite Australian battalions and a regiment of the Field Artillery. In reserve near Canea, Weston could call on the 1st Battalion, the Welch Regiment; the 1st Ranger Battalion from the King's Royal Rifle Corps and the Northumberland Hussars.

Further east at Retimo were more Australians, part of the 19th Australian Brigade, which was under the command of the senior Australian officer on the island, Brigadier (later Major-General) George Vasey. He was a tough-talking soldier who chafed between the wars at what he saw as deficient military preparedness, then revelled in the chances another war gave him. It was Vasey who, when ordering his men to hold a pass in Greece, was widely reported as telling them: 'Here you bloody well are and here you bloody well stay. And if any bloody German gets between your post and the next, turn your bloody Bren around and shoot him up the arse.' Officers other than Vasey probably said similar things in moments of great danger; the difference was Vasey's words lived on. Vasey, who was in the Canea-Suda area himself, also had at Retimo three artillery batteries, engineers and some machine-gun troops.

Further east again was the fourth defensive area of Heraklion, the bailiwick of mainly British soldiers under the command of Brian Chappel, a man as quietly spoken as Vasey was outspoken, and who had chosen a professional army career ahead of the life of a scholar at Cambridge. He had battalions from the Leicestershire, York and Lancashire, the Black Watch and the Argyll and Sutherland Highlanders regiments as well as one Australian infantry battalion.

Greek forces were distributed among each of the defensive areas — there were three regiments among the New Zealanders, for example — and one historian noted that despite misgivings about their performance from Allied officers, they put up a stubborn fight. They were especially adept, apparently, at acquiring weapons and other equipment from dead paratroopers.

As the battle developed, ground zero became the area assigned to the 22nd Battalion, the men of the southern North Island commanded by a noted disciplinarian, Les Andrew, who had won the Victoria Cross in the First World War. Andrew was known as 'February' to his troops because his favoured punishment for transgressors was 28 days' confinement to barracks. For all that, as was remarked by many later writers, he had the respect and admiration of his men and received a touching farewell when he eventually left the battalion to return to New Zealand. The defensive area assigned to the 22nd was bounded on the north by the sea and between the beaches and the foothills lay the aerodrome, the object of all desires. The western boundary was the bed of the Tavronitis River, which was mostly dry and likened by the battalion's historian, Jim Henderson, to some of the braided Canterbury rivers. To the east lay the village of Pirgos, which was sometimes also called Maleme. The flat land in the battalion's area was mostly covered by olive groves and the hillsides were terraced with stone banks and planted in grapevines. The area was also dotted with small ravines.

Companies, platoons and even sections could not see each other because of the terrain, and supporting fire could be mounted only at great risk of firing on one's own. The lack of effective wireless communication, and the continual breaking of telephone wires, meant some units fought almost entirely in isolation of each other, not seeing and in many cases not knowing.

It was the 22nd that bore the brunt of the German onslaught. When recalling the terrific blitz from the air that preceded the paratroopers and the glider-borne troops, Cox said he was told by one First War man: 'I thought nothing could beat a barrage of 5.9 shells, but this lot certainly did.' Another survivor of the First War said his first experience of bombing and strafing in the Second was worse than the Somme or Passchendaele.

Cox was an interested observer as the battle unfolded. He talked about the Germans making a new type of war with the parachutists floating down — though some of the men on the ground likened the sight to opening day of duck shooting season — but once they were on the ground, it was an old type of warfare. 'For the parachutist on the ground is after all nothing more than a better armed type of infantryman,' Cox said in a radio broadcast.

'When he's unbuckled his parachute and collected his gear, he's got to fight on his feet without any machines to protect him, just as our troops have. Even his planes — and this is a very important point — could not help those first parachutists in the early hours for the fighting that began the moment they got on the ground was deep in olive groves and swayed backwards and forwards without any settled front. The Messerschmitts and Heinkels which hovered overhead couldn't fire without running the risk of hitting their own troops.'

One of those who made the duck shooting comparison was Charles Pankhurst who, as a Riverton farmer, would have been well used to the opening day of the season on the first Saturday in May. This was the third Tuesday, but never mind. Pankhurst recorded in his diary:

I thought the end of the world had come as the air seemed full of the parachutes, but, once I got something to shoot at, I lost my fear. Duck shooting must be tame compared to parachutist shooting. As they drifted down … we blazed away with our rifles and there were not many to reach the ground alive. Those who did were nearly all mopped up…

'Mopping up' seems such a mundane expression for killing or being killed, yet it wasn't just the phrase of the frontline soldier (not that there was much of a front line on Crete). The same expression was used by the 23rd Battalion commander, Doug Leckie, in his recommendation for a bravery award for one of his platoon leaders, Rex King. The battalion's second in command, Tom Fyfe, was killed in the first phase of the attack, apparently by Germans who landed in unoccupied territory and had time in which to organise themselves. King led his platoon to find them. 'Lieut King showed great initiative, bravery and leadership in that he, in the Maleme area on 20 May, led his platoon in mopping up operations with great success and was responsible for many casualties among the enemy,' his citation said. One of King's victims was understood to have been Fyfe's killer. Later in the year, when King was in a prisoner of war camp in Germany, he learnt that he had won the Military Cross.

Another of the 23rd's platoon leaders was the irrepressible Sandy Thomas, who tossed a coin with King to decide who would lead the counter-attack into Galatas a few days later. He too won a Military Cross on Crete and was equally active on the first day. He was sent to 'mop up' (battalion historian Angus Ross's phrase this time) Germans who were on high ground overlooking both the 23rd and 22nd Battalion positions. They killed 29, took three prisoners and lost two men killed themselves. As Thomas later remarked: 'Before long every man in the platoon was wearing a Luger revolver and a pair of Zeiss binoculars, and our morale was extremely high.'

Amid the darkness of battle, there was some light. Artist Peter McIntyre sat behind a stone wall and sketched as the paratroopers drifted down and as bombs and bullets whistled about. He was trying a watercolour when, as he recorded later, he was approached by a tough-looking New Zealand infantryman. 'He was about to pass on when he saw that I was painting a water colour,' McIntyre wrote. 'He did a double take and stared for a while. I looked him fair in the eye but he just shook his head, said "She's right, Dig. P'raps *I'm* nuts," and went on his way.'

Cox was right about the parachutist being better armed, especially compared with the Crete defenders whose equipment was still far short of what was needed. A document captured during the battle listed the battle equipment for the parachute troops. It filled a full page of old-fashioned foolscap with single-space typing. There was the personal stuff such as clothing, helmets, identity disc and such like, then everything was itemised under headings: In combination pockets. In haversack. On the belt. In trouser pockets. On the person. In pockets of flying tunic. Everything from machine pistol to toilet paper, pencil with its own special point protector to string and spare shoe laces.

Whether a paratrooper, one of the soldiers from the gliders, or the glider pilots, the priority on the ground was for each to establish where he was in relation to the enemy — usually referred to just as 'Tommy' or 'the British' — and where in relation to his own men. Roethmaer, the glider pilot who didn't have time to write to his mother, thought the men he ferried to Crete were lucky. They survived the rough landing and could still fight. 'Things didn't go as well with everybody,' he wrote in his diary. 'For the most part there were 50% casualties. In one machine ... there were eight men dead and two severely injured ... Our leadership failed miserably. Much could not be attempted for the majority were disabled or dead. That is how things went with us on the first day.'

Throughout the first day, the Allied soldiers watched Very flares fired by Germans burst in the sky. Most of them were white, which was one German, or one unit, signalling to another, 'I am here, rally around me.' Only occasionally were there red or green flares, which were a call for assistance from the aircraft. So interwoven were the positions of friend and foe that air attacks on the first day were not as common as they later became (and as they had been in the warm-up).

One unit of paratroopers flirted with the accepted proprieties of war when it landed on or near a field hospital in the Canea area that was defended by the 18th Battalion. Both the hospital and a nearby ambulance unit had been bombed and strafed in the lead-up and then became the target of troops once they were on the ground. The hospital's commanding officer, a Wellington doctor, John Plimmer, was shot and killed when he challenged the parachutists. The patients, about 40 of them, and about a hundred staff were herded from the hospital to the field ambulance and, according to some reports, were used as a protective screen by the Germans. Some of the more serious of the bed patients were allowed to remain in the hospital, although that, Dan Davin believed, probably depended on the temper of the individual parachutist. Eventually, realising their precarious military position and the dubious morality of their situation, the Germans tried to rejoin the main body of their unit near Galatas. Along the way, they ran into members of the 19th Battalion and after a short fight, the patients and hospital staff were freed. The hospital was eventually re-established and a red cross prominently displayed. It was not harassed again, although patients and staff had to join the long haul to the coast and evacuation. (Plimmer's death was described in the *Medical Journal* as a severe loss and 'a great blow to all who knew him'. At a memorial service in Christchurch in 1951 for doctors killed in the war, Freyberg specifically mentioned the loss of Plimmer 'for personal reasons', although he didn't elaborate.)

The Germans were later accused of a war crime for attacking the hospital and using patients as a screen, but nothing came of it. Their defence was they saw the hospital as a military camp and even New Zealanders later conceded the hospital should probably not have been sited where it was. The 'human shields' aspect was put down to a mistake by some New Zealanders, but not before it had been written of around the world. Some Germans were also accused of wearing New Zealand battledress, but that too was a misinterpretation of a heated moment. There were many of them. Heated moments. Misinterpretations.

There was also heroism. Some of it was noticed and rewarded, some noticed and not rewarded, some not even noticed. Heroic deeds became commonplace. One extreme example on the first day was that of Lance Corporal John Mehaffey of 15 Platoon of the 22nd Battalion. A 24-year-old clerk in Waipukurau when he enlisted, he was sitting in a slit trench with other members of his section when a German hand grenade was lobbed into the trench. Mehaffey whipped off his helmet, placed it over the grenade then stood on it. Both his feet were blown off. He died soon after. Only one man of 15 Platoon survived the first day. He was Bruce 'Doc' Fowke, who told the story of Mehaffey and nursed him and two others until they died. Mehaffey was recommended for the Victoria Cross, the only decoration that could at the time be awarded posthumously but, in the words of Haddon Donald, 'our military secretary, sitting comfortably back in Maadi camp in Egypt, turned it down'. Thirty-three years later, in February 1974, an army sergeant, Ken ('Huddy') Hudson, died in similar circumstances. A soldier on a training exercise at Waiouru would not let go of a grenade he had accidentally primed and Hudson grabbed his hand and tried to throw the grenade. But it exploded, killing both men. Hudson was awarded the George Cross, the peacetime equivalent for servicemen of the Victoria Cross, for 'devotion to duty and courage of a very high order'. An exceptional act in peace but not exceptional enough in war, it seemed.

While some in other battalions could talk of duck shooting and delight in acquiring souvenirs, 22nd Battalion bore the brunt of the German onslaught. Throughout the first day and into the night, platoons and companies of the battalion fought isolated and separate actions, in many cases not knowing where the others were. Even the official historian for the battle, Dan Davin, who was on the island as an intelligence officer and who spent eight years from the end of the war studying the battle and trying to work out who was where and who did what, acknowledged the amorphous nature of the fighting, especially on the first day. It was during the confusion on the first day that Davin was shot 'just when I was rather enjoying myself'. His wounds ensured that, for him, the fight was over and he spent a few days in hospitals before being evacuated to Egypt.

The 22nd Battalion's commander, Les Andrew, took much of the blame for failing to hold Maleme and therefore for failing to hold Crete, but Davin acknowledged he was handicapped by 'hopelessly bad communications' and found it more and more difficult to operate his battalion as a unit. In other words, the various elements of the battalion fought as disparate units and for much of the time lacked the coordinated control they should have had.

Of all that the defenders of Crete lacked — equipment, military hardware, food, men — an effective communication system may have been the most critical. For the most part, troops had to rely on the First World War method of field telephones, with lines subject to all sorts of interference from the air and from the ground. It was continually relaying lines under heavy fire that earned Cyril Bassett a Victoria Cross on Gallipoli 26 years before. Not much had changed. Arthur Helm, a loquacious signaller and a well-known identity in Wellington for many years later, remembered that he spent much of his time on Crete crawling around looking for breaks in lines. The lines slung from telegraph poles were such obvious targets they were disposed of on the first day. The hastily convened inquiry in Cairo into the Crete campaign concluded that the British Army (which meant the Dominion armies as well) was 'painfully behind the German army in the development of signals communications'. Wireless sets were few and barely manageable because of their size. They had to be carried by cars and, of course, there was a shortage of them. 'Many sets had to be abandoned because they could not be manhandled,' the inquiry found. It also had scathing comments about the lack of preparation. Lines should have been buried rather than laid on poles, but no attempt was made to do this until the Germans were almost on top of them. Even lines which were buried once the Allied soldiers took over were still cut in bombing raids and Les Andrew reckoned they needed to be at least six feet (two metres) deep to survive. Freyberg, frustrated by criticisms of delay in reacting to the loss of Maleme, said it had to be pointed out there were no wireless sets and only a few telephones.

For much of the time during the first 24 hours after the Germans landed, Andrew had only fleeting and intermittent contact by telephone with his companies and he had just one wireless set for contact with James Hargest at brigade headquarters. By sod's, Murphy's and any other law that determines if anything can go wrong, it will, that one wireless set went on the blink soon after the first paratroopers landed and it took two hours to fix. It seemed cruelly apposite given the Greek location that Andrew and other battalion commanders were reduced to the age of Pheidippides, the youthful hero of Ancient Greece who ran from the plains of Marathon to Athens to gasp out the joyful news: 'Rejoice, we conquer!' and then promptly keeled over and died. The soldier runners who had to be used on Crete did not have great distances to cover, but the risk to their lives was constant. And if they got through unscathed, they were often too late because they'd had to make detours or because they'd got caught up in a fight along the way. At one point in the alarm and confusion about what troops were where, a runner was sent to look and report. He returned to his platoon after some hours and said there was no one where there should have been. Disbelieving, the officer dispatched the poor runner back to have another look.

Andrew had another burden. Within the 22nd Battalion's defensive area of responsibility were some Royal Air Force, Fleet Air Arm and Royal Marines men whose primary task had been to service their aircraft (by 20 May an endangered species) and to guard the aerodrome. But these men were not under Andrew's command. He could ask and politely suggest they do something, but he could not order them. Andrew asked (who he asked was not clear) if they could be brought under his command, but the request was refused. There were a few armed men among them and they did fight but, as Davin remarked, 'no clearly concerted plan is discernible'. It seems likely their commander was Eric Weston, who was in charge of the Royal Marines and in charge of the whole island before Freyberg arrived. It is possible to read between lines in various reports and deduce that Weston had a bad case of the pip.

As the day wore on, the strength of the German invasion became increasingly apparent; at the same time, the thinness of the defences became equally obvious. Andrew's battalion was understrength and under pressure.

Andrew and his headquarters staff waited in vain for a counter-attack from 23rd Battalion. They were so concerned about its non-appearance they sent up flares indicating they needed help in a hurry and even resorted, such was the hopeless state of communications, to semaphore flag signals. The risk to the exposed signaller as he waved his arms around can be imagined. Germans did not provide the only ducks that day.

Without a battalion counter-attack, Andrew opted for the most desperate of measures, a counter-attack by a platoon, already reduced in numbers, of his C Company, which was in charge of the aerodrome perimeter. Twenty-eight men of 14 Platoon set out under Haddon Donald. With them were some Englishmen from the RAF tents and two tanks which Andrew had been keeping as the best trump card he had, though it didn't amount to much. The first tank shed a track and its crew surrendered to the Germans. The second was able to turn and lumbered back, but its turret could not rotate and was effectively useless. Haddon, who had been shot in a thigh, loaded some wounded men onto the lee side of the tank and told the driver to retreat. 'This we did under a hail of bullets and mortar bombs and eight of the 28 who had started got back unscathed along with five wounded.' The counter-attack was a disaster.

It led to a fateful, and much discussed, conversation between Andrew and Hargest on the repaired wireless. Andrew told Hargest the counter-attack had failed, he had no further resources and in the absence of support from 23rd Battalion, he would have to withdraw. This prompted Hargest's much repeated response: 'If you must, you must.' Andrew did not mean withdraw from the aerodrome position, but back to a ridge held by one of his companies. He believed Hargest understood that.

The 23rd did not send a battalion-strength counter-attack because Doug Leckie, the battalion's commander, had apparently been told by Hargest that 'everything is in hand' and because Andrew's increasingly desperate communications, the Very signals and the semaphore, were not seen through smoke and dust that covered the aerodrome area. It became clear, clear at least after the event, that Andrew on the one hand and Hargest, Leckie and others on the other, had two different views of the battle. Andrew was in the thick of it and, having lost contact with most of his companies, had the bleakest view. Hargest, Leckie et al. had quite a rosy view of a situation that was deteriorating, but they didn't know it.

Soon after the 'if you must, you must' comment — or perhaps in the same conversation — Hargest told Andrew that he was dispatching two companies to help him out, one from the 23rd and one from the 28th. Andrew, not unreasonably, would have expected them to be dispatched more or less immediately. But twilight became darkness and still they had not appeared. By the time they did, it was too late. The precise movement of men and platoons that night is not clear, even now. Davin called the narrative confused. The effect of the night's movements was that New Zealand soldiers withdrew and that the critical Hill 107, which had previously been at the centre of the 22nd's defensive system, became nothing more than what Davin called an outpost.

Te Rangiataahua Kiniwe Royal, known as Rangi to all, was one of the most notable Maori officers. Commissioned in the First World War, he worked tirelessly and prominently for Maori welfare; he'd played rugby for Auckland and was said to have been close to New Zealand selection until injury ruled him out. He commanded the Maori Battalion company sent to Andrew's aid and told his story at brigade headquarters the following morning. He said he had been told to get his company to Maleme to assist the 22nd and that, on the way, he should pick up guides from 23rd Battalion headquarters as well as a section of the 6th Field Ambulance. He'd been told by his battalion commander, George Dittmer, to take a circuitous route that had been reconnoitred, but, once having started, Royal took his men across country in a direct line towards a bridge that had been lost by the 22nd. They reached 23rd Battalion headquarters at about 9 pm, having killed about 30 Germans along the way and having been joined by the Field Ambulance. The Maori cooled their heels for about an hour before the guides arrived and the whole party set off. Royal told his men to speak only Maori so that other New Zealanders would know who they were and wouldn't fire on them and so the Germans wouldn't understand them.

When they got to the edge of the aerodrome it was obvious the Germans were there in considerable numbers and the guides pointed out where one of the two 22nd Battalion headquarters had been. One German called out in passable English: 'We are coming to get you!' Royal recounted what happened next:

> The boys of B Company wanted to fight and to tackle the Germans on the drome but I said 'No', that our job was to find the 22nd Bn and that if a battalion could not hold the aerodrome, then a company had no show. I consider that if we had had 22nd Bn and A Company 23rd Bn there for a proper attack, we could have cleaned up the place very easily for although the Germans had sentries posted … it was obvious the remainder were asleep and more or less undressed. The Germans were lying in gun and other pits around the drome wire. My sergeant-major got three of them in one pit with a grenade; one of them was seen standing up, pulling on his trousers.

The guides next led Royal and his men to a farmhouse where they thought 22nd Battalion headquarters had also been, but the place was empty — both of New Zealanders and of Germans. They retreated through a village that had been cleared of Germans by the 21st Battalion and there they ran into what was left of the 22nd's B Company — with Andrew at its head.

Royal said:

> They had just come up out of a gully on the west of the road. Colonel Andrew explained: 'We asked for reinforcement and assistance from brigade early in the afternoon but none came. The position deteriorated further and we had to pull out.' Those may not have been his exact words, but they give the sense of what he said to me.

Royal delivered his verdict:

> The thought in my mind was that the battalion nearest to 22 should have been used for some early counter-attack; mine had had to come

the furthest distance. I also think that as events turned out, brigade headquarters was too far away from the aerodrome to be able to appreciate the situation.

So the aerodrome was lost and Crete was lost. According to Davin, everything thereafter was about recovering positions rather than holding them, counter-attacking instead of holding defended positions. In the immediate future, everything thereafter was about getting as many men off the island as possible; of relying on the navy to save the New Zealand Division — not to mention all the others there — from destruction. In the longer term, starting almost as soon as the evacuated troops landed in Alexandria, it was about who was to blame, whose fault was the loss, whose career could be sacrificed.

Freyberg was in something of a lofty isolation. Some of the blame fell upon him, some of his subordinates talked about him behind his back, but he had to carry what he knew in silence. A few years after the battle, he wrote that holding the aerodrome would not have defeated the Germans. 'I consider it would have delayed the end in Crete, but no more.' Even Davin, one of the foremost Maleme-was-the-key advocates, acknowledged that even if the Germans had been forced off Maleme, or not got a foothold on it in the first place, such was the German domination they could have switched their considerable attention to others at Retimo or Heraklion.

It's worth considering the view of a British officer in London, Oliver Stewart, made public in the *Observer* newspaper in Britain on 25 May and therefore still at the height of the battle. Given the lack of communication, he could not have had any better knowledge than anyone else. But first of all he warned of what Crete could mean in terms of a still-expected invasion of Britain 'Crete is but a beginning. For us, it must be looked on as a sinister experiment, the details of which we shall neglect at our peril.'

Then he added: 'Whatever may be the view of the air staff, my own opinion is that without air support we shall not be able to hold Crete against the scale of airborne invasion now launched by the Germans.'

5

The King and Us:
the rescue of King George

'This place has become no fit abode for important people.'
— Bernard Freyberg to Archibald Wavell

In peacetime, Win Ryan was an Auckland accountant. In war, he became a King's bodyguard. But even more than that, the man sworn to protect the regal personage could also have ended his life.

Ryan, a platoon commander in the New Zealand Division's 18th Battalion, saw his duty with clarity. His overall commander, Bernard Freyberg, had told him to always be by the side of King George II of Greece, never to let him out of his sight, and at all costs not to allow him to be taken prisoner by the Germans.

Ryan felt keenly the burden of responsibility. What would happen if capture became inevitable? What would Ryan have to do to prevent it? Ryan knew very well what the implications and the complications were.

In a letter in 1952, 11 years after he was discharged from his royal duties, Ryan wrote that he joked with his immediate superior officers that in the event of certain capture by the Germans, 'it might become necessary to take drastic action'. One, a colonel, responded he hoped it would not be necessary but he, as Ryan recalled, 'again made it clear that he was not on any account to be taken prisoner'.

Fortunately for Ryan (and the king), no drastic action was necessary. The pair seemed to have got on famously in their harrowing trip from Freyberg's headquarters area in the north of the island over the White Mountains to the south and the embarkation point where they were taken off by a British destroyer.

The king was just one more worry for Freyberg and one more point of disagreement between him, the commander-in-chief, Archibald Wavell, and the British Government. The king and his prime minister, Emmanuel Tsouderos (himself a Cretan), had left Athens ahead of the German advance and sailed to Crete where, being Greek soil, they intended to stay as long as they could as the representatives of the legitimate Greek government. It wasn't just the king and the prime minister — there was a whole retinue of staff and relatives as well as remnants of the British Embassy in Athens. Freyberg wanted shot of the lot because, as far as he was concerned, they were just more non-fighting personnel to feed and protect. In any case, since Freyberg knew what was coming, the king would be far better off well away from Crete.

Freyberg had an early meeting with the king, the prime minister and the British ambassador to Greece, Sir Michael Palairet, and they agreed that once Freyberg decided the danger of them staying was too great, off they'd go. But doubts were raised about how it might look if, at the first sign of attack, the king cut and run; but a dead king would have been no use to anyone and a king in German hands — even if he was a relative of the First World War's Kaiser Wilhelm — was too much to contemplate. Wavell and the Foreign Office told Freyberg the king had to stay because his continued presence was important to Greek people everywhere and to Britain's allies. Freyberg was charged with ensuring the king was not exposed to 'undue risk', whatever that might have meant to men in pinstripe suits in panelled offices in Whitehall.

Palairet and Wavell sided with the Foreign Office and Freyberg was left to fume. He arranged for the royal party (which included the king's sister, Princess Katherine, and his cousin, Prince Peter), to move to accommodation within the perimeter of his headquarters.

The king was no obscure Greek bearing regal gifts. He was a cousin of Prince Philip of Greece and Denmark who was serving in the Royal Navy and who would later marry Princess Elizabeth, the heir to the British throne. King George II, like Philip and Elizabeth, was a direct descendant of Queen

Victoria. His reign in Greece was far more turbulent than any British monarch of recent times has experienced. The cradle of democracy was rocked violently for much of the twentieth century. George, then a prince, was first forced into exile in 1917. The king, Constantine, was first ousted and then restored and when the Greeks were beaten in war by the Turks in 1922, Constantine had to abdicate again. George succeeded to the throne in 1922 but went into exile the following year while politicians tried to work out what was best for the country. A republic was formed and between 1924 and 1935 there were 23 changes of government until, in 1935, the pendulum swung again and George returned as king. The Germans chased him out in 1941, the communists took over for a while after them and then there was a regency and, finally, George again. But he died soon after his third restoration.

In Crete, aside from his many meetings with those politicians who were there and visiting as many of the Greek people as he could, George II also had his portrait painted. It was Freyberg's idea rather than the king's. Official war artist Peter McIntyre received a plain, if surprising, message from Freyberg one morning: 'Report Force Headquarters, paint portrait of King of Greece.' McIntyre kept a copy of the order for posterity, describing it as 'something of an epic in field orders'. He duly did as he was bid and when the preliminary sketches were finished and Freyberg and Tsouderos went on to other business, the king asked for a sketch of just him. They chatted away about Britain and the army while McIntyre did his work and then he left:

> As I left the King's suite the guards sprang to attention. I thought the King must be behind me, so I stepped aside and stood to attention beside the guards, only to find that the salute was for me. I slunk off down the broad marble stairs feeling very much like Charlie Chaplin in those early films.

The sketching was done on 19 May, the eve of the devastating German attack. McIntyre later renewed acquaintance with the king in Cairo and the pair joked about the fateful day of their previous meeting.

By this time, the king had a fair idea of New Zealanders: respectful but not obsequious, not afraid to say what they thought was worth saying. George II had direct evidence of this. As related by Tony Simpson in his book about Crete, the king was headed for Royal Air Force headquarters (or what was left of it) at Maleme when his car was stopped by an 18th Battalion soldier on guard duty, Peter Butler. Unimpressed by the king's epaulets and decorations, or even the ensign flying from the bonnet of the car, Butler asked for identification. The king replied he had none. 'Sorry,' Butler is said to have replied, 'no proof of identity, you can't go any further.' The king said he really wanted to go and under what circumstances, other than proof of identity, could he go. Butler thought for a minute and said he could go under arrest. 'All right, I accept — arrest me,' the king said. So the car of the king of Greece proceeded on its way with an army sergeant from Whangarei riding on the running board. They reached their destination and an RAF officer asked Butler what was going on. Butler explained and the officer, aghast, said: 'But you've arrested the king of Greece!' Undeterred, Butler hung around until the king had finished his business and then hitched a ride back to his guard post. Along the way, Butler told the king where he'd been in Greece and Crete and what he thought of the Allies' chances of holding off the Germans.

Jim Henderson, the author of the 18th Battalion's *Official History* volume, said Butler, who was part of the battalion's headquarters company, was noted for his one-man patrols during the fighting that followed.

German aircraft filled the skies over Crete for days before the 20 May invasion and while Freyberg and his senior officers knew more or less precisely what was coming, most other people on the island could guess. The island and its inhabitants, temporary and permanent, were being softened up.

Already, the royal party had been moved away from Freyberg's headquarters because of the amount of German attention it attracted and was installed in what was described as a farmhouse on a hill overlooking Maleme. They were joined there by some of the British diplomats and hangers-on as well as Ryan's platoon. Jasper Blunt, a British colonel who had been military attaché in Athens, was put in charge of arrangements to get the king safely to an embarkation point and off to Egypt. As later transpired, Ryan was not all that thrilled with Blunt's attitude but, as the junior officer, he had to put up with it.

Among other notables from the British Embassy in Athens was the head of chancery, Harold Caccia, who later became head of the Foreign Office and retired as Lord Caccia. He at least would have been familiar with New Zealanders and their ways because his mother Fanny had been born and brought up in Hawke's Bay. Also in the group was Major-General Tom Heywood, who had been chief of the British military mission in Greece and was described by a friend as 'John Bull with a monocle'. Pat Savage, a British Army cipher officer who liaised with Cretan communications staff in a mixture of English, Greek and German, was also with the group, but they slipped away without waking him. He was still there at the end and saw out the war in a German prison camp.

At some point in mid-May as the threat of invasion turned to reality, the British and Greek groups split in two. One contained the king, Prince Peter, Blunt and Ryan's platoon, and the other comprised mainly Heywood and the rest of the diplomats. By this time, Katherine had already been taken to Egypt.

The king and his party watched the invasion unfold from their farmhouse. They saw the bombers and fighter aircraft fly in just after dawn, and at around eight o'clock they watched as the parachutists drifted down and as the troops on the gliders headed silently for their destiny. Parachutists landed within three or four hundred metres of the farmhouse but apparently didn't know the important personage was so close to them.

Prince Peter later found out that among the parachutists was a section charged with finding the king. 'Der konig! Wo ist der konig?' (The king! Where is the king?) they apparently shouted to startled locals when they landed. Either no one knew or no one told. 'We survived as if by a miracle,' the prince wrote, 'and Freyberg was proven right in believing that the parachutists would land in order to arrest the king. We discovered later that all the information the German administration had gathered concerning the king's whereabouts had been supplied by a Greek, the honorary consul in Germany.'

One of the parachutists recalled in a 1980 British-made documentary that he had been one who landed near where the king was. He said:

'We saw his house, but we didn't know the king was in it. It was a farmer's house, a normal farmer's house. On the next day, the 21st, we saw a long, long column of civilians leaving the house. It was the king and his government but we didn't know it and we didn't shoot at them because we thought that they were civilians who didn't wish to fight — so we left them.'

Freyberg meanwhile cabled Wavell in Cairo: 'This place has become no fit abode for important people.' He told him the king and his party had nearly been captured and had left for the south coast where by arrangements Freyberg had already made they would be picked up by the navy. (While communications were chaotic at best and non-existent at worst on Crete, Freyberg and his staff could easily send and receive messages to and from Cairo because of a private company's undersea cable that left Crete at Suda Bay. It was of no use communicating on the island, though.)

Tsouderos, the Greek prime minister, remembered that the hasty departure from the farmhouse was not orderly; it was so disorderly in fact that the party was separated into two groups and the king's, which included Blunt and the soldiers, went the wrong way. Tsouderous, whose half of the party included various Greek and Cretan soldiers, could see the king's group in the distance and could see it was heading east, towards Suda and danger. Even worse, they saw that the king and his men were fired upon by some Greek soldiers who thought they were Germans. Fortunately, the thrill of the chase spoilt the Greeks' aim. 'No one was hit although the king very nearly was,' Ryan wrote. 'A bullet hit the rock he was leaning against.'

Tsouderos dispatched one of his men, a cousin as it happened, to catch the king's group and point it in the right direction. This was duly done and the two groups reunited at a village called Therissos. This place, coincidentally, was the starting point of the Cretan revolution in 1909 against Prince George of Greece (cousin to the king 32 years later).

The whole group had swollen in size and brought some unlikely alliances. 'Our retinue consisted of one hundred or more people and was an amazing combination,' Tsouderos wrote. 'New Zealanders, Greek soldiers, local police, Cretans young and old in local dress and many escaped prisoners.'

The Germans had apparently opened the prisons and the prisoners, in distinctive blue and yellow striped clothing, hot-footed it for the hills, no doubt as surprised to join the king's party as he was to receive them.

Ryan's sole concern was the king's safety and he was not happy with such a large group. He sent one section of his platoon ahead to clear the way, split a second section so that soldiers were either side of the king's immediate group, and had the third bring up the rear. The third section kept the king's group in sight at all times but also had the effect of keeping the odds and sods well behind. Ryan wrote:

> I remember the blue and yellow striped convicts coming up to the party, and also many gendarmes. All these were held back by the troops and eventually chased off. This procedure was regularly adhered to throughout and at times force became necessary. On one occasion when an extra large party approached I had to call back the side section and advance section to force them away. No shooting took place although at one stage it seemed inevitable.

The convicts collectively were on the Allies' side. They wrote a letter while still in prison that somehow was translated and found its way to Freyberg:

> Sir: Most unfortunately our dearest Greece succumbed to the higher forces of the Hitlerian regime and the Italian barbarism. Fortunately, however, our island, thanks to its powerful ally, is still free … We, too, the convicts look towards you with gratefulness and hope for the future of our nation, and kindly ask you to stand by our King and Government so that they will take care of us when we get out of prison and see that we also do our

little bit in winning the sacred struggle. We wholeheartedly put ourselves under any service, dangerous or not, provided that the cause of our Allied effort is fulfilled. Trusting that we shall enjoy your proper attention. We remain, respectfully yours, the convicts of the island of Crete.

So tough was the task Ryan's men were set that he had to send some back to rejoin the battalion (although it was no picnic where they were either). The soldiers had been on short rations for some time, had been through difficult times in Greece and in the hills and mountains above Maleme; the escort role meant they covered twice as much ground as the group they were protecting. Some men could do no more.

The party was jeered at as they passed through one village because the women, old men and young boys thought they were healthy men fleeing from the fighting. On learning the truth, they were most apologetic and did all they could.

Some of the soldiers felt they were a bit hard done by. Protecting the king was all very well and noble, but they thought they were missing out on some booty. Ryan said New Zealanders coveted German Lugers or cameras and the men with the king thought they were missing out while the rest around Maleme were benefiting. At one point when an injured soldier required an escort back down to the battalion, there was no shortage of volunteers.

This lust for loot even reached the ears of the king. As Ryan recalled, viewed from aloft and afar, Maleme looked quite peaceful.

[It] gave not the slightest indication of the severity of the fighting there and, eyeing the parachutes, the batman who was in attendance on the king and with us observed to His Majesty that we were losing a great deal of lawful loot on his account. The king laughed and said that things were not as good as they seemed.

He gave the young soldier his field glasses for a better look and remarked that, in his opinion, the Allies were already losing heavily and the Germans were reinforcing.

By this time the party was climbing into the White Mountains which form the spine of western Crete. Over 30 of its peaks are over 2000 metres, with the highest 2453 metres, and one estimate said Ryan's royal party was at its highest not far short of that. They were certainly above the snowline — remember, this was late spring — and to supplement their meagre rations, they melted snow for drinking.

At one point George II told Ryan that so hurried was their departure that he had left behind a suitcase containing state papers and valuables which would be better kept from German hands. Blunt and a section led by one of Ryan's sergeants, Jim Seymour from Te Awamutu, headed back down. They had a detailed list of what to fetch and were also accompanied by an interpreter. Seymour later said he found going down was harder on his tired and undernourished body than going up, but the small party eventually made it to the farmhouse. Reports about what happened next differ — Seymour, perhaps with tongue firmly in cheek, reckoned he knocked on the door and discovered the house was full of Germans. 'His request to enter was denied and he was sent on his way,' one report said. The official version merely recorded that Seymour saw from a distance that the house was occupied and the party retraced its steps into the mountains — 'tired, thirsty and hungry'. Blunt had meanwhile tried to get back to Canea to find out if evacuation arrangements had been made because he could not get through on radio, but he too was turned back. Eventually, up in the hills somewhere, Blunt was directed to a civilian telephone line which, amazingly, was in working order, and he was able to get through to Creforce headquarters and was told the navy was expecting the king.

The trek over the mountains continued, some of the soldiers at times having to manhandle their donkeys over the frozen and slippery surface. One night was spent outside a shepherd's hut on a ridge. A fire was kept burning through the night, Ryan figuring if the Germans saw it they would have thought it quite normal anyway. The soldiers in just shorts and shirts felt the cold keenly. Ryan wrote:

> Deep pockets of snow lay in crevices and during the night more formed. Colonel Blunt gave the king his sleeping bag which, being an old campaigner, he had brought along with his greatcoat. Guards were posted as usual and

these were reinforced by members of the platoon moving about from time to time keeping warm. We had our only meal of the trip here — apart from a large white cheese gathered from a cave. A sheep was caught and stewed in a tin. It was milked first and everybody who partook enjoyed it.

So difficult were the conditions and in such poor condition were some of the men that Ryan decided they should return to the battalion. Seymour was put in charge of the return party that comprised 11 men and the mules and donkeys. They eventually made it back to find that many good friends were dead. The general evacuation was already under way so Seymour and his tired men once more began the trek over the mountains. They were among the last of the long-suffering 18th to be taken off.

The royal party began the descent to Sfakia the morning after the sheep meal, but there was no elation. There were doubts whether the rendezvous with the navy would come off and, in any case, the soldiers had to contemplate the return trip to the vicinity of Maleme. In their tired and hungry condition, it was not something they relished.

The other half of the whole party, that comprising Caccia, Heywood and the other diplomatic refugees from Athens, had meanwhile had a much easier time of it. Rather than trekking over the mountains, they were taken to the south coast by car and by boat and rested up in a cave during the night. They reached the agreed meeting place of Aghia Roumeli well ahead of the king's party and settled down to wait. As Caccia recalled in a speech in 1982:

'After we had arrived at Aghia Roumeli, our first task was to find out whether the king would, in fact, succeed in reaching us before darkness fell. A few of us set off up the Samaria Gorge in search. Before we had gone many miles, a runner … came toward us shouting, "The king is coming! The king is coming!"'

Ryan led the king's party down the bed of a stream to meet the British. He was not all that impressed. Heywood, the 'John Bull in a monocle', walked forward and asked the king if he would like a whisky. 'We would, wouldn't we, Ryan?' the King replied. 'Sire,' said Heywood, clearly not thrilled with sharing with a lowly 'colonial' lieutenant, 'it is *my* bottle.' Ryan commented: 'Personally, all I wanted to do was sleep.'

Ryan thought that the diplomats' party was so well equipped and had travelled so comfortably the king should really have been with it. The two groups together, the senior men conferred in a huddle while Mary Palairet, the wife of the ambassador, boiled potatoes in their jackets. (The Palairets were a well-known English cricket family — one of them co-managed England on the 1932 Bodyline tour — and Mary was the daughter of a cricketer, Herbert Studd.) It was during this impromptu conference that they learned the Germans had such command of the northern side of the island there was no chance of the Fleet Air Arm getting a Sunderland to the south coast to pick the king up. The navy would, however, make an attempt sometime during the night.

Heywood told Ryan that his troops would not have to clamber back over the mountains but would rather embark with the king and stay with him until he was safe in Alexandria.

The naval attaché from the embassy in Athens was Charles Turle, a rear admiral who at nearly two metres tall towered over all the others. (He had played rugby for the South London club Blackheath, doubtless as a lock and lineout leaper.) He was on the beach and supervised the flashing of SOS signals out to sea. After a while, a light far out to sea was seen. Encouraged, the land party flashed SOS again. And, again, there was a returning light. But there was no way of knowing the source of the answering light.

In the end, Turle and Caccia — the one tall, the other stocky — clambered into the boat that had carried them along the coast and set out to look. A corporal with a Tommy gun went too, just in case. They chugged out into the bay and, after a while, the skipper-owner said he would need to turn back because there was hardly any fuel left. Carry on a bit more, Caccia told him. It was all very well for him if the light turned out to be a German's. He and Turle had diplomatic protection. The others didn't.

After a few minutes, the small boat was caught in the cone of a searchlight accompanied by a roar: 'Who the bloody hell do you think you are?' Having been assured of who they were, they were hauled on board the British destroyer *Decoy*. Commander Eric McGregor, the captain, said he had no intention of taking his ship closer to shore until he was assured he was not on a fool's errand.

Another destroyer, HMS *Hero*, was nearby and the two eased into shallow waters where boats were sent ashore to pick up the royal party, the diplomats and the soldiers. Ryan and his New Zealanders, now assured of the safety of the king, could have spent the voyage chatting to one of the *Decoy*'s officers. He was 29-year-old Terry Herrick, a member of a well-admired Hawke's Bay family and later one of New Zealand's most distinguished naval men. He won a Distinguished Service Cross for his 'gallantry and resource' during the naval operations off Crete.

Ryan was just relieved that his job was almost over. 'Although the crew closed up to a number of alarms, the *Decoy* was not attacked on the way to Alexandria,' Ryan wrote. 'The vessel proceeded at high speed from Crete and joined the main fleet comprising two battleships plus cruisers and destroyers early in the afternoon.'

He was no stranger to naval vessels. He had been a member of the Royal Naval Volunteer Reserve in Auckland and was said to be an authority on naval customs. He had a yacht of his own and, according to the *Observer* newspaper, 'his knowledge of practical seamanship would have been very useful had it been necessary for him and his party to make a getaway in a small boat'.

Ryan closed his letter about his royal duty, saying he had no doubt that the king and Prince Peter liked the company of the New Zealanders immensely. That at least was evident from body language in both still photos and newsreel shots when the king was once more with the New Zealanders in Cairo. Ryan was not as impressed with the British officers: 'My own opinion of the senior British officers concerned is very low and I consider they would have been far more use off the ration strength of the island during that particular period.'

Ryan was not the only New Zealand officer to express concern about British officers during the battle.

Soon after arriving in Egypt, George II sent a personal letter of thanks and appreciation to Prime Minister Peter Fraser, who was in Cairo. He talked of the 'courage, coolness and devotion to duty' shown by Ryan's New Zealanders.

Later in 1941, Ryan and each member of his platoon were decorated by the king with the award of the Royal Order of George I in various grades. Ryan received the Knight's Silver Cross with Swords and Seymour and another sergeant, Les Smith, the Commemorative Gold Medal with Swords. A temporary war correspondent, Bill Jordan, wrote from Cairo of what he called 'the most unusual spectacle' of the ceremony at which the New Zealanders were decorated. The Maori Battalion formed the centrepoint of the parade. 'With the striking snap and precision which characterises the drill of the Maoris, the battalion accorded King George a royal salute,' Jordan wrote. 'After the inspection the members of the battalion removed hats and grounded arms preparatory to entertaining the visitors in true Maori fashion.'

Several haka followed, including one led by the composer of the Maori Battalion marching song, Anania Amohau. Another was based on the soldiers' physical training and, according to Jordan, an English officer watching remarked that the haka was 'excellent PT'. The ceremony ended with the massed singing by both Maori and Pakeha of 'Haere Ra', and Jordan wrote that the king and his party were deeply moved.

(Jordan, who had been a reporter on the *New Zealand Herald*, later became one of New Zealand's most intrepid clandestine soldiers, being dropped into both occupied Greece and France to liaise with and train resistance groups.)

King George II spent most of the rest of the war in Britain and in 1945, after more political turmoil, a Greek regent was appointed pending a referendum on the continuation of the monarchy. George returned to Athens as king in September 1946, but died the following April. Seven months later, his cousin Philip, who had renounced his Greek title, married Princess Elizabeth.

6

Fighting right to the end

'It is a strange and grim battle.'
— Winston Churchill

Without the ability to see into the future, without the magical power of being able to look back over their shoulders to see what really happened, the defenders of Crete knew they had to counter-attack. They knew that as long as the aerodrome at Maleme was held by the Germans, it could be used as a ferry terminal for troops sent from mainland Greece. Already, on the first day after its loss, aircraft queued up like taxis at an airport. Other landing strips at Retimo and Heraklion were still in Allied hands, but the Germans could have attacked them and such were their numbers and such was their total authority in the air, they probably would have fallen too. And the Germans had the men and the machines to bulldoze an airfield wherever the land was flat enough.

During the day on Wednesday, 21 May, Bernard Freyberg was still concerned about the possibility of a sea invasion. This was, after all, the orthodox way of invading a country; it was what he had seen at Gallipoli, it was what he and others expected at Crete, and it was what happened throughout the Second World War. The unorthodox was the invasion from the sky that had happened the previous day; logic, in the minds of men who could live only in their own times, suggested what happened on the 20th would be followed up by seaborne reinforcements.

So while Freyberg and his brigade and battalion commanders planned the counter-attack on the aerodrome at Maleme, they also had to be conscious that ships carrying even more Germans could come from the north. Once again, Allied troops had to be spread thinly. The defenders of Crete were also conscious that German air control was not just over Crete but also, axiomatically, over the Aegean between Crete and Greece. Overnight, one British destroyer, the *Juno*, was sunk and another, the *Ajax*, was damaged by near misses.

Generalmajor Julius 'Papa' Ringel had been made commander of all Axis troops on the island and the diary of his 5th Mountain Division recorded for 21 May: 'On the evening of the second day of the invasion, the situation seemed to be balanced on a knife-edge … a heavy, concentrated British counter-attack would force the defenders to fight for their lives.'

As it turned out, the counter-attack was neither heavy enough nor concentrated enough. Its timing was also up the chute. The plan called for the counter-attack to be mounted by the 20th and 28th Battalions, the 20th on the right and the 28th on the left; the 20th was to advance to the airfield itself while the 28th was to continue beyond it.

There were some mutterings that two battalions, as understrength as they were, were not sufficient, but, in any case, there was a qualification. The 20th was positioned to help deter a seaborne invasion if one came and therefore its commander, Jim Burrows, was told not to move until it was relieved. Therein lay the hitch. The relief was to come from the Australian 2/7th Battalion (in the Australian naming convention, the '2' indicates Second World War). There was nothing wrong with the Australians. They were a battle-hardened unit, unlike most on Crete, and had experienced aerial attacks in North Africa and Greece. The battalion commander was Theo ('Myrtle') Walker, a quiet Melbourne accountant who, according to one biographer, was considered fearless by the men he commanded. Walker went to the Creforce conference that nutted out the details of the counter-attack and afterwards went to reconnoitre the area where his battalion was headed. According to the official Australian historian, Gavin Long, Walker was accompanied by Brigadier Lindsay Inglis, who had charge of the New Zealand 4th Brigade. Long said Walker told Inglis he did not like the plan — 'to attempt to bring forward by night a battalion that lacked its own transport, was 18 miles away, and not connected to headquarters by telephone, in time for it to relieve another battalion that was to make an attack the same night'. Inglis's response was that a well-trained battalion could carry out such a relief in an hour. Events soon proved who was right.

The battalion not having its own transport was the most critical issue. Henry Marshall, a major who was Walker's deputy, wrote in his diary: 'During the afternoon ... the transport arrived in dribs and drabs from all sorts of sources ... the drivers were all unnerved by bombing and the threat or sound of planes and were sheltering away from their trucks ...' Marshall worked from memory because he wrote his diary later in the year when he was in a prison camp in Germany.

The battalion's war diary was more immediate and more pointed:

Convoy arrangements faulty and considerable difficulty experienced in finding trucks. Most drivers 'bomb happy' and could not be found. Recce plane detected movement and tps [troops] and tpt [transport] bombed heavily. Considerable delay. Last truck moved at 2200 hrs. (The transport drivers displayed no eagerness to carry on with the job. A plane five miles away was sufficient to start a stampede. As a result we were considerably delayed getting trucks away.)

The drivers were not Australians, but locals hired for the purpose. One Australian thought most of them were Cypriot. In any event, the first of the Australians started heading west between five and six o'clock in the late afternoon and the last company by about eight o'clock. Gavin Long thought the relief of the 20th Battalion had been completed by about 11.30. But this doesn't square with the 20th's own version of events, which had Burrows champing at the bit as the hours passed and that the leading Australian elements did not arrive in the 20th's area until about 1 am. Whatever the timings, Inglis held Burrows back until the Australians arrived; when they did, he and his men were let off the leash. But it was a disorderly move forward — Burrows did not have his whole battalion with him. He decided to go with just two companies and left instructions for the other three to do their damndest to catch up. They did.

The two battalions had the road between Platanias and Maleme as their halfway line and along it three light tanks from the 3rd Hussars under Roy Farran moved in Indian file. But not for long. They came under fire from a Bofors gun on the aerodrome — probably one the Germans had captured — and the first tank was hit, the guns of the second jammed and the third, under orders not to go on alone, hightailed it for home. 'We didn't see the tanks again,' Burrows commented drily. He meant that night. Farran and his tanks were to play a more prominent role a couple of nights later in the famed counter-attack at Galatas.

The two battalions continued their advance, although C Company of the 20th got a little behind the 28th because it was held up by some fierce fighting, some of it hand to hand, in the village of Pirgos.

It was during this counter-attack that the fame of Charlie Upham began to spread. He was already a well-known figure in his battalion; by the end of the counter-attack he was a well-known figure throughout the division and beyond. His succession of heart-stoppingly heroic actions during the attack contributed greatly to his first Victoria Cross. Much of what Upham did could be seen by Burrows, who had placed his headquarters alongside Upham's C Company, and if it couldn't be seen, it could be heard. 'One voice I got to know very well,' Burrows wrote. In an amazingly short time, Upham was involved in at least three decisive actions. 'All of these operations were not only carried out with outstanding courage, but were handled with the skill and quick thinking of a fine platoon commander.'

The problem with the counter-attack was that the more it was delayed by getting rid of Germans along the way, closer came the dawn. And Burrows and all those involved — and towards dawn the attack included elements of the 22nd and 23rd Battalions as well — knew that if they could not reclaim the aerodrome by the half-light of dawn, their chance was lost. They knew they would have no show in daylight when the German aircraft arrived to complement the increasing firepower on the ground.

The Maori Battalion had made progress. Like Upham's company, they confronted the Germans on the edge of Pirgos and ploughed through with grenade and bayonet. Burrows could track the Maori progress: 'It was easy enough to see how far they had progressed both by the flashes and the explosions and also by the truly fearsome clamour that went up every time an assault was made on an enemy post.'

Maori etched their names deeper into New Zealand military lore that morning and during the days that followed. Humphrey Dyer, a staff officer attached to the Maori Battalion, described a spontaneous charge by the Maori during the failed counter-attack as the finest action he saw. 'I believe that for sheer inherent courage, it was unsurpassed in the Middle East.' About 100 metres in front of a group of Maori soldiers, the Germans erected a Nazi banner supported by two poles. A sergeant from the 23rd Battalion was with the Maori looking at the banner with its familiar red background with the white circle and the black swastika. Dyer asked him what he was doing there. 'The Maoris can fight,' he said, 'I'm staying here.'

Dyer wrote what happened next:

As a man, the Maoris rose where they lay, a scattered bank of dark figures under trees. With knees bent, and leaning to the right, they slowly advanced, firing at the hip. They did not haka. Instead, there rose from their throats a deep shout — 'Ah! Ah! Ah!' — as they advanced firing. The Huns with their fat behinds to us going for their lives down the gully and then our job to hold the Maoris in.

Their ammunition spent, the Maori continued the charge, now with bayonets levelled, still uttering their menacing mantra.

'When one considers what the Maoris had been through,' Dyer wrote, 'and the position and state we were all in and think of the spontaneous nature of that charge — the ancestral fighting urge was a truly magnificent thing.'

Some Maori who thought that enough was enough soon discovered that it wasn't. The battalion commander, George Dittmer, like Burrows conspicuous throughout the fighting, came across some of his men taking cover from the heavy German fire. 'Call yourselves bloody soldiers,' he said with emphasis, and moved on. The taunt found its mark. The men rose and followed their leader.

As the sun rose on another Cretan day, the German aircraft came in a constant stream: some fighters strafing and diving with their piercing whistles, some bombing, some landing and disgorging yet more troops who, properly equipped, went straight into battle. The end became inevitable. By mid-afternoon, with both the 20th and the 28th Battalions pinned down and unable to advance further, and with failed communications again ensuring no one had a full picture of the battle, it was apparent it was all over. Charlie Upham and his platoon sergeant, Dave Kirk, indulged in more heroics as they made sure that all of the 20th's companies received the order to withdraw. It was another paragraph in Upham's VC citation; it was in Kirk's citation for his Distinguished Conduct Medal.

Upham was quoted in the 20th's *Official History* volume as saying: 'With another hour we could have reached the far side of the drome.' But they didn't have another hour; the late start had seen to that. The Germans showed they did not like fighting in the dark, especially against the Maori. They were unprepared for the battle that was unleashed on them: some were in bed, some without boots, some eating, one was captured wearing just his identity disc. But in the daylight, with aircraft overhead and NCOs and officers to lead, the German fighting man was a different proposition.

The 20th historians, Dave Pringle and Bill Glue, likened the counter-attack to Inkerman, the battle in the Crimean War that was fought in so much fog commanders had no idea what was going on and all that maintained the momentum was the initiative of individual soldiers. But Inkerman was a victory for the British and French and was said to have sapped the will of their enemy, the Russians. For these Allies nearly a hundred years later, their Inkerman was a loss.

On the night of the 22nd, it was decided to abandon further attacks on the Maleme aerodrome and to withdraw further west. The withdrawal was duly carried out with Maori forming the rearguard, and they were last out at about 6.30 am on the 23rd. The aerodrome had effectively been handed over to the Germans. It was an acknowledgement by Freyberg that Crete could not be held.

But even if the counter-attack had succeeded, even if the Australians had been able to keep to the timetable and if Upham had got his extra hour, what difference in the long run would it have made? It would have meant the Allies held Maleme but would almost certainly have faced an immediate counter-attack with all the air might the Germans could bring to bear. But even if Freyberg's men could have held out, and held out again, for how long could they have held the island, never mind a small, flat part of it? The Germans, despite their seaborne supplies going to the bottom, were still being constantly supplied by air and still would have been if Maleme had been lost to them; they would have gone elsewhere or flattened more land. But the Allies were slowly being strangled of supplies. The navy, for all its success during the night, was still losing ships at an alarming rate and warships could not double as merchantmen indefinitely. The naval commander, Andrew Cunningham, showed clearly enough a week later that the navy had reached its limit.

The counter-attack, like the defence of the island overall, could have been no more than a delaying tactic.

While the New Zealanders waited for the Australians to arrive, while commanders from both fretted at the delays, they at least had the distraction out to sea of what they assumed, correctly as it turned out, was the Royal Navy engaging with the seaborne assault. From shortly before midnight, the firing of heavy guns could occasionally be heard, the rhythmic sweep of searchlights could be seen and, every so often, the glow of a ship on fire could be seen far out to sea. This was the beginning of the 'seaborne invasion' long threatened and which had preyed so much on Freyberg's mind. The Germans had total control of the air but Britannia still ruled the waves — at least for the time being. In that first engagement with German vessels taking reinforcements and equipment to Crete, at least a dozen caiques — the distinctive Aegean fishing boats — were sunk, along with some steamers. An Italian torpedo boat protecting the flotilla was badly damaged.

There was another naval engagement a few hours later in which more caiques, carrying fresh German troops, were sunk or chased back to Greece. The British naval attack was not unopposed. The second was in daylight hours and the flotilla had constant air support and the navy suffered. On 21 May, the destroyer *Juno* was sunk and the cruiser *Ajax*, a name so familiar to New Zealanders for its association with the Battle of the River Plate, was slightly damaged. The next day, the cruisers *Naiad* and *Carlisle* and the battleship *Warspite* were damaged. The destroyer *Greyhound* was caught on its own and sunk and the cruisers *Gloucester* and *Fiji* went to help. They were both sunk as they withdrew after picking up the *Greyhound*'s survivors. (The padre on the *Fiji* was Kit Tanner, who had played five rugby tests for England. He died after repeatedly entering the water to rescue survivors and ensure wounded were transferred to rescue craft. He was posthumously awarded the Albert Medal.) On the 23rd, Lord Mountbatten led a five-ship flotilla to bomb Maleme, and while they were withdrawing from that, Mountbatten's *Kelly* and the *Kashmir* were both sunk.

Mountbatten, rich with royal blood, later wrote a vivid letter to his sister, the Queen of Sweden, about how he tried to turn the *Kelly* this way and that to avoid the diving Stukas, but there were too many and they had all the advantages. He described how the ship went under the water still at full speed ahead and how he clamped his mouth shut with one hand so he wouldn't gulp sea water down into his lungs. He thought he was breathing his last but eventually bobbed to the surface to be confronted by one of his Cockney petty officers, who said, with an innocent air but a smile: 'Extraordinary how the scum always comes to the top, isn't it sir?' Injured sailors were put in the one raft that had been unleashed and Mountbatten and the others clung to the sides until they were rescued by another of the ships in the flotilla, the *Kipling*. (In one of those small-world coincidences, the commander of the *Greyhound* was Roger Marshall-A'Deane, a British officer who married into the A'Deane family in Hawke's Bay and took the name of his wife, Margaret. Marshall-A'Deane was apparently standing with Mountbatten when he saw sailors in the water still needing help; he dived in and was never seen again.)

Winston Churchill in a portrait distributed with the *Weekly News* in 1936.

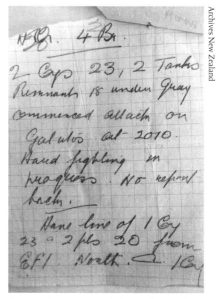

Rex King pictured in 1939 when captain of the New Zealand rugby league team.

A page from Howard Kippenberger's notebook describing the Galatas attack.

Freyberg at his desk in the New Zealand Division's camp at Maadi near Cairo.

Left: German paratroopers get a trim before the battle.

Below: New Zealand machine-gunners relax before the battle.

Tired men sleep on the deck of the ship taking them from Greece to Crete.

The man who planned it all, General Kurt Student.

This German parachutist did not have time to disentangle himself.

Left: One of the first makeshift
German graves erected on Crete.

\

Below: German aircraft flying in.

Above: A much-used photograph shows Jack Griffiths making sure it's only a photo being shot near his boss, Bernard Freyberg, during the attack.

Right: Peter McIntyre in action later in the war.

A sketch by Peter McIntyre of parachutists landing near a New Zealand hospital.

A group of the New Zealanders who saw the king to safety. Front and centre is Win Ryan.

Maori in their 'pt haka' put on for the king.

The story of the *Kelly* inspired Noel Coward to write, direct and star in a film loosely based on it, *In Which We Serve*, which was made the following year. Coward spent a fair part of 1943 in the Middle East and even wrote a diary based on his exploits. He recounted how he met an 'immense young New Zealander', Sandy Thomas, at a Cairo party 'and he told us,' Coward recorded, 'lucidly and with brilliant economy of words, a fantastic story. He is obviously a lion-hearted young man. This became more and more apparent as he so persistently deprecated his own exploits.' Coward didn't let on about the nature of the story, but it was probably Thomas's escape from the Germans in Greece and the time he spent among monks.

Meanwhile, the fighting on Crete had become a series of counter-attacks and rearguard actions. Since losing the aerodrome on the first night, Freyberg's forces had only been able to react; the Germans set the tone for all that followed. It seemed a need to do something, or to be seen to be doing something, born out of desperation and frustration, kept the soldiers going.

It wasn't just soldiers. Sailors and airmen who had ground roles at Maleme also got caught up in the fighting. One naval officer recalled:

> We were a motley collection about 200 strong. We didn't know where our own people were; we didn't know where the enemy were. Many people had no rifles. Many people had rifles and no ammunition. Everyone was desperately tired, thirsty and hungry … if anyone fired at you, he might be a) an enemy, b) a friend who thought you were the enemy, c) a friend or an enemy who didn't know what the hell you were or d) someone not firing at you at all.

There was the frenzied, insane attack at Galatas on the second night by a collection of Greek civilians and soldiers led by a 24-year-old British officer, Michael Forrester, clad in what seemed to be only a yellow-khaki army jersey. It was so many sizes too big for him that it fell to his knees and covered his shorts. In this bizarre garb, shouting all manner of imprecations, he led the Greeks up the hill. There were soldiers among them, it is true, some with their First World War rifles and some with American Springfields they'd found somewhere, some with rifles without bayonets and some with bayonets without rifles. But there were also Cretan women in their ankle-length, heavy dresses brandishing knives or meathooks or whatever else looked suitably menacing, and old men and boys (the fighting age Cretans were still in Greece), brandishing sticks, axes, anything they could find, all the while galloping full tilt up the hill. One Greek had a bread knife with a blade with a serrated edge tied to his rifle barrel as a makeshift bayonet. The Germans, being sensible, well-trained soldiers, turned and ran. They could handle their own kind, but not this.

Howard Kippenberger, in charge of the composite 10th Brigade which included this polyglot force, if force it could be called, was stunned and stared. Forrester, yet another of the special breed of young Englishmen, had been with the military mission in Athens and joined Freyberg's staff, whereupon he was told to get over to the remnants of the 6th Greek Regiment and try to rally them to prevent the Germans taking Galatas. Kippenberger had been waiting for Bill Carson to lead his artillery men to deter the Germans 'when a most infernal uproar broke out across the valley. Over an open space in the trees near Galatas came running, bounding and yelling like Red Indians, about a hundred Greeks and villagers including women and children, led by Michael Forrester twenty yards ahead.'

It was improvised fighting such as this that was characteristic of Crete. And it was such courage by Greeks that prompted Winston Churchill to say earlier in the year when the Italians had been beaten back in Greece: 'Hence we will not say that Greeks fight like heroes, but that heroes fight like Greeks.'

Supporting and covering the Greeks were men of Petrol Company and its commanding officer, Captain Harold Rowe, was indignant, according to Dan Davin, that there were thoughts the company may not have been able to do what the Greeks did. 'Div Pet are and will remain in their original positions,' Rowe told Kippenberger. So they were, but they had no bayonets and were five rifles short of their numerical strength. They were mainly drivers and technicians, they had had no training as infantry fighters, but there they were, fighting and holding what they were asked to hold. The Petrol Company and the Greeks were later joined by what remained of Divisional Cavalry, an armoured unit much reduced in strength commanded by John Russell. He was a military man to his toenails: his father was Guy Russell, who commanded the New Zealand Division for most of the First World War; his grandfather and great-grandfather had been career soldiers. Russell was killed in action in the Western Desert in 1942.

The role of the Petrol Company in such a fierce battle as Crete was typical of units which were not frontline troops. Circumstances turned them into a fighting spearhead, even though they had neither the weapons nor the training. Over the 10 days or so of fighting on Crete, the company lost 25 killed or died of wounds, 62 wounded and 120 left on the island to fend for themselves as best they could. Only one officer and 49 men of Petrol Company made it back unharmed to Egypt. Three of the company's casualties were brothers — Ivan and Colin Standen were both killed on Crete and Aubrey Douglas Standen, known as Ben, was left behind wounded and spent the rest of the war in prison camps in Germany. Three other sons of Marion and Arthur Standen of Wellington served in other units of the 2nd NZEF.

Some men on Crete gave up their own chances of freedom for the sake of others. This was the case for the 23rd Battalion's medical officer, Ron Stewart, padre Bob Griffiths and two orderlies, John Walsh and Bill Buchanan. When the battalions of the 5th Brigade had to withdraw from the Maleme sector, priority was given to the walking wounded and they were helped out in darkness. But about 60 stretcher cases remained in the 23rd regimental aid post, and the four men saw it as their duty to remain with their charges, which included some Germans. It was a selfless act of devotion to their jobs, especially given they had no idea how ruthless the Germans might be with them, and they were described as 'brave and courageous gentlemen' by one of the 23rd officers, Bert Thomason. But historian Angus Ross saw pragmatism ahead of sentiment. Given the continuing needs of the battalion, he wrote, and the problems replacing these trained men, it was an unnecessary sacrifice. All four were captured and sent to prison camps, but Buchanan escaped at

Salonika by tunnelling under the wire. (Stewart took up postgraduate studies in Britain when he was freed in 1945 and spent the rest of his life as a general practitioner in Gore. When he died in 1983, his obituary in the *Medical Journal* said of his time as a prisoner: '… he was a magnificent medical officer and a tremendous help to all his colleagues in the four years of their incarceration'.) Two other doctors who were captured in order to save their patients were Fred Moody and Selwyn de Clive-Lowe, the capture of the latter leading to an extraordinary coincidence. His brother Trevor, also a doctor, was captured in North Africa later in 1941 and was initially taken to Crete where he was held captive in the same building in which Selwyn had previously been held. Another cleric who chose to remain behind with wounded was Walter Hurst, the first padre appointed to the 22nd Battalion. He spent the rest of the war as a prisoner. Hurst later became the dean of Wellington Cathedral and set up Samaritans, the welfare organisation.

The nature of the terrain and the fighting led to many instances of personal initiative. A few men of the field punishment centre had acquired German light machine-guns and considerable ammunition. This proved an invaluable supplement to their meagre armament, but the booty was so difficult to carry around they considered abandoning it. Then one of them hit on the idea of borrowing a donkey and, to do this, three of the men crept into German-held territory. They found and captured their quarry which immediately became a beast of burden for them. They headed back to their battalion and along the way stumbled into a fight, in which their recently acquired arms proved useful. They then rejoined the 22nd Battalion, to be greeted by its commander, Les Andrew, with the remark: 'What have you been pinching this time?'

It was obvious to all that the battle, if not already lost, was being lost and it was just a question of how long the Commonwealth soldiers could hold out. During one withdrawal to new positions, Sandy Thomas, then a 23rd Battalion lieutenant, wrote about trudging mile after mile but with discipline maintained. 'Everyone was tired,' he wrote. 'All were vaguely resentful, although none of us could have put a finger on the reason.'

The Germans continued to pour reinforcements into Maleme so while one side was gradually running out of its supplies and equipment, deficient to begin with, the other was gradually building its up. Five days after the initial parachute landings, equipment such as motorcycles complete with sidecars was unloaded at Maleme and the aerodrome had become a base for the first squadron of fighter aircraft. German firepower became greater than it had been in the frantic first days while, for the New Zealanders, firepower was becoming just a memory: machine-gunners of the 27th Battalion didn't have machine-guns and the artillery had either to abandon or destroy its guns in retreat. Practically all the defenders on the island, whatever branch of service they may have been, by then were fighting as infantry.

Some of the New Zealanders looked back nostalgically to the fighting on the first day when they had captured a German with a big Nazi flag. He told them it was to be used as a ground signal for the dropping of supplies. Thomason and Thomas of 23rd Battalion spread the flag out and weighted it down, then waited to see what would happen. Not long after, transport aircraft roared over and dropped containers carrying mortars and bombs, snipers' rifles, machine-guns, hand grenades and even food. Such bounty from above was a thing of the past.

The village of Galatas and its surrounding slopes became an increasing focus of the defensive effort as the Germans moved in and for a time established a gap between the 18th and Composite Battalions. Kippenberger was worried that if the gap widened or became permanent, New Zealand forces would be separated and some perhaps cut off. All available men were sent in to help plug the gap. Among them was a platoon of signallers led by a harassed and doubtful lieutenant. He was both surprised and relieved when his small group ran into an equally small section and he saw, in the fading light, what he thought were the red patches of the infantry. 'I suppose you are on the same errand as I,' the signals man said to the other. 'What about your taking over and disposing my men too? I'm only a signals officer and I'm afraid that I don't know much about infantry tactics.'

The other officer stared, then laughed: 'Only a signals officer! What the hell do you think I am? I'm only a bloody bandmaster!' Signallers and the other group, comprising bandsmen and the Kiwi Concert Party, dissolved into helpless laughter, according to the Divisional Signals *Official History*.

It was around this time that Kippenberger went to a conference at divisional headquarters where, he thought, the atmosphere was not cheerful. 'I saw some of the Twentieth platoons moving back, looking dazed and weary to exhaustion, and for the first time felt the coming of defeat.'

At least one who did not feel a pending doom, or at least did not show it, was John Russell, who was described by a brigade major, Brian Bassett, as a sheer joy. His cheerful manner and light speech was such a tonic that Bassett recalled that every time the phone went at brigade headquarters, he hoped it would be Russell calling. One call from Russell went: 'Hello dearie, got any cigarettes? Oh, by the way, there are about a hundred Jerries coming up the road at us.' Told that reserves would be sent, Russell's reply was not to bother, he'd sort it out.

There were smaller battles within the one overriding battle, that for Crete. There was Ruin Hill, Pink Hill, Cemetery Hill, none small to the men who fought and died in them, but still skirmishes set in the frame of the bigger picture. All were in the Galatas area and that was a name that was destined to live on and, as so often in martial memories, because it was where men made a statement, even though it was a loss.

Even the Germans marvelled at the resistance and resilience of the New Zealanders. While there was only one Allied war correspondent on the island, Robin Miller of the 2nd NZEF, there were three German reporters. One of them, Kurt Meyer, wrote home:

Not a New Zealander takes as much as a step backwards; one lanky fellow heaves himself out of his slit trench. He has taken out two hand grenades, one in each hand, while that in his left explodes prematurely and tears the hand off, the other he throws at the feet of the advancing Germans who are not more than three strides from him.

(At least 10 war correspondents, including seven Australians, had been fleetingly on Crete. The group, which included the *Sydney Morning Herald* reporter Gavin Long, who later became the editor of the Australian official histories, overnighted there on their way from Greece back to Egypt. They no doubt fumed into their beers at Shepheard's Hotel in Cairo at the lost opportunity. One of the best of war correspondents, Alan Moorehead of the *Daily Express*, was in Addis Ababa when he heard what was happening on Crete. He made desperate efforts to get there in time, but got only so far as the next-door island, Cyprus.)

The Germans were winning this part of the war, there was no doubt. The 18th Battalion, sent to shore up the cooks and batmen and Petrol Company men of the Composite Brigade, were grossly understrength and sorely stretched. Bill Carson arrived with some artillery drivers to lend a hand. Whatever branch of arms they were, they improvised as infantry against the best Germany had. The 18th Battalion, the specialist infantrymen, were under severe pressure. They began to retreat in the face of the unrelenting enemy fire. In places, an orderly withdrawal was a rout; in other places, the unwounded plodded along supporting the wounded; other wounded just lay where they fell, and were captured. The cheery Russell's force was isolated and in danger of remaining so.

Kippenberger, who sprained an ankle as he dived into a ditch when the paratroopers were landing on the first day, leaned on a walking stick in the road and surveyed the retreating troops, some of them in his view on the verge of panic. This was when he waved his stick and shouted: 'Stand for New Zealand! Stand every man who is a soldier!' One of his biographers, Denis McLean, called it an appeal to the elemental spirit. 'But behind that lay an understanding,' McLean wrote, 'deeply chiselled into Kip's own make-up by his experiences 25 years before on the chaotic battlefield of the Somme, that what bonds soldiers is the reminder that all are in it together, that a man does not let his comrades down.' As things turned out after Crete, it was a pity some of Kippenberger's fellow senior officers did not remember that.

In these circumstances was born the frantic charge at Galatas that has lived on as a mental battle honour if not one on an unfurled standard hanging in a church somewhere. Freyberg called it one of the great efforts of New

Zealanders in the defence of Crete. Kippenberger wrote later he knew it was no use trying to patch the line any more — 'obviously we must hit or everything would crumble away'.

They hit all right. There were the trained infantrymen led in platoons either side of the road up to Galatas by Sandy Thomas and Rex King; there were the small tanks commanded by the free-spirited Englishman Roy Farran; there was Bill Carson and some of his gunners; there was Mike Forrester, the blond Englishman, still in his poncho-sized jumper; there was John Gray, the 18th Battalion commander who not long before Kippenberger thought had aged 20 years but he charged up the hill like a young private; there was the Danish cook who somehow had become a fighting New Zealander; there were some of the concert party men and some of the bandsmen.

Of course, not all men are cut out to be heroes. Thomas, who proved himself heroic, wondered before the charge if his men were as afraid as he was. The answer was yes, they were. Thomas was able to conceal his fear and replace it with adrenaline-pumping action. But some men could not. One 23rd Battalion man was arrested by a senior officer for refusing to take part; another cowered under an olive tree, sobbing his heart out. The story of Thomas threatening to shoot an English soldier, and then the soldier being shot by another New Zealander, has often been told.

Haddon Donald told of one of his men a few days earlier who, shaking and wild-eyed, was taken to a cave where he would be protected from the constant German air attention. When Donald's men returned to retrieve him, the soldier was dead. There was not a mark on him. They immediately imposed the layman's post-mortem diagnosis that the poor chap had died of fright.

Thanks to the charge that fully occupied the attention of the Germans in the village, Russell and Harold Rowe of the Petrol Company were able to extricate their men from their difficult situations. The attack was a success and the Germans were driven out of Galatas. But it was a temporary reprieve, just a respite from the norm of increasing German dominance. Kippenberger or other commanders did not have the men or the weapons to hang on to Galatas. They discussed it, but it simply wasn't feasible. After the spectacular attack, Kippenberger joined a conference called by the brigade commander, Lindsay Inglis. Also there was Bill Gentry, staff officer from Freyberg's headquarters. They knew that if nothing was done, the Germans with air superiority would retake Galatas the following morning. They also knew that if nothing was done, it would be a step nearer defeat. Inglis was keen for an attack in force and asked George Dittmer, the commanding officer of the Maori Battalion, which, like all the others, was much depleted. 'I'll give it a go,' Dittmer responded, as Inglis must have known he would. But Gentry, ever the pragmatic professional, ruled it out. For all their losses, the Maori were the freshest of the New Zealand battalions, and if they were used to hold Galatas, they could not be used to hold the broader line. The Maori would also have been asked to advance at night through olive groves interspersed with ravines on a front that was too wide. So Galatas was conceded; it was another card in the pack to fall. The end was coming.

The frantic Galatas attack cost the 23rd Battalion dear. All of C Company's officers and most of its non-commissioned officers became casualties; by the next morning, only about 30 men were left standing. When the time came eventually to quit the island, the battalion had suffered 299 casualties from a strength at the start of the battle of 571.

Ian Stewart, the Welch Battalion doctor who wrote one of the more readable books about Crete, introduced a poignant note to the Galatas tale. As the New Zealanders moved off, he wrote,

> behind them Galatas lay in silence, save only for the small muffled sounds of the wounded. Towards midnight a Cretan girl, about twelve years old, stole out from the broken masonry. She crouched over the bodies in the gutters, covering them with rugs and carpets and returning, where she found response, to offer drinks of sweet goat's milk.

The Royal Air Force continued to do what it could with bombing missions from bases in Egypt, but in the overall scheme of things they were largely ineffectual. Their lack of effectiveness did not detract from the courage and skill of their crews, who must have known the against-the-odds difficulty of their task before they set off. The New Zealanders on the ground cheered when they saw the big Blenheim bombers with the red, white and blue roundels roar in over their heads; they were so used to the big black swastikas when they looked up at the sound of aircraft engines. Then they groaned when they saw smoke trail from a Blenheim as it sought refuge after being hit by anti-aircraft fire. One Blenheim, one of a flight of four, was seen to dive and turn towards the mountains after bombing Maleme. It never made it back to base. One of its crew was a 25-year-old New Zealander, Stuart Niven.

A more disastrous raid was mounted four days later. Of six bombers involved, two collided after take-off. The remaining four bombed Maleme, but only two returned to their base. The other two aircraft were lost over the North African desert; the crew of one baled out and made it back two days later, but the other crew perished. Blenheims from a different squadron were sent the same day to bomb German positions in the Suda Bay area. One returned early with engine trouble while the other two carried on and, unable to find the positions, they bombed the aerodrome anyway. They became separated on the return journey and one of them crashed in the Qattara Depression, a superheated desert wasteland that troops in the North African fighting did their utmost to avoid. The crashed Blenheim was found by searchers three days later, but it was only on the sixth day that two of the crew, one of them a New Zealander, were found in the desert. The body of the pilot, Murray McKenzie of Canterbury, was never found.

Possibly the most tragic of the air losses was from one of the last planned raids on Crete, on the night of 29–30 May. Two Wellington bombers collided on take-off; both aircraft caught fire and their bombs exploded. Of the 12 airmen, six died including the captain of one of the aircraft, 21-year-old Henry Goodall, whose parents lived in Tauranga.

As the impossibility of holding Crete was underlined time and again, the view from afar was a little different. Officials in Cairo and London did not appreciate the gravity of the reality, partly because the communications lack meant they could not be fully informed and partly because of what they wanted to believe. Even on the 23rd, when there was still much fighting to be done but the final outcome was apparent, Churchill cabled Freyberg: 'The whole world watches your splendid battle on which great things turn.' It was a grand Churchillian phrase, but the whole world was as ignorant as he was of what was really happening.

Some strange decisions were reached in Cairo. A staff officer there dispatched a battalion of the Argyll and Sutherland Highlanders to the south coast of Crete, thinking the Scots would be ideal defence against further parachute attacks. He seemed not to have been told there had been no parachute attacks in that area and none was expected anyway because of the terrain and the distance from other German troops. And no one bothered to tell Freyberg that the troops were being sent; he only learnt of it when they arrived.

On the morning of 27 May came another of the let's-get-stuck-in-attacks seen twice at Galatas, the first by Forrester's Greeks and the second ordered by Kippenberger and led by the 23rd Battalion. The attack on the 27th came to be known as the Battle of 42nd Street because it occurred in an area where the 42nd Field Company of the Royal Engineers had camped while forming part of the Crete garrison late in 1940. The sappers bivouacked beside a narrow lane and called it 42nd Street, the name jointly inspired by their own and by the title of a popular film and song from 1939:

Come and meet those dancing feet
On the avenue I'm taking you to — Forty Second Street
Here the beat of dancing feet
It's the song I love the melody of — Forty Second Street.

It was a different rhythm being tapped out on 27 May. (Although typical of the confusion of much of the fighting at Crete the date of the battle was recorded by the Australian battalion that fought in it as 26 May. The battalion's war dairy was typed some time after the fighting so presumably the mistake crept in during the transcription of hurried notes written at the time.) It wasn't so much the date that was important as the deed. It showed that yet again, when the Allied troops had conditions in their favour and the ammunition and equipment to do something about it, they could outfight the Germans.

The Australians, the 2/7 Battalion, and the New Zealanders, mostly the Maori Battalion, held a rearguard line at 42nd Street near Canea, when the German 141st Mountain Regiment approached. They saw the Germans coming and attacked. Precisely who ordered the attack was not known and it was described later as a spontaneous charge. No one knew for sure whether the Maori or the Australians charged first, just that both seemed to charge at the same time. Dan Davin tried to sort out who did what when, but he gave up. He recorded that the Australian version was quite reconcilable with the Maori version.

The Australian diary says the Germans were about 250 yards away when the charge began; when the Anzacs had closed to a mere 50 yards, they went to ground and shot at virtually point-blank range. The Germans, not expecting any attack never mind one so ferocious, broke and ran, and the New Zealanders and Australians gave chase. 'It was crazy, crazy, crazy, the most thrilling few minutes of my life,' an Aboriginal member of the 2/7th, Reg Saunders, later wrote.

Jim Burrows of the 20th Battalion did not take part but like most soldiers on the island, soon heard of it. Back in New Zealand in 1943, he told a Christchurch Boys' High School reunion about it. One of those in the charge was an old boy of the school and Burrows reported how the old boy screamed out 'School! School!' as he ran hell for leather at the Germans, bayonet at the ready. Not far away was an old boy of the school's great rival, Christ's College. He heard the cry from the sporting field that had transferred to the battleground and responded in the only way he knew how: 'College! College!'

The air was infected with enthusiasm for the fight. The 2/7th's commanding officer, Theo Walker, wanted to join in and asked one of his men to give him his rifle and bayonet. This he could not do. Walker later recalled saying: 'I know that I should not be here, but I must be in this with you boys.'

Rangi Royal, according to the Maori Battalion history, led his men 'brandishing a bamboo walking pole like a taiaha in one hand and a revolver in the other'. Greeks, fighting like heroes again, joined in with the Maori and there were even some Spaniards there, part of a small Spanish contingent in the Layforce commandos. The Maori were, like the battalion's marching song extolled, fighting right to the end.

One of the Maori Battalion company commanders was Humphrey Dyer and, 12 years later, he wrote to another of the company leaders, Fred Baker: 'Suddenly something blew up in front and heavy MG [machine-gun] fire opened on us. There was a yell on our right and we went forward with C Company on our right shouting "Charge!"' Dyer said men of the 19th Battalion, on the left of the Maori, initially hung back, but when they saw what happened, they too joined in.

Dyer told how they overtook some Germans and bayoneted them — 'I got one at a couple of yards in Wild West style' — and some shamming dead were shot. Dyer thought some of his men no doubt remembered how some of their mates were shot at Maleme by Germans who pretended to be dead. Then he told Baker: 'Huns now running hard and we after them shouting, "Charge! Charge! The bastards are running!"'

What Dyer did not write, then or later, perhaps because he felt he could not, was what he shouted at his maximum adrenaline moment. 'Come on, you black bastards,' he exhorted the Maori. This comment was retold with much ribaldry and included in the booklet for the 22nd Battalion's 50th anniversary in 1990.

(Dyer, who had been a professional soldier then a schoolteacher before rejoining the army, later had command of the Maori Battalion but resigned his post in North Africa after he refused to obey an order from a superior officer, Lindsay Inglis. Inglis sent a general order to all units that captured enemy equipment had to be accounted for and handed in and could not be retained for personal or battalion use. Dyer, a Pakeha, protested that it was in keeping with tradition that Maori earned the right to keep booty won from the enemy. Inglis reported Dyer to Freyberg and the big boss had no choice but to support his brigadier. Dyer resigned and was replaced by Eruera Love, who became the first Maori to be the battalion's commanding officer. Dyer later wrote a book in praise of the Maori warrior, *Ma te Reinga: by way of Reinga; the way of the Maori soldier*.)

Forty-second Street gained a place in Australian folk culture. The 1970s TV soap opera *The Sullivans*, which told of how the Melbourne Sullivan family was affected by war, recreated the battle in one of its episodes. Sunbury, a Melbourne satellite town, became Crete for the occasion as one of the Sullivan boys joined in the charge.

Reports of the death toll at 42nd Street vary, but the consensus seems to be about 300 Germans were killed compared with Anzac losses in the low double figures. As the Maori Battalion historian Joseph Cody drily remarked: '... the Maoris were not further molested that day'.

There were some accusations later that war crimes were committed. Some German wounded had been deliberately killed and that some showed evidence of 'stab wounds or broken skulls'. Walker, the Australian commander, rejected the war crimes allegations and Reg Saunders agreed there were broken skulls and men were stabbed — 'it was hand to hand combat and that's what happens'.

John Clark, who helped Angus Ross with research when Ross was writing the history of the 23rd Battalion, wrote to him and told him that '42nd Street was an impromptu show with nothing much to it'. He introduced an intriguing and unexplained element when he added: 'They [the New Zealanders who took part] were under the influence but cleared the Hun from the vicinity.' If Clark meant what any reasonable reading of the phrase would mean, it would have been neither the first nor the last time that men went into battle after drinking, if only to give themselves 'Dutch courage' (if that politically incorrect phrase is still acceptable anywhere but in the Netherlands). Indeed, some of those who made the spectacular attack on Galatas were said by various sources to have had more than a passing acquaintance with Cretan wine. Haddon Donald made no bones of the fact that, denied water, he helped himself to a wine substitute when it was available.

The English doctor, Ian Stewart, thought that 42nd Street 'again revealed the sort of response that might have been obtained from these men earlier at Maleme'. This was a constant theme of Stewart's and not for nothing was his book subtitled 'A story of lost opportunity'. But the soldiers at 42nd Street did not counter-attack in force, as they would have had to have done at Maleme, and did not have to hold what they gained. The Battle of 42nd Street was a short and sharp show of defiance, nothing more. The men by then could do nothing more.

7

An island lost

'It's the New Zealanders! It's the New Zealanders!'
— Voices in the hills

It was a characteristic of the Battle for Crete that it was fought largely in three separate areas: the concentration at least in New Zealand eyes has been on the battles in the west of the island where names such as Maleme, Galatas, Suda and Canea became familiar because that was where the New Zealanders fought. It was also the area of the island on which the German general, Kurt Student, concentrated most of his forces and it was there the Germans gained the foothold that led to eventual victory.

But the battle was for the whole of the island, not part of it. How the battle evolved was determined by several factors: the geographic shape of the island; the lack of equipment, communications and even the necessities of life such as food and water available to the Allied forces under the overall command of Bernard Freyberg; the overwhelming superiority the Germans had in the air. Geoffrey Cox, a New Zealand Rhodes Scholar, journalist and intelligence officer on Freyberg's staff, said in a radio broadcast to New Zealand that the Germans could be beaten in a straight fight, man to man. But they could not be beaten when it was men against machines, and it was the Germans who had the machines.

Freyberg disposed his forces to cover the main centres with their landing grounds and harbours, all situated in the north of the island; that is, closest to the German air bases in Greece. He remarked more than once, as did other soldiers, that from an Allied point of view, Crete was upside down. Freyberg would much rather have had Crete's south coast, with its precipitous cliffs and lack of beaches and towns, facing Greece. Freyberg's forces were stationed to the west to cover the Maleme-Canea-Suda area; in the centre to cover Retimo and in the east to cover Heraklion.

The problems began after the German invasion on 20 May and Freyberg's lack of equipment was exposed. He had no armour and little transport so even if he could have organised a brigade-strength force to act as a mobile reserve, he had no protection for it and no way of getting it from one point to another. The German air superiority, combined with the Allied lack of transport and anti-aircraft hardware, meant that each of Freyberg's defensive areas was forced to fight as self-contained enclaves. Even worse, the poor communications meant that news filtered only slowly from one area to another and sometimes not at all. This lack of communication had the most tragic consequences for the Australian and Greek troops assigned to the Retimo area.

The Australians arrived on Crete from Greece on 29 April and the next day settled into defensive positions at Retimo, where 2300 Greek troops waited. Their existence there was much the same as it had been for others in the Canea area for the first three weeks: defensive positions were prepared as well as they could be and men generally had a relaxing time, aside from the daily strafing, until the invasion on 20 May. The Australians had such a good time that the village of Retimo and a couple of small outlying areas were declared out of bounds to troops 'as a few men early on proved their inability to appreciate the potency of the Greek and Cretan wines'. The cordial relations which developed with the local population paid off handsomely when the fighting began, according to the war diary of the 2/1 Battalion. The garrison's commanding officer, Ian Campbell, knew well the limitations of his command. They were under-equipped, like everywhere else, they had lost key personnel in Greece and the Greek troops for whom he was responsible were both poorly trained and poorly equipped, although they included a highly regarded unit of 800 Cretan police.

And the Australians and Greeks at Retimo, as elsewhere, were up against German forces which were well trained, well equipped and highly motivated.

Two German parachute battalions floated down onto the Retimo positions during the morning of 20 May and there seemed initial success for Campbell and his mixed force when the German commander, Alfred Sturm, and his regimental headquarters landed slap bang in the middle of the happy Aussies. The surviving Germans were in two groups, one to the east defending grimly and the other also on the defensive between the Australians and the Cretan police. Campbell got a message to Freyberg saying he needed reinforcements but was told none was available — he was on his own.

And on his own he remained. The Germans gradually consolidated their positions and gained fresh men and more equipment. The result was that the Retimo garrison was effectively cut off from the rest of the island. The Germans interrupted what communications there were except for one line to Freyberg's headquarters and eventually that too was cut. Campbell learned what was happening on other parts of the island more by chance than by formal channels of communication. To all intents and purposes, he exercised an independent command.

On the third day of the invasion, Campbell and the German commander agreed on a truce so both sides could bury their dead and recover wounded; this was a remarkably similar experience to what happened on Gallipoli 26 years before, almost to the day. The German command headquarters was based in an olive oil factory and, during the truce, an officer emerged from the factory with a demand for unconditional surrender. He told Campbell that the German landings on other parts of the island had succeeded and that the Australians' position would ultimately be hopeless.

'Naturally I refused his demand,' Campbell later wrote, 'and we expended a few more of our precious shells on his factory when the truce terminated.' But Campbell also accepted 80 walking wounded Germans from the factory, which he noted meant the strain on the German rations was transferred to him. But he said that, as a prisoner of war later, he was glad he had.

Campbell and his troops did as much as they could and Freyberg, in a message he was able to get through to him, remarked: 'You have done magnificently.' But for all the magnificence, they were encircled and they could not break the German hold. Freyberg sent reinforcements in the form of the 1st Rangers, part of the King's Royal Rifle Corps who had survived Greece. The Rangers were motorised infantry bereft of their motors and they had no artillery support either; the Germans made quick work of them. Campbell in a letter to doctor and writer Ian Stewart long after the war said he received a message that the Rangers had 'come a gutza'.

Further east at Heraklion, things went much better for the Allies. Brian Chappel, the former Indian Army general who was in charge, had with him more than 3000 fully equipped British and Australian infantry as well as three Greek battalions and ancilliary troops. The Argyll and Sutherland Highlanders, who had been deposited on Crete without Freyberg knowing, had found their way to Chappel's command. Also there was The Black Watch, who were prominent in the first-day resistance that led to something of a stalemate at Heraklion. A regimental history written by Bernard Fergusson (a onetime lieutenant-colonel in the regiment and later New Zealand governor-general) quoted one of the German commanders as saying of the assault on Heraklion: 'My first surprise was when I found that position was held. My second was when I discovered who the infantry were. The battle continued with great ferocity but The Black Watch never surrendered. Had it been any other regiment, all would have been well.'

While such a ringing encomium about an enemy sits easily in Black Watch history, the fighting at Heraklion was neither as prolonged nor as desperate as all that. Fighting in the Heraklion area occurred mainly in daylight hours. As one of Chappel's officers later wrote:

> … for by a tacit and mute understanding no firing took place at night; it would have inconvenienced both sides equally. For this was the time when what had to be done was done, when the casualties were evacuated, the dead were buried, the rations and ammunition distributed, and the men were able to walk about and stretch their legs.

This must have been galling to the men in the fight of their lives further west, had they known of it. Freyberg sought from Chappel reinforcements for Suda Bay, but none other than a couple of light tanks sent by barge were forthcoming. Heraklion, as with most of the rest of the island, was at times isolated because of poor communications and for some of the time messages between Chappel and Freyberg's headquarters had to go via Cairo. One of the difficulties in post-war analyses of what happened at Heraklion or, more pertinently, what did not happen, was that very few messages survived. Chappel himself apparently said little or nothing about Crete before he died in 1964. He left the army two years after the war and spent the rest of his working life with the Red Cross. As an obituary remarked: 'As a man Chappel was distinguished chiefly for his modest character and reticent disposition and for his loyalty to friends. It was said of him that he spared no pains to conceal the details of a highly creditable military career, even from the closest members of his family circle.' If he was reluctant to tell close family members about what happened on Crete and why he made decisions he did, war historians must have gone knocking on his door in vain.

While the Australians fought as well as they could at Retimo and while office hours were kept at Heraklion, in the west the inevitable came ever closer. It became a question of which came first: the end of the month or the end of the battle. It was almost a tie. Things in the Canea sector which bore the brunt of the fighting became even more confused and there was a time when battalions did not know to which brigade they belonged or who was giving orders to whom. Decisions by James Hargest were questioned early in the fighting; now it was the turn of Hargest's superior, Edward Puttick, the stand-in division commander, to come in for some criticism; so too one of his brigadiers, Lindsay Inglis, and the Marines general who had preceded Freyberg in overall command, Eric Weston. At one point, Weston accused Puttick of being 'cavalier in the extreme' in countermanding an order from Freyberg. And Freyberg himself thought Inglis had ducked responsibility.

Whatever the senior men did or did not do, say or did not say, those lower down the military command chain kept on fighting and defending, knowing that sooner or later three or four things would happen to them: they could be killed, they could be wounded, they could be wounded and captured, they could be left alone and isolated or, best option of all, they could be evacuated for the second time in a month. They would be beaten again, but at least in a position to fight another day.

Freyberg, for whom dedication to duty was paramount and among his duties was the care and welfare of the men under his command, knew it was time to get out. Quite apart from the increasing number of Germans and their superior equipment, the Allied soldiers on the island were unspeakably tired and at the end of their tether. They were underfed, dehydrated — and turning water into wine may sound fine but it's not what an undernourished body needs — tired and their nerves were frazzled. Many carried wounds that in normal circumstances would have seen them lying on hospital beds.

On the morning of 26 May, Freyberg spelt it out as clearly as he could to Archie Wavell who, like Churchill and anyone else not on the island, did not have a real understanding of conditions and prospects. 'I regret to have to report that in my opinion the limit of endurance has been reached by the troops under my command ... No matter what decision is taken by the Commanders-in-Chief from a military point of view our position here is hopeless.'

Freyberg went on to say it was already too late for all his troops to be evacuated, but quick action would save as many as possible. More than 30 hours later, the afternoon of the 27th, Freyberg received acknowledgement from Wavell that evacuation could begin. It took that amount of time for staff officers in Cairo and politicians in London to realise that for all their hopes and for all the fine rhetoric about 'all costs', the only option was to take the word of the man in command who knew, rather than just thought, what was going on.

And so the process of evacuation began, later than it should have, slower than it could have. Those who compared it with the end in Gallipoli 26 years before knew the differences: the evacuation of the peninsula then was a masterstroke of military planning. Not a man was lost and the Turks had no idea the Allies were going until they had gone. Crete was much, much different. Men stayed to fight rearguard actions while long lines of soldiers snaked over the White Mountains to the congested little south coast town of Sfakia that became the object of all men's desires. The Greek battalions and the Cretan policemen and the civilians fought valiantly to stave off the Germans so their new friends, the British and the New Zealanders and Australians, could get away to fight again.

A new mark of heroism arose as men fought not to kill or to stay alive but stayed and fought in order that others might get away. But war, for all the glories assigned to it, is never only about sacrifice and selflessness. As the march to the sea became a rush, and as the navy ships came and went, came and went, and the last one came closer, some men discarded their military discipline and their humanity. Friend fought friend, Brit fought Australian fought New Zealander, mate cheated mate. The valorous Clive Hulme spoke about how he was set upon by Aussies.

For the evacuation of Crete to have succeeded, however, such shortcomings in human behaviour had to have been in the minority. And of course they were not exclusive to Crete. Men can never know how they are going to react in moments of extreme stress on a battlefield until they have to. Ian Stewart, on Crete as a doctor, saw it clearly: 'During the fighting, as in all fighting, some men had lost forever, in 10 minutes of action, a reputation acquired in 20 years as a peacetime soldier.'

Some men were magnificent under stress. Small groups of soldiers or individuals not attached to any unit for various reasons made their way slowly along the long and winding road over the mountains. Sometimes they stopped and made their own little camps, blocking the path of formed units which were following. In one of the gorges on the southern side of the range, such men gathered. It was an area known as Komitadhes Ravine, but pretty soon it was known as Rhododendron Valley, perhaps because of its flora but also perhaps a nominal echo of Gallipoli — the Australians and New Zealanders in 1941 would have known of the part played by Rhododendron Spur in 1915.

Individuals and groups gathered in the ravine, for the most part hungry and thirsty, many of them wounded, certainly all of them footsore and tired beyond belief. There were complaints about why they were on Crete and who was to blame, and there were concerns about what would happen to them.

Men such as these stragglers needed to be organised and an artillery major, Mervyn Bull, became the chief organiser. He was a schoolteacher by profession, a good bloke by inclination. He first started collecting disparate groups of New Zealanders together then added other nationalities to his growing flock. It got to the point that he, tired and thirsty and as knackered as the rest, assumed control and responsibility for the lot. He organised them into parties of 50 and got other artillery officers to compile nominal rolls of each group so a track could be kept of movements. He tried to get food and water for them all but succeeded only in getting enough for one tin of bully beef for each group. He dispatched a lieutenant, Donald Allison from Nelson, to the beach with a group of men to rustle up as much food as he could gather. An officer on the beach established who Allison and the men were and told them to stay where they were and embark on a ship that night. Allison refused on the grounds that his duty was to report to Bull.

Among those who passed through the ravine was Jim Hargest, who by most accounts was exemplary in organising and controlling the gradual movement of soldiers across the mountains. Hargest told Bull that six artillery specialists would have to go that night and Bull and the rest of his men the following night. Bull refused, saying it would be bad for morale if he left the men for whom he was caring. By this time, more than 3500 men were part of the Bull brigade: just about every nationality on the island was represented. Bull, Allison and the others stayed; they received an order from Eric Weston to surrender and sadly raised a white flag. Some of the men, disgusted, pulled it back down again. They spent the rest of the war in prison camps. After the war, Bull became the longest-serving rector at Timaru Boys' High School.

Freyberg by this time was in a cave in the cliffs overlooking Sfakia. There was little left that he could do and he was most reluctant to leave the island while other men remained; his attitude was that of a ship's captain. He sat in the cave with men such as John White, his personal assistant; Jack Griffiths, his aide-de-camp; and George Beamish, the last air force officer on the island.

White didn't stay there long. Freyberg wrote a brief account of his views of the battle and sent White on the next ship to Alexandria with it. His second sentence summed up the prevailing view, a view with which the beneficiaries of hindsight have not always been in accord: 'The troops were not beaten by ordinary conditions, but by the great aerial concentration against us ... The bombing is what has beaten us, the strafing having turned us out of position after position.' He said the defeat was not the fault of the troops.

The way to the beach was guarded and only organised or authorised units could get through. Individuals were not allowed to pass. Arthur Helm, who reckoned he laid and relaid every telephone wire on Crete, was with a unit that had the authority to get to the beach. He and his men had to thread their way past hundreds of waiting, tired men. 'Who are you? Where are you going?' they'd say. 'We had been told not to answer them, but the temptation was too great,' Helm recorded. (It should be noted in a kindly way that, for Helm, silence was frequently an impossible condition. He could talk, as the saying went at the time, the leg off a chair.) 'We told them that we were going to take up a position to fight the rearguard action and invited them to come with us. There were no volunteers.'

Strangely, the mass of men heading for what they thought was salvation was not overly troubled by German pursuit. The enemy aircraft did not fly at night and during the day attacks were sporadic at best. It was one of the few things that went right. The Germans did not leave them entirely alone, though. A small German party of infantry was seen close to Freyberg's headquarters on the slopes overlooking the sea. Two companies of the 20th Battalion were sent off to sort it out. One of them was C Company, Charlie Upham's. He and his men were desperately tired and sore; Upham was so badly wounded and ill with dysentery that in any other circumstances he would have been on a stretcher or hospital bed. The men, like all the others, were thirsty and hungry. But there was a threat to the man they called 'The General' and that could not be tolerated. One company crept around the lower slopes looking for its quarry; Upham's went for the high ground, intending to attack from above. It was a 600-foot climb, an Everest for weary men. Watchers could see them slowly making their way up as the lower company engaged the attention of the Germans. Two hours went by. Sometimes Upham's men could be seen in the distance, sometimes not. There was a sharp burst of firing, lasting about a minute. Then some single shots. Crack! Crack! Then the C Company men could be seen descending. Word came through soon after that all 22 Germans had been killed. No C Company men had been touched.

It was in the nature of the battle itself and of the gradual withdrawal that the formed and more able fighting units would be required for rearguard duty and would therefore be the last down to the beach. Hargest was in charge and he ensured that his men would act and look like soldiers until the last. He was in charge of a brigade, but it was not of brigade strength: it was estimated to be perhaps 1100 men and as they progressed men along the way tried to join them. Some did. Gunners, engineers, bandsmen, medical orderlies — anyone without a unit just tacked themselves onto the Hargest brigade. Some of Bull's strays became Hargest's. Not all were allowed to stay. Hargest had issued orders that anyone without a rifle was a straggler and could find his own way.

Navy ships waiting offshore had already taken on troops and made their way to Alexandria and back when Hargest led his men down from the hills at close to dusk. He wanted them to look like soldiers. He'd ensured there was sufficient water not just for them to drink but to shave as well. (A lumbering old car commandeered for the purpose was sent back to a village to fetch as much water as it could carry.) They wore as close to their full uniform as they could. They carried weapons in the manner prescribed. Ahead of them on the rough track were soldiers who had been waiting and hoping. They resented queue jumpers, who were regarded as low a form of life as water-stealers and cigarette-pilferers. But the word had gone on ahead: 'It's the New Zealanders. It's the New Zealanders.' Men got to their feet and moved out of the way in silent respect. Some saluted in the near-dark.

The embarkation was as confused as the battle had been. No one knew who was going, how many could go, or when. Some were told to stay and mentally they adjusted to life as a prisoner of war; then they were told they could go. And the reverse. Freyberg sent for Hargest and told him he had to choose which of his battalions would have to stay. It was a terrible decision for a man to have to make. He sent for John Allen, a 40-year-old recently appointed officer commanding the 21st Battalion. Hargest recalled telling him: 'I have to choose, John. Your Battalion with its attached troops is the strongest; you yourself are the youngest CO and are freshest — you have to stay.' Allen 'took it like a man'.

As it turned out, Allen didn't have to stay and he continued the fight in North Africa but was killed in action later in the year.

Hargest described his last moments on Crete in a letter to his wife Marie in Invercargill:

> The last time I wrote was two days ago in a cave overlooking the sea in the cruellest area I've ever seen and although I wrote as though I was certain of getting off, I was far from being sanguine — the trouble was that I knew too much of the hazards — the shipping difficulty — the enemy bombers, the probability of a failure of contact. All that dreadful day I stayed at Force HQ as NZ's representative self-appointed, and determined to get every man off with me who could … that's the main thing, I came off with my brigade … our battalions are shattered and equipment gone — our clothes scattered, but we marched down to the boats from the hills as a brigade with our arms in our hands and went aboard. If I never accomplish anything more in this life, at least I've done that and when you hear of the fighting in Crete being among the fiercest in history, at least you can say that was our brigade.

It was on the night of the last day in May that Hargest filed on to the navy's landing craft with his men. The Marines general, Weston, was leaving by flying boat and sent a message for Hargest to join him. 'I declined,' Hargest wrote in his diary, 'but he himself came and said, "You can do no more here; you may be urgently needed in Cairo. I must order you and your staff to come with me." That settled it. We went.'

Freyberg and his staff also went by Sunderland flying boat, Freyberg going only because of a direct and specific order from Wavell. Senior generals don't thumb their noses at more senior generals.

Bob Laycock's Commandos took over the task of defending the rear from the New Zealanders, and when Weston ordered them to the beach, an Australian brigade was given the job. They fought, as they had fought at Suda and elsewhere, with the phlegmatic purpose of their nationality: the attitude of let's get on with the job and worry about it later. Like the New Zealanders before them, the Australians finally made their way down to the beach, filing past the hundreds of unarmed men, some of them wounded, cramming the narrow tracks. One of the Australians called it 'nightmare country'. The spearhead of the Australians made it onto the beach and battalion commander Theo Walker sent some men on to a landing craft. He joined them, but promptly disembarked when he realised the bulk of his battalion were going nowhere. The landing craft full of troops made its way out to the last of the British ships. One of the officers remarked the battalion on shore stood 'quiet and orderly in its ranks'.

The battalion second in command, Ken Marshall, wrote: 'I found Theo and we sat on the edge of the stone sea wall. He told me that things were all up and the navy had gone.' A few hours later, some of Walker's men approached him and said that further along the coast some Australians were flying white flags: 'Shall we shoot them?' they asked. Walker went and saw them, realised how hopeless was their position, told them to destroy their equipment and escape if they could. Walker himself climbed back up the road until he came to a German officer, who happened to be an Austrian, and surrendered to him. The Australian official historian, Gavin Long, reported the exchange: 'What are you doing here, Australia?' asked the Austrian, in English. 'One might ask what are you doing here, Austria?' replied Walker. 'We are all Germans,' said the Austrian.

For the Australians defending at Retimo, things were 'all up' there as well. Surrounded by superior German forces, Campbell knew when to fight and when not. The end of May was a time to not fight. The war diary for the Australian's 2/11 Battalion carried the finality of the fight: 'The CO explained that further resistance by the Bn alone was obviously hopeless. He said every man should be given the option of surrendering to the enemy or making off into the hills with the hope of being picked up from the south side of the island.'

It then made the telling comment: 'At this time nobody had any idea that troops on other parts of the island had been or were to be evacuated.' The bane of the whole battle, poor to non-existent communications, played its last malevolent trick on the Aussies. In one last desperate attempt by Freyberg and Wavell to let the Australians at Retimo know what was going on, an RAF aircraft was dispatched from Alexandria with the intention of dropping orders to the besieged men. But the aircraft never appeared; the drop never happened.

Campbell called a conference of his senior officers and told them the position. When the conference ended, some decided to surrender but some chose to run. Ray Sandover, who commanded the 2/11 Battalion, declared his men would not surrender and he told them it was every man for himself. Go for the hills, he told them. Campbell was commander of 2/1 Battalion and doubled as the brigade commander. A professional soldier, he surrendered his men en masse. Sandover, a citizen soldier, took the more daring action. Thirteen of his officers and 39 men eventually made it back to Egypt. According to Long, the Germans found the Australians friendly and calm 'just as if they had given up a sporting test match'.

At Heraklion, where the fighting was confined to daylight hours, all the Allied troops got away on the night of 28–29 May. They were taken off the jetty in orderly fashion on to destroyers and ferried out to waiting cruisers. It seemed so simple and so successful, compared with what was happening elsewhere. But the success was illusory and the relief of the troops short-lived.

Within half an hour, the steering gear of one of the destroyers failed and the ship nearly collided with another. Troops and crew were hurriedly transhipped to another vessel and the crippled destroyer was sunk by gunfire (to prevent it becoming German property). But the delay proved to be fatal.

The rest of the ships were caught in daylight by the Luftwaffe and without protection from the RAF. One of the destroyers, the *Hereward*, was bombed and beached and its crew and passengers taken prisoner. But the cruisers were the main targets of the estimated 100 aircraft which bombed and strafed the ships at intervals for about eight hours. The cost was ghastly. Of the 4000 embarked amid such serenity at Heraklion, about 800 were killed or wounded in the air attacks; The Black Watch lost more than 200.

The naval commander-in-chief, Andrew Cunningham, upon whom rested the responsibility of getting as many troops away as he could as well as preserving his ships and the primacy of the Royal Navy in the eastern Mediterranean, was at Alexandria to watch the remains of the Heraklion rescue fleet arrive. An eloquent man, he wrote that he would never forget 'the sight of those ships coming up harbour, the guns of their fore-turrets awry, one or two broken off and pointing forlornly skyward, their upper decks crowded with troops, and the marks of their ordeal only too plainly visible.'

Out on a bridge wing on one of the ships, dramatically caught in a searchlight cone, was a piper of The Black Watch playing a lament. It wasn't reported what he played, but it was most likely the regimental lament, 'Lochaber No More':

> These tears that I shed they are all for my dear,
> And nae for the dangers attending on war,
> Though borne on rough seas to a far bloody shore,
> Maybe to return to Lochaber no more.

It wasn't just Cunningham and the senior naval brass who stood on the wharfs and watched the ships coming in, bringing their all-too-few human cargoes from Crete. Also there was New Zealand Prime Minister Peter Fraser, who had been on his way to London but stayed in Egypt while the division — *his* division — fought on Crete. On the day the general withdrawal began, Fraser had his own personal problems but underplayed them as much as he could. He and his party had flown from Cairo to Alexandria to meet ships bringing in wounded New Zealanders. The return journey was in two cars and when one of them broke down, everyone piled into the other: there was the prime minister; his private secretary, Cecil Jeffery; the commander of the 2nd NZEF in Cairo, Brigadier Norris Falla; the head of the Prime Minister's Department, Carl Berendsen; plus two British officials and the English driver. At about 10 o'clock at night, speeding along what passed for a desert highway in 1941, the front offside tyre burst and the car flipped several times, ejecting some of its passengers. Fraser and Berendsen escaped with just scratches and an attack of the shakes. But others suffered moderate injuries, including broken bones. Fraser did not have long to dwell on his own misfortune; the hardship of thousands more was more pressing.

Three days later, on Thursday, 29 May, Fraser was visiting New Zealanders in hospital when he was told that Archie Wavell wished to see him urgently. They met and Wavell told him the next ships evacuating troops from Crete would be the last. Fraser was driven back to Alexandria to meet more men then returned to Cairo for another meeting with Wavell, who wanted him to sign a document that had already been signed by the overall Australian army commander, Thomas Blamey. It was to the effect that no more troops could be brought off and that those remaining should surrender. Fraser refused point-blank to sign. He made his position as clear as the waters running off the Southern Alps:

> I stated that while the United Kingdom with its 45,000,000 people could sustain a heavy loss of men without very disastrous effects, and that even Australia could sustain a large loss much better than New Zealand, it would be a crushing disaster for our country and its war effort if such a large number of our men fell into the enemy's hands without every effort being made to rescue them. I repeated a number of times that a further effort should be made to evacuate as large number of our men from Crete.

Cunningham listened to this plea in silence then said he agreed: the navy should do more if it could. A cruiser, the *Phoebe*, was on its way from Crete to

Alexandria and since it was the most serviceable of those left, although it was damaged, he would dispatch it again on one last trip. Cunningham and Fraser went to Alexandria for the arrival of the *Phoebe* and Cunningham went direct to the ship's commanding officer, Guy Grantham ('Granny Grantham' to the irreverent, although he was only 41). Cunningham told Grantham he and his crew could be replaced if they wished. Grantham said he would consider it an honour to bring more men off, and when he put the option to his crew, not one wanted to leave the ship.

The *Phoebe* went in company with four destroyers, which were going anyway, and the five together brought off about 4000 troops.

In a grateful and poignant footnote to the navy's role, New Zealanders who made it to Egypt voluntarily organised a collection to help the dependants of sailors who had died while trying to rescue soldiers. A presentation took place, appropriately, on the *Phoebe* and Freyberg insisted that a private soldier hand over the money to Cunningham. The man chosen was a private from Field Ambulance, Denis Sampson, who spoke eloquently of how the navy gave men courage and hope. The men raised a total of £820 11s, equivalent in today's terms to about $70,000.

On the day the Germans started landing on Crete, 20 May, nearly 43,000 Allied troops were on the island, including almost 8000 of the New Zealand Division. When the battle was over, 1751 Allied soldiers had been killed or died of wounds (671 New Zealanders), 1738 were wounded and just over 12,000 were prisoners of war (2180 New Zealanders, including 488 wounded). Of a maximum German force of about 23,000, deaths were estimated at 4000 and wounded at about 2600 (an unusually high proportion of deaths to wounded). As with much of the story of Crete, the figures cannot be precise. Even the New Zealand figures, like those of some of the worst fighting in the First World War, cannot be finite. Some men have simply not been accounted for and came into the category of missing, presumed dead. War was never an exact science nor as precise as an accountant's ledger.

Of the New Zealanders who did not get away from Crete on the Royal Navy ships, the majority became prisoners of war. But many, an indefinable number, took to the hills to live off the land, to be helped by the Cretans who paid dearly when caught by the Germans. Many moseyed around the country until they could find a means of escape; a final tally can never be known but it has been reckoned that perhaps as many as 300 men somehow found a way off the island to get to friendly shores, most commonly Egypt. The largest number in one group seems to have been the 62 New Zealanders who were in a total party of 125 that escaped on the submarine *Torbay* in August 1941. Lesser numbers got away on other submarines. Among those on the *Torbay* was the Australian battalion commander, Ray Sandover, who had told his men to get away if they could. He and others hid in the hills until a Cretan took them to a naval officer disguised as a Greek who had been put ashore from the submarine. So many came out of the hills to go that one naval rating, so Sandover told a lunch in Perth after the war, made 33 trips in a rubber boat from the shore to the submarine.

Among the submariners helping were two schoolmates from Wairoa, Philip ('Froggy') Le Gros and Bruce Bennett. Le Gros swam with a lifeline to guide soldiers who had decided to swim out to the submarine rather than wait for the dinghy. The two friends were decorated for their actions. The *Torbay* was commanded by a Scot, Tony Miers (later Sir Anthony), who won the Victoria Cross the following year for an attack on shipping near Corfu.

One of the most remarkable escapes was engineered by a Royal Marines major, Ralph Garrett. He and his men commandeered a disused landing craft and, with about 140 men on board, got the engine working and pointed it south. After travelling just a few kilometres, they fished a New Zealander, William Hancox, out of the water and invited him along. He had been swimming towards an abandoned rowing boat but found the barge a better option. He was the only named New Zealander on board, but said there were about eight others. When the craft ran out of fuel, Garrett had the men use their bootlaces to stitch together blankets for a sail. Steering was by the simple method of two men at a time swimming behind the craft pointing it in the required direction. They made it to North Africa after nine days and, according to one report, two Maori swam ashore and found help. The escape became widely known because the strange craft featured in paintings by the New Zealand war artist, Peter McIntyre, and an Englishman who was appointed artist to the Mediterranean fleet, Rowland Langmaid. (Garrett, who was awarded a DSO for the escape, and his 16-year-old son Stephen were drowned during a duck shooting expedition in Scotland in 1952.)

Every escape from Crete in the circumstances was extraordinary. But there were some who went beyond even that. Brandon Carter, a Pukekohe farmer, escaped first from capture in Greece and then from Crete. He was in hospital in Greece when that campaign ended, and a few weeks later he escaped on a fishing boat to Crete. But the Germans had control by then; he was recaptured and put to work in a kitchen for a time before being imprisoned at Galatas. Carter, from the 27th (Machine Gun) Battalion, escaped again and teamed up with an 18th Battalion private, Dugald McQuarrie, late in June and the pair took to the countryside. They eventually made their way to the south coast where they joined two Australians and the four of them found a dinghy that had seen better days. Holes were plugged with balled up socks and a bigger hole was blocked by the simple expedient of one man sitting on it. Thus shipshape, they set off. Only Carter had had any experience with boats, but somehow they made it across the Mediterranean to Sidi Barrani in Egypt. They beached their craft and clambered out of it. When one of their rescuers went to pull it in, it fell apart. Both New Zealanders were awarded the Military Medal. The following year, Carter was involved in an impromptu bayonet charge in an effort to free captured New Zealanders in the Western Desert and was blinded by shrapnel. His twin brother, Bassett, roared across the desert on a motorbike to get help. Bassett was killed in action at Cassino in 1944; Brandon lived until 1977. When he was invalided home from the war, he was presented with a Braille watch from Freyberg.

As with the battle, so with the aftermath. There were so many stories, so many heroics that they became commonplace. There was much that could never be known. The island endured German occupation until the summer of 1945, but even with peace in Europe, the Germans remained. Shipping was in demand everywhere and there was none to ferry the German troops back across the Aegean to Greece, there to get a train back to their homeland. The Germans were effectively prisoners on the island, but they were allowed to retain their arms for a while because of fears that the Cretan people would seek their revenge. Hundreds of Cretans during the years of occupation were put to death by the Germans for harbouring Allied soldiers or even just on suspicion of doing so. Families were wiped out, villages were razed. The Gestapo had been on the island and showed a savagery and brutality that shocked the regular German soldiery. But now it was over.

In early June 1945, one of the first visitors in peacetime was Geoffrey Cox, who had been there in war. He toured the areas once familiar to him, noticing the changes and in some cases the absences. The small printing shop where he had produced the *Crete News* was gone; there remained just outlines of rooms where Freyberg had had his headquarters; weather and work, he noted, had removed many traces of the battle. He also remarked on the incongruity of the defeated enemy still going about their business — the men in their short shorts, jackboots which almost hid their socks, their red, white and black insignia. They helped the British load mortar bombs and rifles onto barges for later dumping out to sea. The only explosions now were from ammunition dumps.

At Galatas, he noticed little different: 'Only a few gaps are torn in the white village street, but the buildings opposite the church are all destroyed.' The priest and the schoolteacher, with nary a word of English between them, hosted Cox and his colleagues to a slap-up meal of roast pork and chicken and wine; of course, the wine. Dark-eyed Cretan girls pressed flowers on them. Clutched in hands, and shown with pride, were badges from the uniforms of New Zealanders or British or Australians, men who had been helped in the dark days. The priest told Cox through a hurriedly found English speaker where all the New Zealand soldiers were buried around Galatas. Cox wrote:

> I only hope it will be some solace to those who loved these men to know they lie amid scenes as lovely as any in their own land, and that their graves are tended and guarded by a proud people whose friendship is an honour not easily or carelessly bestowed.

A few months later, Freyberg returned to Crete. He had with him Howard Kippenberger and others who had been there in May 1941. The streets were crowded; every house was open to the New Zealanders. They were among old friends. Those bitter days of 1941 had created a bond that even now has not been broken. Sandy Thomas was back on Crete in 2011 and was greeted as the conquering hero and, of course, with his upright bearing and his chest full of medals, that was exactly how he looked.

Canea, the city bombed almost out of existence by the Germans, conferred upon Freyberg its freedom. Crete was his like it never could have been in 1941. The months after the war were an unsettling time in Greek politics and there were fears of a communist takeover. However, as Freyberg remarked, the extremes of Greek politics, both left and right, walked together with him through the streets of the Cretan towns on a carpet of flowers thrown by a grateful population.

One of the group was artist Peter McIntyre and he was amused and delighted at an outdoor civic lunch when a Cretan girl went forward with a present for Freyberg. It was a postcard of a much-reproduced image drawn by McIntyre in 1940 soon after he arrived in Cairo, depicting soldiers at a urinal and warning against too much talk: 'It's wonderful what leaks out,' it said. 'Keep your mouth shut.' A New Zealand soldier hid in the girl's house while trying to evade Germans and evidently left the postcard as a token of thanks. Freyberg passed on the gift to McIntyre, who kept it the rest of his life.

Freyberg and his party had been taken from Italy to Crete by the Royal Navy cruiser *Ajax*, on which some of them had escaped from Greece and which was a partner with New Zealand's *Achilles* in the Battle of the River Plate in 1939. If one of the New Zealand ships couldn't carry the post-war Crete party, the *Ajax* would do just fine. After the feted welcoming throughout the island, Freyberg repaid some of the hospitality with a party on the quarterdeck of the warship. There were New Zealand army men in their best bib and tucker, British navy men in their starched tropical whites … and bearded and baggy-trousered Cretans who not long before had been up in the hills doing their best (which was considerable) to make life a misery for the occupiers.

McIntyre was one of the guests and he told the delightful tale of how the navy served a powerful rum punch that the Cretan brigands, by polite custom, tossed off in one gulp. The quicker the gulp, the quicker the refill. The scene warmed, McIntyre wrote, voices rose and battles were refought.

'Then the Maoris amongst us enlivened proceedings further by stripping to the waist and putting on a tremendous stamping haka that shook the deck. This was too much for the brigands. Fiercely afire with navy rum, they leapt into the fray brandishing their long knives, leaping and yelling.'

Not much more than four years before, they were people from opposite ends of the earth, one unknown to the other. Now they were, and have remained, as blood brothers.

8

Men of valour

'Courage is the thing; all goes if courage goes.'
— Playwright J. M. Barrie talking about his friend Bernard
Freyberg during a rectorial address at St Andrew's University, 1922

It reads like something from a fiction thriller, a type that could have been dreamt up by Lee Child: 'He … sank his teeth into the German's throat until he tasted blood.' But he was no character of fiction, he was no figment of anyone's imagination; he was Alfred Clive Hulme of Dunedin and Nelson, farm labourer until the war came and he donned a uniform.

From first to last, Clive Hulme was a killing machine. Few Germans within hitting distance escaped his deadly accuracy and hot ruthlessness. No sooner had the first paratroopers landed than Hulme was mowing them down.

The bare details of Hulme's extraordinary killing spree have often been told, taken largely from newspaper reports and from the citation, published in October 1941, for his Victoria Cross. But an astounding document among the papers of Angus Ross, the academic who wrote the *Official History* of the 23rd Battalion, provides the full story in much greater detail.

Hulme was sent home wounded after Crete and while convalescing in hospital in Rotorua, he thought he was poorly treated by a reporter for the Auckland weekly magazine, the *Weekly News*. He spoke only reluctantly to reporters after that. The reporter, J. C. Goodwin, was told at the hospital he couldn't see Hulme but he should read a story in the Wellington paper, the *Evening Post*, which reported Hulme's arrival home. Goodwin's full-page article was inaccurate in parts and exaggerated in others, but certainly did not put Hulme in a poor light. He emerged as a modest hero. Hulme's objection was probably no more than he didn't like the public attention. (Ross later commented that a director of Wilson and Horton, the company that owned the *Weekly News*, told him Goodwin was only a temporary employee and disappeared to Australia.)

It was largely as a result of that incident that Hulme, 15 years after Crete, was interviewed by Ross on the last day of January 1956 in the office of his old battalion commanding officer, Brigadier 'Acky' Falconer.

Hulme was a provost sergeant with the Field Punishment Centre (FPC) on Crete when the Germans attacked. He said they had two sets of orders in the event of attack — the first was to rejoin their battalion as soon as fighting began and the second, a verbal order for which there was no written record, was from Brigadier James Hargest that required the FPC to move to 'any sticky spot and deal with trouble there'.

Hulme rearmed the men from the FPC with rifles and grenades and led them in an attack on the first lot of German troops who landed just above the centre. In Ross's words, Hulme and his men 'cleaned them up' and Hulme sent captured maps to brigade headquarters, which showed the results of German reconnaissance. It was clear the Germans targeted areas which they believed were either unoccupied or just lightly occupied. Ross recorded this first sortie of Hulme's: 'Hulme claimed no special credit for the manner in which the FPC men cleaned up their area but he said he later counted 130 German dead in their general area, all killed as a result of the initial battle ...'

Soon after, an engineers lieutenant named Hector (John Ross Monro Hector) saw Hulme and told him his company was being fired on by German riflemen and machine-gunners up a valley to the west of the hill on which the FPC was situated. The lieutenant asked Hulme to sort it out, but Hulme refused, saying his men needed a spell after an exhausting morning. Hulme also warned the lieutenant against approaching the Germans himself. The lieutenant was bent on progress, though, so Hulme and Jim Shatford followed, to give covering fire. Somehow, three Germans were taken prisoner and

Hulme said he was going to shoot them. Hector ordered they should be taken back and handed over to the proper authorities. As they advanced, Hector and his men were all shot and the prisoners made a break for it. Hulme and Shatford then found the Germans responsible and shot 'two or three'. Hulme then tried to help Hector, who was bleeding profusely: 'You were right; tell my OC,' he told Hulme. Then he died. (Hector was of pioneering pedigree: his paternal grandfather was Sir James Hector, the eminent versatile scientist, who married Maria ('Georgie') Monro, a daughter of Charles John Monro, the man credited with introducing rugby to Nelson.)

From this point, Ross reported, timings became a little vague. At some stage during this early period Hulme was required to report to Hargest at brigade headquarters. 'I can use your rifle and want you now to deal with a sniper shooting in the door of an RAP [regimental aid post],' Hargest told him. Drily, Ross reported that Hulme went off and stalked and shot the sniper.

It was soon after this that Hulme donned a German parachutist's camouflage suit, or smock, and over the years this has led to the conclusion that Hulme deliberately disguised himself as a German in contravention of the accepted rules of war. It caused a flurry of publicity a few years ago when it was written Hulme donned 'a Nazi uniform' and there were calls for apologies to the families of his victims and talk about war crimes and similar wringing of hands.

Undoubtedly to Hulme, and a great many other soldiers, the rules of war were something drawn up in comfortable, unthreatened splendour in a hotel in Geneva or The Hague by men with pens and secretaries and who could afford principles and five-course meals. It was a world and a lifetime away from the kill-or-be-killed reality of a close quarters battlefield. They would have agreed with the reason for rules, but knew there was a yawning gap between theory and practice.

As Ross wrote:

This suit gave him a certain amount of protection both through making him inconspicuous and through making him appear to Germans as being himself a German. With it, he wore a paratrooper's camouflage hat. This was like a balaclava in that it rolled up to be worn as a cap … or could be dropped down in a hood over the face with slits for eye-holes. When wearing this outfit, completed by crossed German belts or webgear with egg grenades or bomb pouches, Hulme usually carried three or four Luger pistols and as many German egg grenades as the pouches would carry.

Ross's account of his interview with Hulme was typed, but at the end of that preceding sentence he wrote in hand: '… and no doubt looked very like a German paratrooper'.

On one occasion when Hulme returned to the FPC area, he found a big German going through New Zealand documents. He was, evidently, the biggest German Hulme had seen — nearly two metres tall, broad-shouldered, well-proportioned and very blond: the very model of Hitler's master race. The German was wearing a steel helmet and, Ross reported, Hulme aimed carefully at his brow just below the helmet, fired and killed him. 'Never before nor since had he felt so sorry to kill a German, so fine a man did this particular German appear to be,' Ross said.

Sometimes the killing machine showed compassion. Hulme shot at a German and merely wounded him. He approached to finish him off, but the German dragged from a breast pocket a photograph of his wife and children and showed it to Hulme. Touched, Hulme gave the man water and left him as comfortable as possible to be picked up by other Germans.

Three days after the German invasion, Hulme was heading towards the 23rd Battalion position when he was greeted by an old friend, Bill Green, from Motueka, who warned there was a sniper about. No sooner had the words left Green's lips than they were replaced by a shout of pain — he'd been shot in a knee. Hulme went back to help, but Green motioned him away, saying he would be all right but to make sure he got the sniper. Hulme knew roughly where the sniper was and began a circuitous route up the hill to get behind him. Hulme was almost at the tree where the sniper was when a German aircraft roared overhead, strafing as it went. Hulme dived for cover and so did the sniper — right on top of the New Zealander.

Ross's narrative, as told to him by Hulme, continued:

Neither man had time to engage the other with pistol or other weapon before they fell into each other's arms and engaged in a physical struggle to the death. The German butted, kicked and eventually tried to bite. Hulme responded in kind and sank his teeth into the German's throat until he tasted blood. The struggle went on for some minutes with neither man letting go but eventually the German got a hand loose and into a bomb pouch and was drawing a Luger when Hulme tightened his grasp on him and the Luger went off in the German's abdomen and he dropped.

Just for good measure, Hulme hunted around for the German's sniper rifle and took it to battalion headquarters. One less German, one more spoil of war.

While the retention of Maleme aerodrome was still a prospect, Hulme was sent for by Hargest. Making his way to brigade headquarters, he came across a group of New Zealand engineers being held prisoner by one German sentry. Hulme couldn't use a rifle for fear of hitting one of the engineers but, fortunately, he had a short German bayonet stuck into his belt. He used that instead. Hulme continued on his way and saw a figure out in the open with a Tommy gun — a Thompson submachine gun — blasting away. Hulme immediately took aim but then realised the figure was none other than Hargest himself. Hulme did not bother to inquire what a brigadier was doing on his own in a frontline infantry role. Instead, he carried on to headquarters and was told to go to a village to the east of Maleme and find out enemy strengths both in the village and at the aerodrome.

Ross said he had a 'minor adventure' on the way in which he killed a German, then found numerous Greek women in the village but few Germans. He made his way to the aerodrome proper.

Two unguarded aircraft were on the runway some distance from others. Hulme pulled opened the door of one and threw in a fusee, a type of incendiary. A fire started, Hulme slammed the door and made off. But the fire went out, and there was still no sign of guards, so Hulme returned. 'A little worked up,' as Ross put it, Hulme tossed another fusee into the second aircraft and left the door open. 'To his delight,' Ross wrote, 'both planes caught fire and made a terrific blaze.'

The fire and smoke brought Germans running and Hulme made himself scarce, eventually finding his way into a swampy area and in order to fully hide himself, he lay in the water. There he stayed for most of the rest of the night until he was confident the Germans had given up looking for him. He emerged from the swamp, cold, wet and smelling, and stumbled over the body of a dead New Zealand soldier, a Maori.

Ross took up the story:

Taking out his personal possessions and weapons, he stripped off his stinking wet clothes and put on those of the dead Maori. For a day or two afterwards, whenever he got hot, he could smell the odour of the dead body but at the time it appeared preferable to the horrible smell of the swamp-soaked clothes he had taken off.

The intention of a 23rd Battalion company commander, Major Bert Thomason, was to keep Hulme out of the heroically mad charge at Galatas. 'You've done enough,' Thomason told him, and he took Hulme's rifle and laid it against a tree. But like the Man from Snowy River's pony, Hulme's pluck was still undaunted and his courage fiery hot.

He watched the two lieutenants, Sandy Thomas and Rex King, toss as to who was to go first in the race up to the village. The attack got going, Hulme could hear the blood-curdling, hair-raising, spine-tingling yells of the possessed New Zealanders, and he couldn't stand and watch them go until he could see no more. He snatched his rifle from the tree and ran after them; he passed the rear and caught up with Thomas.

Greek women added their screams to those of the soldiers; rifle fire and tracer bullets seemed thick in the air. Thomas went down, hit in the thigh and hip by shrapnel and a bullet. The attack seemed stalled. Thomas said something to the effect of 'If I had two good legs, I'd go forward to see what was happening.'

Hulme could take a hint. On he charged, into what he later learnt was a schoolhouse, from whose windows a withering fire ensued. Ross recorded what happened next: 'He threw a German egg bomb at the doorway and burst the door open and hurled in quick succession three or four grenades inside. There were shouts and screams of pain from inside but five Germans came running out and ran down the road.' Hulme called for a couple of New Zealanders to shoot them, but they were out of ammunition and the Germans escaped.

Hulme went on and chased another German into a house. He and a private, Wally Dunn, burst into the house but couldn't find the German. A trapdoor seemed to lift slightly and Hulme told Dunn, 'They are down below.' He tossed down two grenades after calling 'one, two, three' and, on 'three', Dunn lifted the trapdoor. To their horror, screams from Greek women and children rose from the cellar. How the women and children fared was not recorded. Hulme and Dunn started to leave the house when the German they'd lost emerged from behind a door. Dunn grabbed Hulme's rifle and bayoneted the German so fiercely that it went through the German and into the stone wall behind. Hulme pulled it out and the German, impaled no more, slipped to the floor.

There was a history between Hulme and Dunn. Hulme as provost sergeant had had to deal with Dunn, who had breached some military law, and Dunn told Hulme at the time he would 'get him' some day.

As they prepared to leave the house, Hulme asked Dunn if he still intended to 'get him' because he had no intention of exposing his back to him. But Dunn said, as reported by Ross: 'Clive, you'll do me. You needn't worry ... I will go first.' The two shook hands and went off in search of more Germans.

Hulme came across about 30 or 40 New Zealanders on the opposite side of the village, pinned down and unable to rejoin the others. Hulme sent a corporal back to find reinforcements, and when the corporal returned and said there were none, Hulme went off himself in search of help. He went back through the village, where dead Germans, New Zealanders and Greeks lay around, and found Thomason, who was with Brigadier Howard Kippenberger. By this time, it was about three o'clock in the morning. Thomason told Kippenberger who Hulme was and the brigadier wrote something in a notebook.

Thomason then told Hulme to go back to the village and bring out the men he had been with. This he did, and he arrived back in time to hear Thomason say to someone that he was not moving until Hulme returned.

About this time, Hulme heard from stragglers from 19th Battalion that his brother, Harold, 'Blondie', who he believed had gone to Egypt, had joined the 19th in action and been killed. According to Ross, Hulme was determined to avenge his brother's death. This contradicts several published accounts that Hulme joined the charge at Galatas in anger because he had heard his brother had died. But as he made clear to Ross, it was only after Galatas that he received the dreadful news.

Vengeance was still the uppermost emotion. Hulme fell back from the 23rd Battalion withdrawal and waited by a tinned food dump — depot was probably a more indicative word but Ross called it a dump — where men helped themselves as they passed by. A small German patrol showed up. Hulme shot the leader in the stomach as he was picking up a tin. Hulme then shot two more before he left to catch up with his battalion.

Some confusion began to set in around this time with men being separated from their units and some unclear about where they were and where they were supposed to be going. Thomason again told Hulme to have a rest but intense fire opened up and some Australians could be seen running back in a panic, as Ross put it. Thomason shouted, 'Shoot them down! Shoot them!' But Hulme and others went to the position the Australians had abandoned and returned fire on the Germans. The Australians reorganised themselves and rejoined them.

Thomason called Hulme back and took him to a conference of senior officers convened, apparently, by Hargest. 'I make no apology for bringing

Sergeant Hulme into this conference,' Hargest told the others. 'He will probably be one of the last out tonight and may as well know from the beginning what is the plan.'

Hulme told Ross that as 'the brass' talked, the odd bullet whistled close by and a nearby hill was identified as their source. Hargest looked at the hill and turned to Hulme: 'You can go,' he said. Hulme climbed round behind the source of the firing and found four Germans looking down on the New Zealand camp. He worked out which was the leader and shot him in the back. Hulme was still dressed in the German camouflage smock at this time and when the other three turned to see where the shot came from, he turned to look too. The three Germans took him to be, as Hulme hoped, one of theirs.

Ross's account related what happened next:

> When the men in front of him looked down again, Hulme picked off one and then another. The last came up towards him and he shot him through the head, blowing out both his eyes — a sight he would never forget. Before he could move, another — the fifth — German came round a corner on his left and Hulme shot him too, making his score on this occasion five.

Hulme by this stage, as he confessed to Ross, had forgotten how long he had been without sleep or proper food and at times he was disorientated. At one point he went the wrong way and entered the town of Suda where he met some retreating New Zealanders, who told him Germans were not far away. No sooner had the warning been delivered than Hulme was challenged in German. He threw himself over a wall into a courtyard and there a Greek priest took him through a house and out into a lane. He trotted along the lane hoping to catch up with his battalion but instead of being found by Germans, he was taken by a British force that had landed not long before. It was an element of Layforce, a commando unit formed earlier that year and named for its commander, Lieutenant-Colonel Bob Laycock. He was the epitome of the English upper middle class, educated at Eton and Sandhurst, a soldier son of a soldier, but it was not his type that seized Hulme.

As Ross recorded:

> They seized Hulme, threw him to the ground, punched and kicked him.
> He insisted he was a New Zealander but they said he was a Hun. They
> were, according to Hulme, Cockney bullies who nearly knocked him
> out. When they searched him and found his pay-book, they declared he
> had stolen it from a New Zealander. They tried him out in various ways
> and eventually accepted his statement that he was a New Zealander
> and let him go.

In fairness to the Cockneys, however bullying they may have been, Hulme at
that stage was still dressed in the German gear.

Hulme was so desperate for water he drank some washing water he
came across and eventually made his way back to the 23rd, where he told
Thomason of his run-in with the Cockneys, and Thomason told him that
Layforce had just landed and been charged with holding the rearguard as the
New Zealanders made their way to the south coast and evacuation. (Laycock's
personal assistant with his force on Crete was the novelist Evelyn Waugh,
who later wrote about the action in *Officers and Gentlemen*.)

Again, Thomason told Hulme to take it easy but, again, events supervened.
Hulme was about to sit down for his first meal in days — tinned tomato
soup or tomatoes, he couldn't remember which — when firing again broke
out. 'Sergeant Hulme!' Thomason shouted. 'Get men up on top of that hill!
Whoever gets men there first, wins!' Hulme told the nearest men to join him
and raced up the slope, meeting some New Zealanders fleeing down. Hulme
reached the top first, braced himself, and took aim at a column of Germans
also heading for the top. 'The leader was ten to twenty yards away when
Hulme bowled him over. Later, he sat on the stone wall, used his feet as a rest
for his rifle, and shot several Germans from that position.'

Mortar fire now found them and an officer shouted that someone had to
silence it. Hulme offered to do so and said he wanted five men to go with
him. None offered so Hulme started to go alone, first checking to see he had

sufficient ammunition. It was at this point he was shot in the right arm and elbow, his right forearm and hand dangling down, useless.

He headed down a road and ran into a bunch of Italian prisoners, one of whom, an officer, bandaged Hulme's arm as best he could. He was directed towards a hut that was crowded with wounded. A medical orderly gave him a syringe and showed him how to use it to ease the pain. Hulme assumed it was morphine, but didn't know. He injected himself and gave some to two other wounded and left the hut.

Ross wrote that Hulme had an encounter with an English soldier that he was vague about — the Englishman thought him a German and tried to shoot him but he, like Hulme, had the use of only one arm. Whether it was the effect of whatever the substance was he injected himself with, Hulme told Ross he wandered off, feeling 'a bit queer' and talking to himself. He came across a German mortar which he thought may have been the one he had been asked to silence. Two Germans arrived carrying mortar bombs and Hulme thought his time was up. He jabbered away to them and approached them and found that they were more frightened than he was. They had no personal weapons so Hulme shot them both with a Luger, using his left hand. He then kicked the sights of the mortar as hard as he could to render it useless and resumed his journey in the rough direction of the south coast.

At one point, Hulme was given some water by a Greek woman and, at another, asked some Australians for water but they just ignored him. He eventually fell in with other New Zealanders and even rejoined Thomason and some of the 23rd. Thomason told Hulme to organise the stragglers into a decent group and march them in some sort of order or else clear them off the road.

Thousands of men were making their way to the south coast and hoped-for evacuation, some of them in properly formed units, some in ad hoc groups, some alone, some hitching rides on the few vehicles available.

As Ross related, 'Hulme says he made a great effort to boost the morale of the stragglers by telling them that they could make it and that if the Germans came up from the rear, they could fight them off.' As some of these men had no arms, Hulme gave away two of his last Lugers and also secured arms from the roadside for those who were prepared to take them.

At last he reached the track down to Sfakia. There were queues of anxious, tired, hungry men, many of them wounded. They knew that if they couldn't get on a boat, they would likely have to fend for themselves on Crete and in all likelihood be taken prisoner. The character of men in such circumstances was tested like never before, army discipline confronting personal instinct.

Some pushed and shoved their way up the queue. Others just stood mute, resigned to their fate, whatever it may be. There was some fighting in the lines. Two men carrying a wounded mate on a stretcher dropped the stretcher and just left him on the side of the track. Hulme and Bill Cook, also of the 23rd, picked it up as best they could and shuffled down the track.

A piquet (a picket, a small guard detachment) was stationed at the gates to the embarkation point and only wounded were being allowed through. Hulme and Cook and their stretcher were allowed and they got their stretcher on to a navy pinnace. But then things went wrong.

In the story that Hulme told Ross, someone shouted that this was the last boat for the night. It caused a panic. 'A mob of Aussies at the gates suddenly charged and swept the piquet aside,' Ross wrote.

They rushed at the boat. The naval officer in charge had a big torch … and he beat down on the heads of the Aussies trying to force their way on board. They were not to be denied and pushed their way on, pushing the naval officer overboard. They also pushed the stretcher and its wounded man overboard and Hulme too landed in the water. He came up and after treading water for a time could see the outlines of a naval ship and decided as it was only 120 to 150 yards away to try to swim out to it. He tucked his wounded arm hand into his belt and swam out … he reached the ladder of the ship exhausted and found he could not pull himself up with one hand. As he hung on wondering if he would be crushed between pinnace and ship or what, a sailor came down and in a distinctly North Country accent asked, 'What have we got here?'

The sailor pulled Hulme on board and he then either passed out or went to sleep. When he woke, the sailor was still with him and asked him if he had any German weapons. Hulme told him he didn't then remembered there was still one Luger somewhere. The sailor rummaged through Hulme's clothes and found it. Hulme told him he could have it and the sailor was delighted.

Hulme relaxed for the first time for days as the ship headed for Alexandria. His day was done.

Hulme's citation for the Victoria Cross, made public six months later, said he 'conducted himself with such courage that the story of his exploits was on everyone's lips'. Ross in the *Official History* volume of the 23rd Battalion noted that the commander, Doug Leckie, limped over to see the ailing Sandy Thomas at Galatas. 'He stayed and talked with me for some time, speaking sadly of the Battalion's casualties and proudly of its showing throughout the fighting,' Thomas wrote. 'He spoke at length of Sgt Hulme who … had done wonders.' Jim Hargest, who commanded the brigade of which the 23rd was a part, talked of Hulme showing 'such a complete contempt for danger that it amounted to recklessness'.

Hulme's citation made mention of his killing 33 snipers. He certainly killed snipers, as Ross's words made clear, but more besides.

It wasn't of course only Hulme the men were talking about. The other to share the awe and respect of the men with whom he served, and who also won a Victoria Cross on Crete, was that one of a kind, Charlie Upham. As with Hulme, Upham's heroics were spread over several days and lasted from the time the Germans first landed until almost the point of evacuation.

Upham, widely known throughout his battalion, the 20th, even before the deeds that won him the VC, was known to his friends at 'Pug', with no one too sure whether that came from his facial features or his readiness to use his fists. He was well known too to his officers, especially Howard Kippenberger, the battalion commander. 'Kip' first came across Upham at Burnham, just south of Christchurch, soon after the war began. No leave was allowed one weekend except for special circumstances, and Upham went to Kippenberger to plead his special case. As biographer Kenneth Sandford related it, Upham told his

CO he wanted leave for personal reasons.

'Well, I'm sorry Upham,' Kippenberger said, 'but you'll have to tell me the personal reasons before I can consider it. What's the matter?'

'I want to give a chap a hiding; that's all.'

Upham got his leave and the hiding was administered, apparently because the recipient welshed on a debt.

A few weeks later, Upham and Kippenberger met again. Upham had been recommended for a commission, but to become an officer he had to go to an officer cadet training unit at Trentham. Upham asked Kippenberger if that would mean he'd be delayed leaving New Zealand and going to war. Yes, it would, was the reply. Then take me off the list, said Upham. It was only later when in Egypt that he was commissioned. But only just. He passed out at the bottom of his course into a pool of new second lieutenants. It wasn't that he didn't know his stuff; it was just that the answers he gave in the exams did not tally with the answers required by the British Army types who set the questions. But Kippenberger knew his man and Upham rejoined the battalion in his new uniform, still with his old desire to get to grips with Germans or Italians — either would do.

An *Auckland Star* reporter, Robin Miller, who went to war as a dispatch rider and was seconded as a war correspondent, took up the story:

Charlie Upham thus journeyed with us to Greece with the newly acquired responsibility of platoon commander. Infantry fighting there was rare and he and his men were not favoured by opportunity. He took with him to Crete the beginnings of a severe case of dysentery which was to wrack his body throughout the bitter island campaign, but he refused point blank to retire to hospital. Week after week he was a sick man, day after day his body grew thinner.

Yet, remembering that, think back on things he did on Crete, the feats that made his citation for the Victoria Cross one of the most extraordinary on record. How he led his platoon from one enemy strongpoint to another in a yard by yard counter-attack on Maleme airfield; how he reached into his tunic for a fresh grenade, crawled up to German posts and blew them to pieces; how he helped carry the wounded out and led an isolated company to safety; and later, in the fighting retreat from Galatas, how, though twice wounded, he took his tiny platoon into a fierce battle against an overwhelming force and how, lame, exhausted and more sick than ever, he was still fighting on his very last day on Crete, hounding a German patrol from cover, killing a score of them with a Bren gun and scattering the others in panic.

Miller related how he was on the same evacuation ship as Upham and how they talked for an hour, but not once did Upham mention any of his own endeavours; it was all about the other men.

Five months later, when the VC was announced, 'Charlie took the news like a staggering blow,' Miller wrote.

He was angry and sullen in turn. He hid himself away from war correspondents and photographers who rushed to find him. I remember him saying he did not want the award, that it was not rightly his. When at last he was reconciled to it, I knew he was holding it in trust, as it were, for all the men who fought beside him.

It was Kippenberger who persuaded Upham of his public duty, especially when a New Zealand Broadcasting Service man, Norman Johnston, sought a taped interview to send home. Kippenberger cunningly told Upham to see it as an opportunity to speak publicly, not about himself, but about the men with whom he served.

Upham was known as much for his earthy language as he was for his unremitting courage and determination, and it was only on the third attempt that Johnston was happy with what he got on tape. He thanked people who had sent him messages of congratulations, he thanked his commanders, his NCOs, and his men, those he knew and those right through the division. He talked of the men left on Crete, some killed, some captured, some wounded and captured. He named some of them, including Jack Hinton, who had won a VC in Greece. He thanked the Greeks and the Cretans and urged people to help them after the war with clothes and food and, spoken like the trained farmer he was, stud stock. He ended with these sentences:

'The division over here is going from strength to strength and the morale of our own troops is unsurpassed. You will hear more from us again. We have a great little army up here in the sandhills. I would like the New Zealand Government to know that it is impossible to send over too much New Zealand tobacco to the troops. It is very much appreciated here. Kia ora.'

To those who knew him, it was typically Upham: think of others, do unto others.

Upham would have enjoyed the panic and humour that lay behind the presentation of the VC to him by General Claude Auchinleck, the Middle East commander-in-chief. The ceremony was planned for out in the desert with Upham receiving his VC and Kippenberger a Distinguished Service Order. But on the eve of the great day, the person responsible at divisional headquarters realised they had neither medals nor ribbons to present. A hurried call was made to the widely known Jack Griffiths, who was aide to Bernard Freyberg, the divisional commander. Freyberg had a chestful of medals and Griffiths was asked if an old tunic was lying about and if so, could a couple of the general's ribbons be borrowed. No problem, said Griffiths, but warned they were a bit shop-worn. Never mind, he was told, if they look old it'll just seem like they took a long time getting here. The other possible lender was Lieutenant-Colonel Les Andrew, who also won a VC in the First World War, but he'd gone away on leave somewhere.

While the borrowing was going on, the new DSO ribbon was delivered to the headquarters, but it was promptly lost. So Freyberg's ribbons duly arrived and Auchinleck pinned the red ribbon with blue edges of the DSO to Kippenberger's chest and the claret ribbon of the VC to Upham's. When the photographers and newsreel men were gone, and when the division parade was dismissed, Griffiths retrieved his boss's regalia.

More than 50 years later, when Upham, then aged 84, was in London to receive an award from the Greek Government, *The Times* newspaper recounted the events that led to his becoming the only man to win a second VC. 'It takes more than blind courage to fight like that,' its writer, John Percival, said.

> It takes great skill, cool nerves and the reflexes of an athlete. It also takes a readiness to kill, which most of us, safely removed from the horrors of battle, find chilling.
>
> There were some on his own side who were horrified by Upham's ferocity on that occasion. [Percival was writing about Upham's deeds on Crete]. However, the fact that he risked his life several times the same night, helping to carry wounded men out of the battle, also marks a paradox common to many brave men: savage rage against the enemy; compassion and gentleness for those in need of help.

The Times had not changed its tune. In October 1941, when the VCs to Upham and Hulme were first announced, it remarked on how the bar had been raised by the deeds of these two men in a war the like of which the world had not before seen. An editorial read:

> In the Baghdad of the Arabian Nights it used to be ordered that the story of any notable achievement should be written down in letters of gold. Is gold good enough, we can but ask, for the achievements of the two New Zealanders who have been awarded the Victoria Cross for valour?

It told of how Upham was suffering from dysentery and could eat very little (in fact, sip only condensed milk).

> The ordinary mortal, who knows to his shame how a little indigestion can upset both his eye and his nerve on the golf course, will feel that

on the least eventful of those nine days Mr Upham's courage was superhuman. Courage, moreover, in this case meant something far more complex and intellectual than was demanded, say, of even the officers in the charge of the Light Brigade.

The editorial writer warmed to his task:

The men of Talavera and Waterloo were heroically brave; but there may be some excuse for asking whether the nature of modern warfare has not raised the standard of courage to heights unknown before. If it should be so, and if brainpower, initiative, and resourcefulness are necessary to courage of the highest order, it may be surmised that the free peoples are more likely to produce that order of courage than any others … Out of all this devotion to an ideal, this rivalry in the service of a great cause, there must grow a great glory of courage before which all men and women of good will must feel as proud as they are humble.

Three days after one 20th Battalion soldier, Upham, received his VC, it was announced from London that another, Jack Hinton, had won the VC for his endeavours in Greece. This prompted a tongue-in-cheek note from a New Zealand lieutenant-colonel, Jim Burrows, who was temporarily absent from the battalion and commanded the Southern Training Depot at Maadi Camp in Cairo. 'It would be a convenience to this Headquarters if in future the names of members of the Twentieth Battalion who win Victoria Crosses were published in one list and not on different days as appears to be the present practice.'

Burrows was later astonished to learn that his note was included in an anthology of writing about the war on land.

9

Ted and his bottle

Though the cap is all rusty it outshines the chrome
As it waits for the soldier who never came home
— From 'The Soldier Who Never Returned' by Ross McMillan

When the last of the navy ships turned and sailed across the Mediterranean as quickly as they could for the safe haven of Alexandria, nearly three thousand New Zealanders were still on Crete. Most of them were prisoners of the Germans, destined for prisoner of war camps in Greece, Italy, Austria or Germany. Some were faring for themselves as best they could and plotting ways to get off the island. But 671 New Zealanders were there to stay forever. In the early days of June, some bodies still lay where they fell; others were in quickly dug, shallow graves.

It was only by the end of the war, when the Germans had gone, that it was known for sure who had died. And even then, there was continued worry, anxiety and misery for family and friends at home. Some would never know.

Among those who stayed on Crete was a 35-year-old driver with the headquarters company of the 27th (Machine Gun) Battalion, La Tour Mollet d'Auvergne. The name reflected his French ancestry on both his father's and mother's sides, but to the men of the 27th, he was simply 'Ted'.

His story was neither representative nor typical of the 670 others who died during the nasty, bitter fighting for Crete. Every one of the 671 had their own individual stories, their own tales to tell. They all had people close to them who would see them no more, who farewelled them at some stage in New Zealand or Britain, dreading it might be the last time they saw them. The difference with Ted d'Auvergne was that his tale continues to be told. It is an extraordinary, poignant tale and if it reflects the respect and esteem with which ordinary New Zealanders even today regard their fighting men of long ago, his story may be representative.

For this is the tale of Ted's bottle. The essence of the story is that d'Auvergne was in a bit of a rush in December 1939 to catch a train to get to Burnham, where he would rejoin his battalion and go overseas. Ted had a beer with George Provan, the publican at the Waihao Forks pub south of Waimate and, on the point of having a second, realised he'd better go or he'd miss the goods train which was to take him to Waimate. One or the other said the second bottle, of Ballins XXXX Natural Beer, should be kept waiting for Ted to have it when he got home from the war.

The bottle is there still.

It's in a glass case now and its original label faded and fell off, but a replacement was provided by Ballins. Behind the bottle is a photo of Ted that looks as if it were taken from a football team line-up. At the base of the bottle is the crossed guns badge of the 27th Battalion and around it are poppies, more and more added each Anzac Day.

There have been about a dozen publicans at Waihao Forks since the war and all have honoured Provan's pledge to keep the bottle there 'for Ted'. It's a story that has spread far and wide and the bottle, perched in its case above the bar, has become something of a shrine and a tourist attraction. It has been designated an official memorial by the RSA. The couple who now run the pub, Shane and Sandy Doolan, patiently and repetitively go through the story they must have told hundreds of times. They also provide a folder of photos, newspaper clippings and other documents related to either Ted or his bottle. Some of the details of the story vary, but the broad thrust is always the same: a bottle was kept for Ted when he went off to the war. He was supposed to have it when he got home again. But he's forever in the Suda Bay cemetery and the bottle is, so all the publicans have ensured, still in the pub.

The d'Auvergne family came from the Channel Islands, the British dependency just off the Normandy coast of France. The islands used to be part of the Duchy of Normandy and, in one of those quirky throwbacks, the reigning British monarch is still formally the Duke of Normandy, whatever the monarch's sex. The Queen therefore is a duke. The first d'Auvergne to come to New Zealand was Charles, Ted's grandfather. The day after he arrived at Lyttelton in 1856, he married a fellow passenger, Sarah Ward, and after a couple of years in Auckland they returned to Canterbury and settled in Rangiora in North Canterbury. Their oldest son, Edward, married Lucretia Adele Mollet from a noted Akaroa family in 1893. They had six children, all of them born in Rangiora, the last of whom was born on 21 February 1906, and was named Le Tour Mollet d'Auvergne.

This was a bit of a mouthful for a young boy growing up in rural Canterbury; he may have known that the moniker Le Tour he was saddled with was rich in French history, but it's unlikely many others would have. (The name comes from a line of warrior nobility that originated in the Auvergne region of France, hence d'Auvergne — 'of Auvergne'.) So the mouthful was reduced to Ted, probably because his father was Edward. Ted's mother died a year after he was born, his father remarried in 1913 and the family moved to South Canterbury, first to Makikihi on the main road south of Timaru and then to Waihao Forks where they took over a farm. The place was so-named because it's where the north and south branches of the Waihao River meet on their journey to the Pacific just north of the mouth of the Waitaki River. The forks, the pub and Ted's bottle are on an inland road that roughly parallels State Highway 1 and are 12 kilometres south of Waimate.

Ted was a boarder pupil at Timaru Boys' High School and while there damaged an ear while diving to such an extent that he was almost deaf in that ear. It gave his head a characteristic lean while listening to anyone and the belief in the family was that his hearing should have kept him out of military service. In the 1920s and 30s Ted took over much of the work on the family farm and became well known in the district both as a farmer and for social and sporting activities (the latter including swimming and rifle shooting). The pub served as the social centre for the farming community. In a small book about Ted and his bottle, Jim Sullivan recorded that Ted was fascinated by motors and machinery and he devised a lighting system for the family home at a time when the area did not have electricity.

Ted d'Auvergne enlisted in Timaru 12 days after New Zealand joined Britain in its declaration of war. (The story went that he fudged his partial deafness by standing with his 'good' ear closest to his examiners.) His service number was 7110, which put him among the 'four-figure men' who had a certain cachet among other members of the 2nd NZEF. A contrary view was that the four-figure men enlisted as soon as they could to escape wives or debts, or both. Twelve days after signing up, d'Auvergne and nearly 700 others arrived at Burnham, and swapped their civvies for khaki. One of 30 farmers in the battalion, he was assigned to the headquarters company. The battalion, after some elementary work at Burnham, went south to Cave for more rigorous training (and to shoot their Australian-made Vickers guns).

The battalion was part of the First Echelon of the 2nd NZEF and was put on active service on 14 December 1939 and all troops were given a fortnight's final leave. It was during that final leave that Ted spent his last days on the farm and had his last drinks in the Waihao Forks pub. Back at Burnham, the battalion was inspected by the 2nd NZEF commander, Bernard Freyberg, on the 30th, there was a farewell march through Christchurch on 3 January and two days later the soldiers were ushered on to a train. Military secrecy was high and the blinds in the carriages were down and an officer was stationed at one end of each carriage to ensure they stayed that way. None of the men was allowed to know the destination as the locomotive chugged out of the station. It took neither a genius nor a spy long to work out that the only possible destination could have been Lyttelton; it didn't take many others long to work it out either because when the train emerged from the tunnel, hundreds of people waited by barricades at the wharf for a last farewell. The name of the ship the machine-gunners boarded was supposed to be a secret as well: it was officially listed as 'transport Z.6', but no sooner were men on board than it was obvious to all who could read that it was the Polish liner *Sobieski*.

For those who couldn't read, the Polish crew soon told them what the ship was. It had been built two years before for the North American run and, not having been reconfigured as a transport ship, the men enjoyed something of the life of a peacetime tourist. With another troopship from Lyttelton and the cruiser *Leander* as escort, they sailed up to Cook Strait to be joined by other troopships from Wellington and by two more escort ships, the British battleship *Ramillies* and the Australian cruiser, *Canberra*. The convoy headed west into the Tasman and the last Ted d'Auvergne and all the others could have seen of New Zealand was the white tip of Mt Egmont receding into the distance.

Men on the *Sobieski* had their own troopship newspaper comprising a cover bearing a drawing by one of the gunners and stapled cyclostyled sheets containing shipboard news. It was typical of its type that was pioneered in the First World War. It had letters to the editor of this kind: 'Sir: Please tell me if my husband, Private Pullthrough, is a Glorious Dead. The man I live with won't eat or do anything until he is certain.' Or 'Sir: My son is 2IC of his spittoon. Do I get more money?' But it also contained serious news. The second-last issue, published as the ships neared the Red Sea, reported the death of Bombardier Theodore Ross Kerr-Taylor, well known in Auckland rugby circles as 'Doddy'. He became the first member of the 2nd NZEF to die outside of New Zealand on active service. He was on one of the other troopships, the *Empress of Canada*, and died of complications with a bout of tonsillitis. All the ships in the convoy hove to for the burial at sea and the sounding of the 'Last Post' by a later member of the Kiwi Concert Party, Gordon Kirk-Burnnand.

Egypt was reached in February and almost all of 1940 was spent either training or waiting for action that never came. The battalion's trucks were employed to ferry Italian prisoners of war one way and Australian soldiers the other, and it is likely that d'Auvergne, because he was a driver, was involved. His military record showed that he spent 12 days in hospital with an illness that was not specified.

In March 1941, with the whole division together for the first time, d'Auvergne was in Greece for that brief and forlorn campaign to halt the German advance. Most of the machine-gunners were taken from Greece to Crete in the British cruiser *Ajax*. Among the assortment of nationalities crammed into the warship for the six-hour voyage to Suda Bay were two young Greek women 'camouflaged' in Australian battledress. The Australians accused of smuggling them on board assumed an air of innocence.

Conditions for the machine-gunners on Crete were as chaotic as they were for most troops. Specifically, their tools of trade were deficient. Some had machine-guns with no tripods, some had tripods with no machine-guns. Ordered to set up a defence perimeter around Maleme, some of the gunners fashioned tripods of whatever wood they could find. In most cases, gun crews comprised two men instead of three. The efficiency of the gunners was compromised by the conditions: lack of proper tripods meant their guns could not be aimed accurately and clouds of steam rising from their positions (because water in their water-cooled guns could not be replenished) served as a marker for the Germans.

D'Auvergne seems to have become separated from the rest of his battalion two or three days after the Germans took possession of Maleme. He and three others raced down a terraced hillside as German fire chased them. Jim Sullivan quoted one of the others, Laurie Martin, as saying that when they got to the bottom, Ted was not with them. 'A couple of infantry sergeants were there and they said we weren't to go back to look for him. We just had to keep going.'

The battalion's total casualties on Crete were 122, including 18 killed. It was not known until after the war that Ted d'Auvergne was one of the 18. His father and stepmother were told by a letter dated 21 June that their son was missing. A month later, his name appeared again in published casualty lists, this time as wounded and missing. But then nothing more. No more word. From July 1941 all his father and stepmother, his brothers and sisters, all the people in South Canterbury who knew him, all they could do was wonder. All they had was the ache of not knowing. This applied to Ted d'Auvergne; it applied a hundredfold around New Zealand.

D'Auvergne was remembered in Auckland. In early 1945, a returned soldier wrote a reminiscing column in the *Auckland Star*. He remembered 'long Lefty' and 'little Shorty' who had a champagne supper in a flash Cairo hotel and signed the chit 'Peter Fraser'. He remembered 'Rhubarb' Pye being bitten by a black scorpion and 'Big Larry' who walked 'those bitter miles to Sphakia with eleven holes in him when Crete died'. And he wrote:

> 'We shall remember them' has meaning now. Not the thin sob of a bugle sounding the Last Post, limp flags lowered, an automatic prayer or two. Each recalled event brings them vividly to mind, and for a space they are with us again, grinning, carelessly cheerful. Latour D'Auvergne, of that famous family, a humble number in a machine gun outfit, Alley Sloper and his gun-crew … they're all there, leaving Valhalla for a brief moment to gather in a bar with a 'hoppy' ex-machine gunner and an invalided member of the Long Range Desert Group.

The war over, the last of the New Zealanders was taken off Crete. The Germans went home. Crete was at peace, left with its memories and its newly dead. On Anzac Day 1945, so the hand-me-down story has it, George Provan looked sadly at the bottle kept for Ted and slowly took the poppy from his lapel and wound the stem of it around the neck of the bottle.

Ted's father died in 1946, not knowing the fate of his youngest son. But he'd already had one hammer blow delivered to the heart by the war. Daughter Rata, who had been an ambulance driver in London during the war, died of illness on the way home and was buried at sea in the Bay of Biscay.

By this time, what was left of the family had moved to Waimate. Sometime later in 1946, an envelope bearing Greek stamps arrived for 'Charles d'Auvergne'. It contained a letter, written in excellent English for someone to whom it was a foreign language, which explained what had happened to Ted. It was written by Yakovos Kalionzakis, who was 17 years old when the Germans rained down from the sky on his home. He wrote that he and 'Mollett' fought together against the Germans but that d'Auvergne was shot in the chest. Young Yakovos somehow got d'Auvergne to his house, but he soon died. Ted had with him a letter addressed to his parents and he asked the young Cretan to send it. Apparently, Yakovos buried d'Auvergne as best he could, hid his papers in the house, and went in search of New Zealand officers or the Red Cross, so he could hand over the letter and say what had happened to its author. But, instead, Yakovos was taken by the Germans, the letter was confiscated, and he was shipped off to a prison camp in Germany.

Remarkably, he remembered the name and address he had seen on the letter d'Auvergne had entrusted to him and when he was home again in Crete in late 1945, he picked up his pen to add another chapter to the d'Auvergne tale. By this time, he had also been in touch with the war graves registration people and told them where d'Auvergne was buried so he could be re-interred in the Suda Bay military cemetery. Apparently realising he would need some sort of proof for his tale, he included with his letter a photo that had been in d'Auvergne's possession. It showed him with a woman whom Yakovos assumed was a girlfriend. In fact, it was younger sister Rata.

Lillian d'Auvergne went to the police with the letter and they advised caution because it was not unknown for fraudulent letters to come from Europe seeking money from relatives of men who had died. But this letter sought nothing. It gave much.

Tragically, the letter appears to have been lost. The d'Auvergne story featured in a television programme, and apparently its makers borrowed the letter and the family has not seen it since.

In 1999, yet another chapter was added to the story. Jim Sullivan wrote that an Akaroa photographer, Kerry Walker, was so fascinated by the d'Auvergne tale that he decided to try to find Yakovos. Until then, the family and others had interpreted the name on the now-lost letter as being 'Takavos Zalionzakis.' When Walker was in Greece, he told his host, who proclaimed that the name was not possible; there could be no such name in Greek. He suggested it should probably be 'Yakavos'. So Walker went to Crete and there in a small village he found the 75 year old who, as a 17 year old, had comforted a New Zealander in his last days and then brought comfort to his family.

With the help of two girls who spoke English, Yakovos verbally confirmed the details to Walker of what had been written in the letter 58 years before.

The *Official History* volume of the 27th Battalion lists d'Auvergne's death date as 'May 1941'; the Commonwealth War Graves Commission gives the date as 2 June 1941. The date, in the end, doesn't really matter. Ted is remembered and the bottle remains. That's what matters.

10

The other side of the hill

'The authorities [in London] would rather lose Crete than lose Ultra.'
— Wavell to Freyberg (perhaps)

The Battle for Crete was a man's battle. That's the way wars were and, generally, still are. The women of Crete were a notable and courageous exception; they fought for their homes and their freedom with a carving knife and, too frequently, became yet another battlefield statistic. But women in the services were not part of the battle; some New Zealand nurses were there before the German invasion but were dispatched to Egypt. There was a woman who had a critical role, however. Her name was Cynthia. But sometimes she was Elizabeth. Sometimes she was Betty. She slept — although sleep in this instance is a euphemism — her way into knowledge of one of the greatest secrets of the war. Her lying down and thinking of England — though she was American — helped provide the Allies with the means of intercepting and understanding most German high command decisions. Cynthia played a critical role in Britain gaining the key to the German cipher machines called Enigma which provided such valuable information to the Allies that it was more than top secret: it was ultra secret. It was Ultra.

As the overall commander of forces on Crete — essentially the island's omnipotent governor for about a month — Bernard Freyberg was the recipient of Ultra signals which contained detail of what the Germans planned, when they would do it and what they would do it with. It was likened to Freyberg playing poker while he knew what cards his opponent held.

Very few people at the time knew what Freyberg knew. The British

For them, the war was over: Allied prisoners on Crete.

A group of Cretans wait to learn their fate.

The London *Daily Mail* reports the end.

New Zealanders on a destroyer docking in Alexandria.

Left: A New Zealand soldier displays a souvenired Nazi flag.

Below: Private Denis Sampson presents the money raised by the New Zealanders to the naval commander, Andrew Cunningham.

Returning New Zealanders at an alfresco lunch on Crete in September 1945.

'Return from Crete' as drawn by Peter McIntyre.

Ted d'Auvergne in uniform.

CONTENTS

MAGAZINE FEATURES—	
Children's Page	19
Pen-friends	21
Short Story	48
Contract Bridge	41
Crossword Puzzle	48
Films	20
Humour	55
Medical	41
Specials	5-9, 22
FARM AND LIVESTOCK	36-40
Main Illustrated Section	23-34

V THE WEEKLY NEWS V

TOWN AND COUNTRY JOURNAL

FOUNDED A·D·1863

WITH WHICH IS INCORPORATED THE WEEKLY GRAPHIC AND NEW ZEALAND MAIL

AUCKLAND, NEW ZEALAND, OCTOBER 22, 1941

CONTENTS

NEWS PAGES—	
New Zealand News	50-54
SPORT	42-47
Realm of Sport	45
Bowling	46
Golf	46
Boxing	47
Turf	42-44
WOMEN'S PAGES	10-18
Social Chronicle	10-15
Domestic Bureau	16
Fashion	17
Home Furnishing	18

Nearly Bayoneted by Charging Maoris

Anecdotes of Modest Hero

SERGEANT HULME, V.C. GOES HUNTING

By J. W. GOODWIN

IT is a brave man who, knowing he is afraid, carries on to shame his fear, and a modest man who, refusing to believe that he has been awarded the highest honour for bravery the Sovereign can bestow, says it should have gone to his brother. These virtues are displayed by Sergeant Alfred Clive Hulme, V.C., who told only his wife that he had been recommended for the coveted award.

None of the many friends he has made in Rotorua, where he is receiving treatment for a wound in the right shoulder, knew until last week that the quietly-spoken, well-built man, with ruddy complexion and fair receding hair, was the sole man now in the country awarded the Victoria Cross during the present war, and one of the select company of 1163 heroes to be similarly decorated in 85 years.

Pursued by Wolves

ASKED if he had ever been afraid, Sergeant Hulme told of a moonless night in the wild mountainous country of Greece near Mount Olympus where he was bringing a number of suspects into camp. Gradually growing more distinct with weariness, a strange sound of snarling and yelping was heard by the sergeant. Curiosity, rather than apprehension, prompted him to ask the cause of the sound. "When I found that we were being followed by a pack of wolves, I covered the last part of the way to camp in Olympic time," he commented.

When the German attack fell upon Crete from the air, Sergeant Hulme was in charge of about 50 men from various units in a bivouac on the top of a ridge overlooking the Mallemi aerodrome. The Germans started dropping parachute troops into two long gullies on either side of the ridge, with the evident intention of taking it. He organised his men into parties and set out to attack German posts on the lower ground, with considerable success. The first night, believing that the enemy would try to rush the ridge under the cover of a machine-gun barrage, he collected more than 60 grenades and made his way through the dark to a point where the streams of tracer bullets were flying uphill over his head.

"I flung all the grenades down the hill into the darkness," he said. "Later other people counted about 120 dead down there."

For three days the sergeant and his men held the ridge, but eventually, after getting a belated order to retire, they departed in the early hours of the morning, having killed great numbers of German parachutists who had been landed on the high ground.

This phase ended, he rejoined his battalion, to find that he had no specific duties. "When the German aeroplanes were over it was a matter of lying still under the trees," he said. "The din was terrific and it was very hard to stay still and do nothing. That was why I started hunting Germans on my own."

Just as a part of the day's work, the sergeant mentioned that on one of the earlier days of the battle he saw a German glider coming down and took a shot at it. He had the good luck to hit the pilot, causing the machine to crash, and all in it were killed. Asked if he had used the bayonet, he said simply that he had killed nine Germans with it and five with his sheath-knife.

The sergeant had warm praise for the men who spent the three days with him on the Mallemi ridge. "They were tough," he said, "and they did everything they were asked, no matter how hard."

Luck on His Side

WHATEVER the qualities displayed by a man meriting distinction, luck enters the story somewhere, and Sergeant Hulme declares that he has had more than the usual measure. Once when disguised as a German paratroop he was saved from a Maori bayonet—"and anything that gets in front of a Maori bayonet goes west, and for good," he declares—only by the rare chance that he was recognised in time by a sergeant of the charging forces. On another occasion, his experience in wrestling, in which he gained some distinction as an amateur in Nelson, enabled him to match his skill and strength against the strength and gun of a German sniper and to be the victor. In a campaign such as Crete, he explained, where man was pitted against man rather than army against army, to be victor was to be the sole survivor. He had dodged behind a tree to escape enemy fire when a sniper dropped from the branches behind him. Sergeant Hulme heard the thud and, whirling round, grappled with the man. They struggled together on the ground, each trying to prevent the other grasping a weapon; the German managed to draw his revolver, but a trick of ju-jitsu learnt years before by an idle chance, enabled Hulme to twist the gun round so that his adversary shot himself.

Of the many adventures related by the V.C. winner, his encounter with the Maori battalion is typical in illustrating the inspiring qualities of initiative, skill and endurance for which the award was made.

Stalking Snipers

EQUIPPED with a Mauser—incidentally of the same type as that owned by the fugitive Graham in the Koiterangi man-hunt—six or eight revolvers, and German ammunition captured from a supply parachute dropped by the enemy, Sergeant Hulme disguised himself partly in German uniform and a cape made from a camouflaged parachute. Eyeholes and an aperture through which to fire completed the outfit. On this occasion, instead of stalking his quarry, he decided to "lie doggo" and wait in a valley strewn with parachute equipment until the invaders came within range. He had plenty of provisions, also captured from parachutes whose distinctive colouring the British troops soon learnt to recognise, and was prepared to stay the day if necessary. One German he had shot and wounded crawled away to warn his companions of the sniper's presence with the result that a patrol of 30 Germans later appeared in a widespread V formation making their way up the valley with rifles at the hip. Crouched under his parachute, he had decided that the end was drawing near when a wild shout from the hill behind him arrested his attention. Over the brow came the men of the Maori battalion in an overwhelming bayonet charge.

"I became so excited that, quite forgetting I was still in German uniform, I jumped up and cheered at the top of my voice," related the sergeant. "The Maoris came full at me with eyeballs rolling and tongues protruding, yelling fierce tribal battle cries. Jerry didn't wait; that was enough. But their bayonets shining coldly in the sun were coming straight for me and it was only by rare luck that a sergeant recognised me and held his mates from giving me a taste of the Hun medicine."

Saved from the bayonets of our own forces, he joined the Maoris in their charge when the German hunters became in their turn the hunted. Ever since he returned to New Zealand and even before he came to Rotorua, where so many of the members of the Maori battalion have their homes, he has on every possible occasion paid a tribute to their dash and courage. "They were magnificent," he has said more than once.

Nelson's Own Battle

"GALATOS was probably the most gruesome scene of the whole terrific campaign," stated Sergeant Hulme, in describing what he called "Nelson's own battle." A Nelson officer, Major H. H. Thomason, was in command of the battalion which made the attack, taking over from Major Leckie, of Dunedin, when he was wounded in the leg early in the action. C Company of the Nelson-West Coast Company made the assault, the two platoons to which the company was reduced being led by Second-Lieutenant Sandy Thomas, of Motueka, and Second-Lieutenant Rex King, remembered as a West Coast Rugby League representative. The enemy was in well-fortified positions in the village when the attack was launched and made their chief defence the dropping of hand grenades out of windows. "The Huns were chased out of the village inside an hour. During the battle many of the women and children in the village also lost their lives as they were in the houses occupied by the Germans," he continued. "The casualties amongst the New Zealanders were fairly high, but it was all for nothing, however, because nearly three hours later when we were preparing our defence positions around the village we received orders to withdraw."

Sergeant Hulme enjoys a swim in a Rotorua mineral bath.

It is somewhat ironical that Sergeant Hulme gave his occupation as a labourer instead of a farmer when he enlisted because at the time farmers were considered of greater importance as productive units than fighting men, yet it was farming which gave him the tracking ability as a result of which he disposed of many enemy snipers, thus earning the award.

Shot in Shoulder

IT was sometimes necessary to crawl for over an hour before he reached a suitable position to put an end to sniping activities, using all the secrets of taking cover and care in not rustling undergrowth learned when stalking a refractory cow. "I had a queer-tempered cow which would not come to be milked, so I tied a bell round her neck, but she was so cunning that as soon as I sent the dog to round up the herd she would stand perfectly still and the bell was useless." From stalking a refractory and annoying cow in Motueka, Sergeant Hulme graduated to stalking sources of annoyance and danger in Crete. Such is the initiative and improvisation that has built an Empire and snatched military defeats from the clutches of tragedy.

Sergeant Hulme confesses that his success was not due to prowess in marksmanship, in which he had little experience in the Dominion and none in Greece. His chief weapon was a German rifle with telescopic sights with which "you couldn't go wrong." June 13 was his unlucky day, when on one of his lone patrols he came face to face with an enemy sniper. Both men stopped and looked at each other for seconds before realising the situation and firing at the same instant. The German's bullet smashed Hulme's rifle and lodged in the shoulder. When the smoke cleared, his adversary was nowhere to be seen. "I was sorry that I couldn't bring the Mauser home as a souvenir," he added ruefully.

These are but a few of the exploits of a man who exhibited the most conspicuous gallantry and devotion to duty, yet one of the comments on the day that he received the news of his decoration was that he had just "done his bit." In a campaign where every man was doing his utmost as the emergency demanded, he considered that the distinction between one man's claim to honour and another's was very fine.

Brothers in Army

SERGEANT HULME — who pronounces his name as "Holm" —was one of three brothers who enlisted from Nelson. Corporal H. C. Hulme was wounded in Greece and killed in Crete, and Private G. B. Hulme is still on active service.

"It is absolutely incredible," said this hero, when the news was broken to him by a newspaper reporter, and not until the date and place of his birth at Dunedin on January 24, 1911, were checked did he credit the announcement. His next thought was for the wife and his two children, Denis, aged five, and Anita, aged two. He gave no thought for what the rest of the country thought of him; his family alone mattered. More soldiers have earned the Victoria Cross than have been awarded it, but none have received it who have not earned it, and New Zealand will be unstinting in its praise.

Sergeant A. C. Hulme, with his brother after the V.C.'s arrival in Auckland from Rotorua.

Winner of the Victoria Cross in the Great War, Mr. J. Crichton, greets Sergeant Hulme at the Auckland Railway Station.

The *Weekly News* story that upset Clive Hulme.

Howard Kippenberger with Charles Upham.

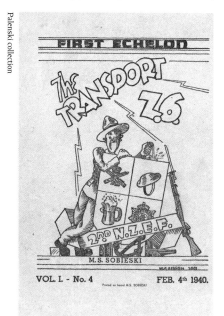

The troopship magazine produced on the *Sobieski*.

War correspondent Christopher Buckley.

Bernard Freyberg and Winston Churchill in happier days after Crete.

Bletchley Park, the place where messages were intercepted and interpreted.

Dan Davin in 1959.

Les Andrew in the 1950s.

prime minister, Winston Churchill, knew all about it, so too his most senior commanders in the field. When Freyberg first landed on Crete and was lumbered with the job of defending the indefensible, the Middle East army commander in chief, Archibald Wavell, took him aside and told him about the Ultra intercepts he would be receiving. He was to read them and destroy them; he was to tell no one what he knew and he was not to deploy his forces based only on what he had learnt from Ultra about German intentions. Even two men closer to Freyberg than any other, John White and Jack Griffiths, knew nothing about Ultra.

Freyberg kept the secret almost until the grave; when he sensed his end was near, he told his son Paul but he had to maintain the secret until told otherwise.

Shelves of books were written about the Battle for Crete, including volumes of the New Zealand *Official History*, before the British Government decided in the early 1970s that the story could gradually — but not totally — be told. The exact text of many of the Ultra messages can never be known; other messages or information about the whole system remain secret.

The relevance to Freyberg and Crete of the cracking of the Enigma code was that since he supposedly knew the German plans, he should have deployed his forces to stop them. Forewarned is, as the tautological saying goes, forearmed. Paul Freyberg, freed at last from carrying the burden of the secret, argued passionately in his father's defence that he could not alter his forces' positions because to have done so would have tipped off the Germans that something in their own communications system was seriously compromised.

The other argument in favour of Freyberg, so obvious that Paul Freyberg did not bother to employ it, is that it is one thing to know your opponent outguns you and has total air superiority; it is quite another to do anything about it.

Throughout military history, or the history of any human activity, one side has wanted to know what the other was doing. This was put into words by the Duke of Wellington in a chat he had with the Secretary of the Admiralty: 'All the business of war, and indeed all the business of life, is to endeavour to find out what you don't know by what you do; that's what I call guessing what was at the other side of the hill.'

The old Iron Duke had it right and Britain, France and, to a lesser extent, the United States, spent much time, energy and money in the 1930s trying to get to grips with what they could learn about a complex encrypting machine — a sort of early computer — the Germans had that was called Enigma. Messages encrypted on the Enigma machines, they learned, were in an impenetrable code. They needed some help and they got it in the form of a German who sold secrets to France and from Poles who had conducted their own investigations into the machines and, most tellingly, had mathematicians who could work it all out.

The existence of the Enigma machines was no secret among people whose minds worked at such a high level. The machines were available commercially and there was even an application to have one registered at the Patent Office in London. The secret was not in the machines themselves but in the way the Germans configured them. The British had a rough idea what the Poles knew, but they wanted to know more. This was where Cynthia apparently excelled.

She was born Amy Elizabeth Thorpe in 1910 in Minneapolis, daughter of a Marine Corps officer. By the 1930s, she was in Washington and married to a minor official at the British Embassy, and it was his transfer to Madrid that led his wife into a secret world. She apparently got involved in clandestine activities during the Spanish Civil War and in 1937 accompanied her husband when he was transferred to Warsaw. It was there she was recruited by British intelligence and encouraged to learn as much as she could from Polish men she met at diplomatic receptions and other bunfights. Among them was an aide to the foreign minister and she learned much from him, including details of a Polish breakthrough in deciphering Enigma. These were passed on to British intelligence.

Betty Pack, as she was then known, made no secret of her methods: 'I discovered how easy it was to make highly trained, professionally close-mouthed patriots give away secrets in bed and I swore to close my ears to everything confidential on our side.' There seems no doubt that she played a vital role in Britain learning more about Enigma, but hers was not the only role and, typical of the secrecy, she had no understanding of the information she passed on. By the time the war began, Polish and French mathematicians in France worked on the deciphering and they were joined there by the superstar code-breaker from Britain, Alan Turing, the man almost synonymous with the Bletchley Park mansion where signals were intercepted and deciphered.

Pack by 1940 had moved on to New York where she was given the code-name 'Cynthia' and set to work prising signals secrets from Italian naval staff in New York and Washington. Her husband died in 1945 and Pack married one of her French informants, Charles Brousse, a press attaché with the Vichy government, and lived with him in Paris until her death in 1963. Her biographer, Mary Lovell, wrote that Pack's contributions 'have been downplayed by some in the intelligence community because of the method'.

William Stevenson, who oversaw British intelligence efforts in North America, certainly didn't downplay her worth. He said her value to Britain and the United States was incalculable, but in the shadowy half-world of intelligence, truth can often be whatever people want it to be. A *Guardian* journalist, William Boyd, who studied the complex wartime spy world, called Stevenson's autobiography 'highly colourful and vividly inaccurate'.

There was no doubting the extreme importance to the Allies of being able to intercept and decode some German messages; it was never claimed they had them all. Where there was some doubt, especially in the early days of the war, was how accurate the code-breakers were with some of the interpretations they placed on messages. There were criticisms that recipients of Ultra information were misinformed rather than informed. It has to be borne in mind that Crete was still in the early stages of the war, even though it was May 1941 and the war began in September 1939. But some of the intervening period had been the much-quoted phoney war and, for months, there was no land contact between the Allied and German forces. In fact, the short-lived campaign in Greece immediately before Crete was the first land fighting between Commonwealth and German forces since Dunkirk.

The Ultra revelation gradually between 1974 and 1977 added a new dimension to discussion about the Battle for Crete. Already, it was controversial because participants and historians argued particular points of view about what should have happened and what could have happened. The knowledge that Freyberg knew more or less with surety when the Germans were going to attack and with what firepower had been suspected for some time, but the identity of the source could be only guessed at. Some people believed a high-placed Greek spy in the Hotel Grand Bretagne in Athens was able to gain information from the German headquarters in the hotel; some reports said the Italians were the source; and others thought high-placed Germans had been got at. Dan Davin, the author who was on Freyberg's staff and wrote the *Official History* volume covering the battle, said the rumour at the time had been that the source was Wilhelm Canaris, the admiral who headed the intelligence arm of the German high command and who was known to have had a fine disdain for the Nazis. Only very few knew the truth.

The British Government in the 1970s decided to make public the breadth of the British code-breaking in the war because of an increasing number of books and television programmes which were either based on wrong information or took a guess and got it wrong. Even the first and most revealing, *The Ultra Secret* by Fred Winterbotham, an air force officer responsible for Ultra distribution, didn't quite get it right. His book unleashed information about the Enigma secrets onto an unsuspecting world. But he wrote that Churchill knew of the plan to bomb Coventry in November 1941 but did nothing about it — what could he have done anyway? — for fear of revealing his source to the Germans. This was later proven not to be the case.

The public release was supposed to make known the truth, the whole truth and nothing but the truth the government wanted known. The intelligence services were still opposed to documents being available at the Public Record Office (now The National Archives) because in principle they wanted nothing written about past operations. Neither did they want past employees, all of whom were sworn to secrecy, bursting into print with lurid tales of information for sex or other exploits in the name of national security.

At the beginning of the 1970s, few people in Britain or elsewhere would have known of the existence of Bletchley Park in Buckinghamshire. By the end of the decade, Bletchley Park was a byword for code-breaking by men and women with brains finely tuned to the most complex of mathematical problems, brains which had been able to sort out the Enigma variations. The war, people came to believe, however wrongly, was not won at 10 Downing Street or the War Office, or even in the White House, but by the clever clogs at the Government Code and Cipher School at Bletchley Park.

When the doors at the fairly new Public Record Office at Kew opened at 9.30 am on Monday, 17 October 1977, people could walk in and read documents which since the war had remained so secret most of the world didn't even know of their existence. As Peter Hennessy, a journalist at *The Times*, remarked, 'Over the next few years the strategic history of the period will have to be rewritten in the light of information about the enemy's intentions now known to have been in the possession of commanders in Whitehall and the field.' That was a little more circumspect than the bold *Times* headline: 'History will be changed by Enigma disclosures'. There could be no such thing; it could not change what happened, merely add to the knowledge or change interpretations. Crete was lost; men died; no amount of political decision making and bureaucratic indexing 36 years later could change that.

But what could change was the esteem in which some men were held. As Hennessy wrote: 'The genius of a Churchill, the flair of a Montgomery and the poise of an Alexander may look a good deal less impressive when it is known just how much advance information they possessed about the enemy's intentions.'

The knowledge put Freyberg's conduct of the defence of Crete under renewed scrutiny. Hitherto, Freyberg's management of his forces in May 1941 had been questioned, but his performance there was more than outweighed by the clouds of glory which trailed him and the New Zealand Division across North Africa and up Italy. But now, the spotlight swung back to May 1941 and focused anew on Freyberg.

The thrust of the argument against him, spearheaded by historian Antony Beevor, was that Freyberg (or someone) misread or misinterpreted information he was given. This particularly applied to a message that warned of an attack on Canea and of a sea landing. Beevor's contention was that Freyberg saw two sentences as one and therefore thought there was going to be a seaborne assault on Canea. This proved to be a serious mistake, Beevor thought.

A supposed obsession by Freyberg about a seaborne invasion has been a constant theme in criticism of him. Beevor was not the first to believe Freyberg had misread messages he was given. That was also the view of an earlier historian, Ronald Lewin, in one of the first books revealing the secrets, *Ultra Goes to War*.

That was published in 1978 and, in the course of research, Lewin wrote to Dan Davin seeking assistance. He said he had difficulty reaching a clear view about the connection between Ultra and Crete and wondered if Davin knew if Freyberg benefited from Ultra. Davin replied that he did not know and suggested Lewin should get in touch with Freyberg's son.

Beevor and Paul Freyberg had a verbal duel via the letters to the editor columns of *The Times* in 1991 about what Freyberg did or did not know; each stated his position and neither agreed with the other. The exchange did tease out one point from another letter writer, Louis Le Bailly, a retired admiral. It contained an essential truth that has often been overlooked:

> To Lord Freyberg and those brave United Kingdom, Commonwealth and Cretan forces must go the credit that never again during the ensuing four years did Hitler manage to launch such a colossal airborne operation. Whatever the tactical location of Freyberg's forces, such was the ferocity with which they fought that the airborne element of the German army, though just triumphant, was virtually destroyed for ever.

The criticism of course, whether with the knowledge of Ultra or not, was always by people after the event and with knowledge of subsequent and consequential events that Freyberg could not have had.

The most eloquent defence of Freyberg's actions was mounted, not surprisingly, by his son Paul, who once he learned about Ultra from his father, spent the last 30 years of his life trying to pin it all down as best he could.

His contention, logical to some but not persuasive to others, was that having deployed his troops, Freyberg could not on the basis of Ultra knowledge change those dispositions. To have done so, to have lessened the emphasis on coastal defence and to have moved at least a battalion to the west of Maleme, would have alerted the Germans to the source of Freyberg's information. That at least was Paul Freyberg's view and it conforms with the Churchill-Wavell position that dispositions could not be made based solely on information received from Ultra.

A few weeks before the Battle for Crete, the Allied naval commander-in-chief in the Middle East, Andrew Cunningham, used a bit of cunning to ensure success in what came to be known as the Battle of Cape Matapan. He learnt of the existence of an Italian battle fleet off Cape Matapan, the southernmost point of Greece, from Ultra. Knowing he could not act on that information, he dispatched a reconnaissance aircraft in the right direction and, lo and behold, it found the fleet. Cunningham was then justified in deploying elements of his fleet against it and inflicting substantial losses on the Italians.

Freyberg was unable to employ similar cunning. He has had defenders other than his son, among them Ralph Bennett, a historian who had the added benefit of working at Bletchley Park. He agreed that Freyberg could not reposition his forces for fear of giving away his source, but wondered also what difference it could possibly have made. A comparison was made between Freyberg on Crete and Bernard Montgomery at Alam Halfa, the battle in 1942 that held up the Afrika Korps' attack eastward toward Cairo. As another military writer, David Hunt, explained:

> Both knew from Ultra the precise details of the German plan of attack, but the former had scratch forces deficient in weapons and no prepared defences and was also under crushing air attack; the latter has sufficient men and heavy weapons, complete air superiority, and the advantage that the key position had already been fortified and garrisoned by his predecessor, [Claude] Auchinleck. That one battle was a near-run defeat and the second a clear victory shows the limitations of knowledge without strength.

One of the most noted of twentieth-century military historians, John Keegan, reckoned that intelligence can be immensely useful and important but is almost never decisive. It's force that wins battles, not knowledge. 'War is ultimately about doing, not thinking,' he wrote. Crete, he said, was an extreme example of knowledge not being enough. He also made the point that while Freyberg knew more or less what German forces would attack and when, he could not have known 'the terrible, superhuman courage of the German attackers … under murderous close-range fire. The New Zealand defenders at Maleme were brave, but not suicidal.'

Keegan also argued that while Freyberg may have misread at least one of the Ultra signals, there were other factors to consider. Keegan thought Freyberg received summaries of the original German signals, a précis compiled by people at Bletchley Park and giving their version of what they considered important. Freyberg did not see the complex and sometimes confusing raw material. It is not possible to know how thorough or accurate the abbreviated versions were because the original are still secret, assuming they even still exist.

Before Paul Freyberg wrote the book about his father, he had written a manuscript about Ultra based on what his father had told him shortly before he died. (Freyberg died on 4 July 1963 in the King Edward VII Hospital in Windsor, not to be confused with the King Edward VII Saint Agnes Hospital in London, a private hospital and formerly one reserved for officers.) In the manuscript, Paul Freyberg described in some detail what his father told him and what the normal procedure with Ultra messages in Crete had been. They were on a thin piece of rice paper and, as already mentioned, burnt as soon as they were read. Sometimes Freyberg alone would read them, sometimes so too would his intelligence officer, Robin Bell. Paul Freyberg subsequently checked with Bell about his father's version of events and they matched in all details.

Paul Freyberg said he also saw his father's secretary John White, aide Jack Griffiths and Sir William Gentry when he was in New Zealand in 1980 and they all confirmed they knew nothing about Ultra while on Crete.

Paul Freyberg wrote in the manuscript on which he later elaborated in his book that his father had indeed planned to reposition his forces because of what he learnt from Ultra, but he first sought approval from Wavell to do so. Wavell refused. Paul Freyberg wrote: 'I remember as if it was yesterday my father saying to me, "As soon as I read Wavell's letter, I knew that Crete was lost".' Hard-copy evidence of the exchange between Freyberg and Wavell, so crucial to Freyberg's defence, appears not to have survived the war. Paul Freyberg believes the letters were probably burnt in Cairo in 1942, along with other secret material, when Rommel approached the Nile Valley.

Both Freybergs believed that Wavell's words were: 'The authorities [in London] would rather lose Crete than lose Ultra.'

It became Paul Freyberg's life's work to find evidence that would justify his father's actions. An Ultra liaison officer was on Crete — he received the signals on the line from London then took them to Freyberg and waited until they were destroyed. The original liaison officer appears to have been George Beamish, the senior air officer, but he lasted only until a specialist arrived. Paul Freyberg wrote to Davin on Christmas Eve 1981 in some excitement to tell him he had discovered that the Ultra liaison officer (LO as he was known) was an Australian, Mickey Sandford, who, sadly for Freyberg's case, had died in 1979. Beevor mentioned Sandford in his book as being the Ultra man but, confusingly, also assigned the role to Ray Sandover. It's possible that Sandover could have been involved but as he was an infantry battalion commander at Retimo, it seemed unlikely. Sandford surely was the man the older Freyberg met and the younger Freyberg had desperately wanted to meet. (It seems likely Beevor or his editor simply confused the Australian names; perhaps to some in England, all Australians look the same.)

Sandford had a remarkably quick rise in the secret squirrel business. In January 1941, he was a successful Adelaide barrister, wealthy son of a wealthy father, Sir James Sandford, who inherited and built on a family engineering business and also involved himself in state politics. His son was Alastair Wallace Sandford, but known as Mickey to all. He enlisted in the Australian Army on 1 February 1941 at the age of 24 years and nine months; he was

185

immediately made a lieutenant and was attached to Australian headquarters; by early May, he was put on the first of a series of aircraft that took him from Sydney to the Middle East, where he was attached to the intelligence corps, and a ship took him to Crete. From then until the end of the war, which he ended as a colonel, he was in military intelligence. His war service in the Pacific earned him the American award, the Medal of Freedom with bronze palm. He lived the rest of his life in Italy but was not forgotten by those whom he served. In 1968, he was made a Commander of the Order of British Empire (CBE). He was described as a British subject resident in Italy, but no mention was made of why he deserved such an honour.

For all its supreme importance and secrecy, a surprising number of people made their entrances and exits on the Ultra stage. One of them was an Anglo-Irish brigadier, Eric Dorman-Smith, who revelled in the unfortunate nickname of 'Chink'. He was known for his bravery in the First World War, for developing a friendship with Ernest Hemingway and his literati set in Paris in the 1920s, and for having caustic views of the hierarchy in the British Army. In early 1941, Dorman-Smith was on Wavell's staff in Cairo and in the second week of May was sent to Crete to brief Freyberg on some aspects of Ultra and to act as postman for Wavell. The commander-in-chief wrote Freyberg a letter asking how he was getting on with various British officers and asked if they were pulling their weight or whether Freyberg wanted changes. It was a chatty, if serious letter.

A Dorman-Smith biographer, Lavinia Greacen, quoted him as saying that he was impressed by Freyberg's courage but depressed by his tactical sense and was in the 'Bear of Little Brain' category. This patronising put-down was repeated by Beevor in his criticisms of Freyberg. Neither Freyberg nor his son has been recorded as responding to this, but the general may have appreciated a quote from A. A. Milne, a contemporary of Freyberg's great friend, J. M. Barrie: 'When you are a Bear of Very Little Brain and you Think of Things, you find sometimes that a Thing which seemed very Thingish inside you is quite different when it gets out in the open and has other people looking at it.' He could at least console himself that Winnie the Pooh has endured more in public memory than Dorman-Smith. In any case, Freyberg would have found himself in good company. Dorman-Smith, who adopted his original Irish name of O'Gowan after the war, was said to have 'had a sharp and ever-ready tongue which he did not hesitate to unleash on those, and there were many, who were slower in thought and speech than himself'. By most accounts, Dorman-Smith did not progress as high up the army ladder as his brain deserved because of his ability to annoy the wrong people at the wrong times.

Another author, a younger British historian, Saul David, took up the Beevor argument when he wrote a compilation book about supposed military blunders. David gave himself a wide remit, from the Holy Roman Empire to the First Gulf War, sweeping past all manner of fights which, like all fights, had to have had winners and losers. David briefly touched down on Crete and delivered his verdict that Freyberg's greatest mistake was his belief in a seaborne invasion. David also described the German invasion as a reckless gamble that succeeded because 'of the ineptitude of the defenders, particularly the New Zealanders'. Inevitably, this brought immediate protest from New Zealand, most notably from Sir Leonard Thornton, a celebrated military figure who had been on Crete. He vigorously defended both Freyberg and New Zealand troops and wondered on what evidence David based his flawed arguments.

A more specific rebuttal of the Beevor argument, repeated by David, that Freyberg had misread Ultra signals came from Freyberg's wartime secretary, John White. He was constantly by Freyberg's side on Crete until he was dispatched to Alexandria at the end of the month with Freyberg's version of events (just in case the general didn't make it). It wasn't Freyberg who was mistaken, White contended during this little flurry of evidence-based outrage in 1998, but Beevor. 'The copies of Ultra signals he read did not include the first message General Freyberg received from the War Office (the Joint Chiefs of Staff) on 1 May 1941. The message began: "German attack Crete by simultaneous airborne and seaborne expeditions believed imminent".' White, who became Sir John, said following paragraphs set out the expected scale of attack and ended: 'Estimated both troops and shipping ample for seaborne operations and lighters for tanks ... Scale seaborne attack dependent on extent to which enemy can evade our naval force.'

But whatever Freyberg learnt from Ultra and however he deployed the forces at his command may be the great red herring of Crete. He may have had the knowledge, but he did not have the means. In a message to Whitehall in 1948, not made public until 1980, Freyberg wrote: 'From our point of view, given the same circumstances, Crete could not be held. I am of the opinion that it could not have been evacuated. Therefore, we had to stay and fight.'

Freyberg elaborated on this in a separate message to Churchill that began, 'My very dear Winston ...' He hinted that the German invasion of Crete was driven by Goering's ego rather than any strategic imperative.

> They used the whole of their Luftwaffe to take Crete, but in doing so wrote off in an operation of no vital importance this most precious and highly trained force. It was, in my opinion, a doubtful and costly success for the German force. But Goering, it appears, felt that he must have a personal success and the Luftwaffe was used.

Regardless of what Freyberg knew or did not know in advance, and what he could say about what he knew, he told Churchill the Germans made two mistakes:

1. They landed their airborne troops on the top of our garrisons in the only possible way in which we could kill them, and they suffered very heavy casualties when they could have landed five to ten miles away from our garrisons without any casualties. They could have made their own aerodromes, built up a front unmolested by us because our troops and our guns were immobile and we had little or no heavy equipment.

2. They brought in their seaborne force by night instead of by day, which enabled our ships to intercept and sink them. Had they come by day the British navy could not have got near them because of their heavy and accurate air support.

Was Crete a disaster? Freyberg said no. 'I am sure history will say it was a considerable feat of arms by tired, disorganised and ill-equipped troops. The only alternative was to scuttle away with part of our force, leaving the balance, including unarmed Palestinians and Cypriots, to their fate.'

11

The blame game

'The problem is to decide what is the proper measure of criticism.'
— Howard Kippenberger

One of the British war correspondents in the Middle East theatre during the war, Christopher Buckley, wrote a book about the failed campaigns in Greece and Crete. Written in the 1940s, when barely a book about Crete had been published, he wrote: 'The battle of Crete will be [a] matter of discussion as long as the ways and means of making war exercise their strange and terrible fascination upon mankind.'

Buckley did not live to see how right he was. An Oxford-trained historian, he was correspondent for the London *Daily Telegraph* and was killed in his next war, in Korea, on 12 August 1950 when the vehicle in which he and two companions were travelling hit a landmine. The correspondent for *The Times*, Ian Morrison — a son of the Australian adventurer and journalist, George 'Chinese' Morrison — and an Indian Army colonel who was a friend of Morrison's, Unni Nayar, also died.

Buckley had sent his Greece and Crete manuscript to various people, including Bernard Freyberg, for comment, and it now forms part of the papers of Dan Davin in the Alexander Turnbull Library in Wellington.

Buckley's views formed a part of the first wave of comment on Crete; he was an element of the immediate aftermath. Comment, criticism and analysis have continued ever since with peaks in interest coming with the publication in New Zealand of the official histories, especially Davin's *Crete* in 1953, with the publication of other landmark books, especially those by Alan Clark

(1962) and Ian Stewart (1966), and the revelations about the existence of Ultra in the 1970s. Interest in and comment on Crete, especially from a New Zealand perspective, have never waned. In 2011, the year some of the remaining 1941 soldiers went back to Crete for 70th anniversary commemorations, one of the more prominent of the fighters, Sandy Thomas, pointed his finger of blame. He said Crete was lost because of the commanding officer of the 22nd Battalion, Les Andrew. Thomas was not the first to finger Andrew and probably won't be the last, although in all likelihood the last of the prominent participants.

It wasn't so much what Thomas said that was pertinent but the fact that it was the latest example of trying to find someone or something to blame, as if the events of Crete could not be explained without the presence of a scapegoat.

The aftermath that has come in lapping waves has all swirled round the same essential rocks of contention: could Crete have been held? Why wasn't it? Whose fault was it that it wasn't? What more could have been done? Should there have even been a battle there? There are many other related questions, and some extremely militarily detailed ones which follow one from the other, but the whole issue comes down to two basic questions: Could Crete have been held *by the forces that were given the job?* Answer: No.

Why not? The Germans had complete air supremacy against an under-equipped ground force. Everything else that happened stemmed from that.

The aftermath, the inquisitions both formal and informal, began almost before the last Allied soldier was back in Egypt. Some were centred on purely New Zealand grounds and others had a much wider focus.

Brigadier James Hargest has been frequently blamed as one of the biggest contributors to the loss for his inaction, indifference even, on the first night when Andrew told him he had to withdraw from his position overlooking Maleme aerodrome: 'If you must, you must.' The folk tale has grown up that Hargest when he got back to Egypt hot-footed it straight to Prime Minister Peter Fraser and put all the blame on Freyberg and anyone else he could think of. It's part of the Hargest historical narrative that as a Member of Parliament he used his influence in 1939 to overturn a recommendation that he not be given a senior army position. (Twelve other MPs had signed up for the war and four of them, like Hargest, gave their lives. And two of them, like Hargest, had also served in the First World War.) The picture has been painted of a tired, ageing and unwell man being overwhelmed by the events which unfolded around him and then seeking to blame others.

The picture becomes a little blurred, though, when it is learnt that that one-man crusader, Clive Hulme, came across the lone figure of Hargest — a brigadier, no less — in a field, alone and unprotected, popping away furiously at the Germans overhead. It blurred again when it was learnt that officers and men alike thought Hargest was magnificent in the crisis of trying to get as many men to safety as he could.

And what really happened in Cairo? Well, in Hargest's own tale related in his diary, he did indeed quickly meet up with Fraser. But also there were Freyberg, Archie Wavell, the navy boss Andrew Cunningham, and the RAF Middle East commander, Arthur Tedder. They discussed the possibility of sending more ships to Crete to get off more men but, by then, Cunningham refused to risk more of his depleted fleet. (This was the same fleet of disappearing ships that would have had to have supplied troops if Crete had been held.)

After that meeting, according to Hargest's diary: 'I bought a few clothes & joined Mr Fraser & the Gen at the NZ Forces Club for lunch.' After that, they cleaned themselves up — Freyberg and Hargest had still been in their unchanged Crete shorts and shirts — and went to Alexandria to meet the last of the troops. It was only the next day, back in Cairo, that Hargest and Fraser met without Freyberg also being present. Hargest and Fraser were joined by Carl Berendsen, the head of the Prime Minister's Department, and Fred Waite, a lieutenant-colonel in charge of soldiers' welfare, for dinner. Hargest said: 'I told my story. I hope it will bear fruit.'

Hargest's criticism of Freyberg, or at least a view that differed from Freyberg's, seemed to centre on the disposition of New Zealand troops during the retreat in Greece rather than on Crete. If he also disagreed with Freyberg about where troops were positioned on Crete, and told Fraser so, he did not have the knowledge that Freyberg had.

There was no hint that something might not have been quite right when he was awarded a bar to the Distinguished Service Order for his performance in Greece and Crete. Recommended by Edward Puttick, who had temporary command of the division, and approved by Freyberg, the citation talked about Hargest's 'devotion to duty, coolness and tactical skill'. The phrase 'great skill' popped up and the rearguard action he organised 'was largely instrumental in securing the same embarkation of our troops at Spharkia'.

I digress here on the rest of the war for this 'tired, old man' with the brigadier-general's three pips and crown on his epaulettes. Six months after Crete, Hargest was captured when his brigade headquarters at Sidi Aziz in what became known as the second Libyan campaign was overrun by Germans. Soon after his capture, he had a perfunctory conversation with the Afrika Korps commander, Erwin Rommel. Hargest did not salute him but bowed instead, and Rommel chided him for the lack of military courtesy. Hargest knew he was in the wrong but pretended otherwise. Rommel complimented Hargest on the fighting qualities of the New Zealanders.

'Yes, they fight well,' Hargest agreed, 'but your tanks were too powerful for us.'

'But you also have tanks.'

'Yes, but not here, as you can see.'

'Perhaps my men are superior to yours.'

'You know that is not correct.'

Hargest was taken with other prisoners by submarine to Italy and was incarcerated in a castle near Florence, home for the rest of the war, it was planned, for senior Allied officers. But Hargest and another brigadier, Reg Miles, escaped and Hargest eventually made his way into Spain and then to England. He crossed France on a train posing as a member of the crew, a pretence sustained by the real crew when the train was stopped and searched by Germans. One of the Frenchmen from the train guided Hargest — on foot — through the Pyrenees and to the Spanish border. When they were about to part company, Hargest emptied his pockets and gave the Frenchman a pile of French and Swiss money. The Frenchman protested that he did not guide him for money, but Hargest said he had no use for it anyway. Hargest wrote his own book about his exploits, *Farewell Campo 12*, and so too did a French author, Gabriel Nahas, in *La Filière du Rail*.

Rather than return home, as he probably could have done, Hargest sought continued military work and was attached to the 50th (Northumberland) Division for the Allied landings in Normandy in June 1944 as a New Zealand observer. As such, he was the only NZEF soldier involved in D-Day. The job was expected to be merely observation and liaison, but Hargest got himself involved in spotting for artillery and found other ways of making himself useful. It was while searching for mortars that the mortars found him. His Royal Army Service Corps driver, Stan Coo, recalled stopping at a crossroads on the edge of a French village not long after the invasion. Hargest left the vehicle, walked round a corner and into a salvo of mortars. Coo went looking and found Hargest on his hands and knees. 'That was a close one, Coo!' he remarked. Hargest had 14 wounds in his body, arms and head, but none of them serious. They were serious enough to get him sent back to England for treatment, though.

While there, he learnt he had been given a job dear to his heart: that of being in charge of all repatriated New Zealand prisoners of war. It was his job to oversee their health and welfare and ensure they could be sent back to New Zealand as soon as possible. But since there weren't many prisoners to take care of in mid-1944, Hargest thought he'd return to France for a while. It was a fatal decision.

Coo drove him into a field to see the colonel in charge of some infantrymen who were engaged with the Germans. Hargest completed his business and the pair were on their way from the area when the Germans saw the vehicle and mortar fire started. Coo was in the act of turning the vehicle when mortar bombs exploded alongside.

'He got the lot,' Coo later recalled. 'He was a big bloke. He completely obliterated me.' As a result, Coo was not touched. He drove 'like the hammers of hell' to the nearest forward aid station, but the medical staff there could do nothing. Hargest was dead.

The blame game

The questioning of Hargest's role on Crete, the wondering whether he was too old for a young man's war, whether he was too 'First War' for the Second, did not come until later. It did not come until men were home, until books were written and opinions expressed. Before the later judgements, there were the untainted ones. Some of those who later pointed an accusing finger did so reluctantly; others were less reticent about apportioning blame for a situation that was beyond any man to control. Before all of that, an editorial writer for the *Auckland Star* put into words what many people must have been thinking:

> There is in some men a rare quality of patriotism which precludes the thought that they have done or could do enough in the service of their country. Brigadier Hargest MP was one of them. The spirit which took him to Gallipoli was undimmed by his experiences there and in France, and by the succeeding years, disillusioning to many soldiers, of peacetime and politics. When war came again he stepped forward as naturally as many men of half his years, and with their quiet eagerness. After serving in the campaigns in Greece and Crete, and in Libya, he was captured, but the enemy could not hold him. He escaped from Italy to safety in Switzerland and again, although officially discouraged from making the attempt, through France into Spain. The full story of that journey has never been told, and when pressed to tell it Brigadier Hargest would say that it amounted to nothing by comparison with the achievements of others who had served under him. Back in London, he sought opportunities to resume active service and in the course of it, he has been killed. He would not complain of dying on the soil of France, whose people, at their own mortal risk, had made possible his escape, and for whom he cherished admiration and gratitude. New Zealand has cause to grieve for the death of a son whose patriotism was deep, wide and sustaining, and to reflect that the prestige which its fighting men enjoy abroad owes much to the spirit and example of such men as he.

Fraser eventually went off to London from Cairo still brooding about the

195

disasters which had befallen his division and wondering whether Freyberg really was the man to run it. Fraser was especially annoyed with Freyberg for not telling him he thought the Greek campaign was ill-advised. Fraser talked to the chief of the imperial general staff, Sir John Dill, in London about Freyberg and he cabled both Wavell and Wavell's successor, Claude Auchinleck, for their views. Wavell, with whom Churchill had become increasingly impatient, had by this time been moved to India. Both the senior British generals sent back replies with warm commendations of Freyberg.

Churchill also sought answers on another front. He wanted to know what happened on Crete and why it wasn't held and, at his behest, an inter-services committee was set up to meet in Cairo and find the answers. Put in charge of the inquiry was a Coldstream Guards officer, Guy Salisbury-Jones, about whom, ironically, Wavell had had doubts and asked Freyberg if he fitted in all right on Crete. Now the table had been flipped over. Salisbury-Jones would have been conscious of the invidious position in which he found himself because he and his fellow committee members were junior to men upon whom they sat in judgement.

As it turned out, the niceties of military chains of command and hierarchy were never upset. The report of 70 pages when it was produced later in the year found no fault with any of the senior men charged with defending Crete. It was critical of the inaction in planning for the defence of Crete in the period between November 1940 and May 1941 and of the lack of cooperation between the services. Its overriding conclusion was: 'Perhaps the major lesson of this campaign was that to defend with a relatively small force an island as large as Crete, lying under the permanent domination of enemy fighter aircraft and out of range of our own, was impossible.'

Wavell was apparently on his way to India when he read the report and was not happy with it. He thought parts of it compromised the secrecy of Ultra — but had to be careful to whom he made those comments — and that, overall, the committee went way beyond its remit. 'The committee have throughout treated the problem of Crete as if it was an isolated problem for which the whole resources of the Middle East were available and there were no other problems to consider at the same time,' Wavell wrote in an angry letter to the War Office.

He attacked the committee on several other points, including its observations about lack of preparation being beside the point because 'no possible preparations in Crete could have conjured up six squadrons of fighter aircraft when they were not available in the Middle East'.

The War Office suppressed the report and it did not become public until 1972.

Hargest was not the only brigadier to talk behind Freyberg's back. So too did Lindsay Inglis, a peacetime lawyer whose suggestive nickname among the troops was 'Whisky Bill'. Inglis was apparently irritated that he was criticised on Crete for not obeying an order from Freyberg. Inglis felt Freyberg was wrong and told Fraser so, and Inglis went to London to do further damage.

Dill, the senior army man in London, had asked Wavell to send to London someone senior who could explain what happened on Crete. Freyberg's intention was to send Hargest, but he was unwell at the time so he sent Inglis instead. It was not a good move. It was not part of the plan for Inglis to see Churchill, but he contrived to do so and gave him his version of events. The effect of this meeting was that Freyberg got blamed by Churchill for the defeat and blamed by Wavell for doing the dirty on him which led to his being sacked. Relations between Freyberg and Inglis were never cordial after that and in 1944 Inglis, after an angry exchange with his boss, went home. Ian Stewart, the English doctor who wrote such a compelling account of Crete, had a disdainful dismissal of Inglis, saying he was 'adept at proving to his own satisfaction that any failure with which he might be associated could not relate to any inadequacy of his own'. The quasi-official *Oxford Companion to New Zealand Military History* said of him: 'His conduct after the battle was disloyal and unprofessional.'

Inglis distinguished himself when he led the division in the breakout at Minqar Qaim a year after Crete when Freyberg was wounded. But he did his after-war reputation not much good at all when he appeared at a war crimes trial to speak in defence of the German who planned the Crete invasion, Kurt

Student. It was not a good image: the man who talked about his boss behind his back supported his enemy in court. Inglis was a military court president in Germany and when he read reports of Student's trial he volunteered to give evidence 'in the interests of British justice'. His evidence centred on his belief that the Germans did not use Allied soldiers as screens and that the Germans did not deliberately bomb a tent hospital because 'they were obviously trying to hit a crowd of troops on the beach'. Allied soldiers, including New Zealanders, swore affidavits that they had been used as a screen and that some members of their units were killed by New Zealand fire. Student, who was not on Crete but directed operations from Athens, was found guilty of three of eight charges and sentenced to five years' jail. The findings and sentence were never confirmed, however, and Student saw out his days in freedom.

Inevitably and rightly, the Greece and Crete campaigns were discussed in Parliament in Wellington, first of all in a secret session that reaffirmed the division's continued presence in Europe and then in a normal session. It was 'normal' for the time because the broadcasting procedure for Parliament then was that it could be heard throughout New Zealand and the South Pacific. Members could choose, or the Speaker could choose for them, if they wanted their dulcet tones heard beyond New Zealand. John A. Lee, who lost an arm in the First World War, asked that his views on the New Zealand presence in both Greece and Crete not be heard in the South Pacific. What he had to say was for domestic consumption only. But when Lee sat down, Speaker Bill Barnard then had to wonder out loud what he should do about members' speeches which referred to Lee's remarks: let them go or cut them off? Walter Nash, the acting prime minister, gave a polished political answer which in essence said: that's up to you.

The gist of Lee's argument was that New Zealand troops should not be sent into a fight they did not have a reasonable chance of winning: 'New Zealanders will fight with anyone on earth, if necessary, but that does not justify sending anybody anywhere except when they have a chance of beating the other fellow.'

Since Lee had demonstrably proven his courage and his worth in battle, he was listened to with the respect he had earned. But that didn't necessarily mean agreement. Lee's comments especially annoyed Sir Apirana Ngata who, although he didn't say so, had had one son captured in Greece and another wounded on Crete. Ngata said if the House agreed with Lee, Wavell and Churchill should be told: 'All right, we will pick and choose where the fight shall take place. We will go in for safe battles, but if there is a risk, for God's sake do not send any New Zealanders there.'

Ngata talked at length about discussions he had on the East Coast with Maori. They were not happy. Talking about Greece, 'they did not like the business at all. When it came to the affair in Crete they liked it even less.' Ngata said his advice to them was simple. They should ask the prime minister to cable the authorities in Europe to send the Maoris home

'because, I said, "Evidently your idea is that they should go abroad as tourists and observers for the Maori and Polynesian races and to report that Egypt is a country infested with fleas, and that the people and customs are dirty while in England there is a magnificent people." That was the kind of information contained in the letters from our boys for about 12 months until our boys were brought face up against the Hitler war machine. Evidently some of our people did not like it. Well, if any member of this House does not like what our boys are doing overseas, I suggest that the member should endeavour to get the authorities to send them home.'

Ngata also worried about the Home Guard, the 'broomstick business' as he called it, and how it had too many men who did not know what to do. Ngata knew what to do: 'Their real duty is over there … the old Maori warrior did not hang about his meeting house waiting for the enemy; he went out on to the hills and ranges to meet him. That is the proper place for New Zealanders to be just now.'

Two years after Crete, Ngata produced a small book, *The Price of Citizenship*, written in memory of Maori who had died in the war and as a lesson to Maori and Pakeha about what he described as 'the deep-seated call of the blood, of the camaraderie of kin and clan and of that pride in race, without which peoples cannot continue to live on earth'.

Maori in the First World War were initially spared frontline duties, but this time they asked for a full share, he wrote. The men of the New Zealand Division realised the value of the Maori fighter and that he was an asset to the country. Ngata then asked: 'Have the civilians of New Zealand, men and women, fully realised the implications of the joint participation of Pakeha and Maori in the last and greatest demonstration of the highest citizenship?'

E tama ma, i hira ai

Ahau ki runga ra!

(Heroes who have by doughty deeds, lifted my flame on high)

Les Andrew, the officer commanding the 22nd Battalion, joined Hargest after the war as being held most responsible for the Germans taking Maleme aerodrome and, therefore, Crete. Andrew went from being a hero of one war, when he won the Victoria Cross, to a scapegoat in the second, even being accused of losing his nerve, whatever that imprecise diagnosis may mean. It was Andrew who drew his forces back from commanding positions on Hill 107 overlooking Maleme and thereby provided the opportunity the Germans needed. Andrew's culpability, if such it was, went beyond army talk into the public domain with the publication in 1953 of Davin's book. Davin, probably out of his respect for men with whom he fought, trod carefully over eggshells as he moved towards a difficult conclusion that Andrew was wrong. Even having reached the conclusion, he tried to soften the blow:

'Ultimately ... the withdrawal from Maleme was to entail the loss of Crete. It would be unjust to Lieutenant-Colonel Andrew to suggest that he should have foreseen this as clearly as the advantage of hindsight enables us to see it 10 years later.' Davin even included a footnote saying that if Maleme had not been lost, there were still other options open to the Germans. Davin at least acknowledged the benefits of hindsight; few other scapegoat seekers bothered.

Howard Kippenberger became editor in chief of the New Zealand war histories in peacetime. It was a good appointment. He had a lifelong interest in military history and was fond of quoting precedents from battles won and lost; he had the mind of a trained lawyer and the experience of a fighting soldier. But he also had the luxury of being able to influence the writing of the histories and to express his own opinions which never became subject to public scrutiny. Kippenberger's influence on Davin's book was pronounced, and it is assumed he had a similar influence on the other histories while he was in charge. It's worthy of note that Geoffrey Cox, a gifted writer who was on Crete throughout, began writing one of the official histories at Kippenberger's behest but withdrew from the task, citing pressure of work in Britain.

The 50-volume series of *The Official History of New Zealand in the Second World War* became an important part of New Zealand's collective memory of the war. The volumes are in effect the official memory and stand in marked contrast to the government's ambivalence towards an official record of the First World War. It was as if Kippenberger, with the willing assistance of Peter Fraser, wanted to make amends for the errors and omissions of 1914–18. Print runs varied, but 4000 seems to have been the average for each volume as they appeared at regular intervals through the 1950s and 60s. Copies of each of the battalion and other unit histories were sent free to each of the participants. Some of the writers employed by Kippenberger were on the government payroll, but he had to come to terms with others. Davin, for example, was paid £1200 to write the Crete volume (according to the Reserve Bank's calculations, that was equivalent to about $81,000 in today's terms).

Davin's circumspect criticism of Andrew may have been influenced by this paragraph from a letter Kippenberger wrote to Davin:

The problem is to decide what is the proper measure of criticism. In our notes we have criticised without any inhibitions, sometimes as [William] Gentry says, coldly and bitterly. That is all very well, but you cannot write so freely. This is an Official History, not a new shocker from [Ralph] Ingersoll or [Basil] Liddell Hart.

(Ingersoll was an American soldier-writer and Liddell Hart was an English military historian; each was noted for his belief in the correctness of his opinions.) As an example of Kippenberger's 'cold and bitter' criticisms, he related to Davin how on 8 August 1915 the Wellington Battalion

> fought almost to extinction to hold Chunuk Bair … when relieved, they were still holding … 'throughout that day, not one had dreamed of leaving his post'. There is no sign of any weakness among the men of 22 Bn but Colonel Andrew was not Colonel [William] Malone. Maleme was as vital as Chunuk Bair and this was a case where it was the duty of an infantry battalion to fight to a finish.

Andrew's decision to withdraw was inexcusable, Kippenberger wrote. So Kippenberger would also have disagreed with John Keegan who, as mentioned in the previous chapter, described the New Zealanders as brave but not suicidal. Kippenberger wanted his men to be suicidal. Would they, if they could, still have regarded him fondly as 'Kip'?

Kippenberger's tongue-lashing extended to his superior officer, Edward Puttick, who had command of the division on Crete, and (of course) to his fellow brigadier, Hargest. Puttick, he thought, did not grasp the importance of the Germans gaining a foothold on Maleme 'and, like Hargest, sat still staring in all directions, including skyward, until his gallant troops were overwhelmed. I have many things for which to be grateful to Puttick, much friendship with Hargest and Andrew. These are violent criticisms which I believe to be just.'

Others disagreed. One unnamed former officer wrote to Andrew after the publication of Davin's book and said he felt Davin was unfair to both Hargest and Andrew.

> In your place I know I would be deeply hurt at the verdict of an author who, in my opinion, is incapable of being a war historian and in such a case it would comfort me to know that many of my friends and

comrades, who were in a position to know, were on my side and still considered me a soldier of outstanding stature.

Andrew himself spoke little about the war. Davin's biographer, Keith Ovenden, called Andrew enigmatic and remote. In 1955, Andrew wrote to the 22nd Battalion historian, Jim Henderson, and said that despite Davin and Kippenberger, he could still hold his head high. 'Chaps who were there know what I did in Greece and on Crete. I'll abide by their judgement and I know why the alleged Official History was issued in that way.' He did not elaborate on that last phrase. When Andrew died in Palmerston North Hospital in 1969, newspaper reports covered his military career at some length but did not mention his alleged shortcomings on Crete. One report from New Plymouth included the sentence: 'His exploits as commander of the battalion during the battle for Maleme airfield on Crete became a legend in the 2nd NZEF.'

More than 30 years later, Andrew was in the gun again. In a television documentary, Sandhurst-based New Zealand military historian Chris Pugsley took the Kippenberger line and said the road to defeat began when Andrew 'lost his nerve', a comment since repeated by people less experienced in military matters. This prompted an angry reaction from a former 22nd Battalion soldier, Barney Wicksteed, who moved the blame from Andrew to the 23rd Battalion commanding officer, Doug Leckie. Andrew had sought help from the 23rd but, according to one view, Hargest told him the 23rd were busy with their own problems and, according to another, the 23rd didn't reply to Andrew's call. Andrew, according to some accounts including Wicksteed's, walked to the 23rd headquarters three or four kilometres away and found Leckie 'had cracked up' and refused to emerge and give orders.

Wicksteed said of Andrew:

We who served under him all held him in the utmost respect and would do anything for him. I had quite a lot to do with him after the war with battalion business and he told me that he had called the battalion that was supposed to be primed for a counter-attack should it be necessary and couldn't get any sense out of them at all. He found later that their commanding officer, who had served in World War I, when the shooting started and with all that noise … it had got him down.

I asked Andrew: 'Why didn't you tell them?' He replied: 'This officer was a friend of mine and a very fine fellow and I wasn't going to say that and upset his family. Just let it go.'

Keith Elliott, a 22nd Battalion non-commissioned officer who won the Victoria Cross for his gallantry at Ruweisat Ridge in 1942, had a telling comment:

In every battle in which I've taken part, if you lose, a scapegoat must be found. The rule applied equally in Trentham and in England when we were on exercises. The lawyer or schoolteacher who could talk the fastest won the battle — but not so when the hardware was flying.

Lloyd Cross, a major in the 22nd, related at the battalion's 50th anniversary how livid Andrew was when awards and decorations for the Greece and Crete campaigns were published. 'When Les saw that out of 38 recommendations only one was awarded (Colin Armstrong, MC) he was so enraged that he ripped off his VC and said that we would be known as the clean-breasted battalion.' Cross said Andrew was extremely brave but 'felt very emotional whenever any soldier under his command was killed'. The book written about Crete in the early 1960s by the English doctor, Ian Stewart, is probably the most comprehensive outside Davin's *Official History*. It may not be coincidence that Stewart and Davin were friends, that Stewart had the run of Davin's papers when writing his book, which was published by Oxford University Press, where Davin happened to be the editor. There is a sense that Stewart wrote much that Davin himself would have liked to have written but could not do so because of Kippenberger's overarching role. An example that leads to that suspicion is this from Stewart:

Commanders do not bring wisdom and insight to every phase of their direction. Often their decisions remain wavering and contradictory until the issue is decided by chance or by some single stroke, fatal or triumphant. Later every blemish fades when touched by the accolades of victory, or all appears blameworthy when marked by the stigma of defeat. In extremity their resources may prove no less surprising than their lapses when fortune has favoured them. These simple truths would scarcely merit restatement were it not that some historians have ingenuously sought to apportion absolute merit and blame between Wavell, Freyberg, Puttick, Hargest and other leaders in Crete.

Stewart was of the firm, even dogmatic, view that had Maleme been held, the island could never have been lost. But he doesn't blame just Andrew or just Andrew and Hargest. There were many mistakes by many commanders. But, writing in the 1960s, he had knowledge that those commanders, especially Freyberg, did not have. Although he was on Crete, he also seemed to have underestimated the debilitating effect of constant dive-bombing and strafing. It is inconceivable that anyone who has not been subject to such aural and physical harassment could begin to comprehend how bad it could be. Christopher Buckley, who was not on Crete, wrote that the defenders could have shown greater resistance by leaping out of their slit trenches and firing at the attacking aircraft. Easy to say perhaps, much less easy to do.

The truth about Crete, if such a thing can be known, lies somewhere between claim and counter-claim and somewhere amid the immediate post-war rush of trying to protect the reputations of some former soldiers while seemingly not caring too much about others. Much judgement has been reached in the peaceful, comforting quiet of hindsight while the men who were being judged had to contend with the danger, noise and confusion of battle; there is much misuse of the knowledge of hindsight in the story of the Battle for Crete. Some historians and others have also had the time and luxury to indulge themselves in the 'what if?' game, a game that shifts historical analysis from non-fiction to fiction. For the soldiers who fought and died, or those who lived with the consequence of their actions or the actions of others, there was no 'what if?' There could only ever be what was.

For the sake of pursuing logical outcomes, however, what would have happened if Maleme had been held on the night of 20–21 May? There would have been a hill full of dead New Zealanders and nothing much to show for it; a bit like the Chunuk Bair that Kippenberger wanted. Even if the hill wasn't lost that night, even if New Zealanders clung to it until they could cling no more, could Crete have been saved, could Crete have been an Allied outcrop in the Mediterranean for the rest of the war, another Malta? How could it have been? How was the island going to be supplied, reinforced, defended? The Germans had the air power and they had the closest air bases (in Greece). The navy, by Andrew Cunningham's own assessment, could do no more. He'd lost too many ships and men already.

Crete was lost as soon as Churchill insisted it could not be. It did not have the defences it should have had, it had no air cover and the troops charged with holding it were on their way back from being tossed out of Greece; there were not enough men and there was not enough equipment. Freyberg knew that. That was why he said he realised from the beginning the problem was a clear-cut one: Crete could not be evacuated immediately — 'Therefore, we had to stay and fight.'

And stay and fight the New Zealanders and their allies did until they could fight no longer. They were tired, hungry, thirsty, many of them ill, many of them wounded, all of them in a place they had no desire to be. It is they who form the bedrock of the Battle for Crete and who should be remembered; what men did in the name of their country and in the name of camaraderie and duty is what ought to be remembered; finding blame, looking for a scapegoat, embellishing one's own reputation, these things detract from the real worth of Crete. Stories such as the soldier who plonked his helmet on a grenade then stood on it to save the lives of his mates; the doctors and padres who refused to leave wounded men and spent the rest of the war in prison camps; men such as Upham and Hulme and a thousand others who did not get the decorations to show their valour; the men who were called upon to do jobs for which they were not trained and for which they lacked the tools; the blokes who stood on the cliffs and watched the ships and their mates sail away; the ordinary soldier, Private Anonymous, who was thrust into circumstances he could never have imagined and did the best he could. The real story of Crete was about selflessness, not selfishness.

Afterword

'How long will the war last? For the rest of our lives.'

— Dan Davin, *For the Rest of Our Lives* (1947)

More than a year after Crete, in August of 1942, a New Zealand expatriate came across his fellow countrymen in the North African desert. It was a year after consecutive defeats, a year after humiliating retreats, a year after being blamed for not doing the impossible. The New Zealand Division was re-equipped and enlarged, reinforced by fresh troops from home. But there were still many men from Greece and Crete in the ranks. But they were different men. Once they were in despair, now they were confident; once they had not known victory, now defeat was behind them.

'They were mature men, these men of the desert, quiet and shrewd and sceptical,' John Mulgan, the New Zealander who was now a British officer, wrote. 'They had none of the tired patience of the Englishman, nor that automatic discipline that never questions orders to see if they make sense. Moreover, he added, they 'had confidence in themselves, such as New Zealanders rarely have, knowing themselves as good as the best the world could bring against them ...'

More than a year after that encounter in the desert, there was another. This time it was with the Australian war correspondent, Alan Moorehead, who worked for the *Daily Express*. They were in the west, in Tunisia, fighting in the Middle East theatre nearly at an end. This is what Moorehead wrote:

> At last we cut around a field of cactus and joined the main road north of Sousse. With the main road we hit the New Zealand Division coming

head-on towards us — in the way the enemy would see it coming. They rolled by with their tanks and their guns and their armoured cars, the finest troops of their kind in the world, the outflanking experts, the men who had fought the Germans in the desert for two years, the victors of half a dozen pitched battles. They were too gaunt and lean to be handsome, too hard and sinewy to be graceful, too youthful and physical to be complete. But if you ever wished to see the most resilient and practised fighter of the Anglo-Saxon armies, this was he.

In the weeks and months and years that followed Crete, the men of the New Zealand Division reshaped and burnished their reputation. They earned respect from friend and enemy alike for the way they fought for Churchill's impossible dream on Crete; although it was a lost cause, they fought with purpose, with sleeves rolled up, there to do a job and they'd damned well do it no matter what.

They were called many things. Churchill called them 'that ball of fire'; Germany's main radio tease, Lord Haw-Haw, dismissed them as 'Freyberg's little circus'; Hitler was even said to have made reference to them as 'poor country lads, who don't know what it is all about and whose bones will bleach along the desert ways'. But Rommel was different. 'The best division in the Eighth Army,' he said.

A captured German document contained an appraisal of the division:

The New Zealanders, most of whom volunteered for service in Europe out of a sense of adventure, are trained and led by General Freyberg, a dangerous opponent. They are specialists in night fighting, they fight on a wide front and their method of attack resembles the German method. The New Zealanders have learnt to follow up closely under the heavy artillery barrages which they use; by this means they are able to take their opponents off their guard and gain their objectives without heavy losses. They are also capable in difficult country of fighting without tank support.

Archie Wavell, the Middle East commander-in-chief during Greece and Crete, wrote to Freyberg: 'I have seen the New Zealand Division grow under you from a magnificent body of men into as fine a fighting formation as ever went into battle for the British Empire and the cause of freedom.'

Roy Farran, something of a free-spirited British officer on Crete, wrote about the New Zealanders: 'Just to look at their confident, smiling faces was good for the spirit. They had been beaten out of Greece by overwhelming odds, they were ill-equipped and underfed, but it takes more than that to daunt the finest fighting troops in the world.'

There was some bitterness after Crete; 'higher ups' were blamed for getting them into a fix they should not have been in, although numerous writers, both at the time and later, noticed that Churchill and Freyberg seemed always to be beyond criticism from the troops. Much easier to point the fingers at anonymous 'powers that be'.

Crete memories would not have entirely faded, but they would have receded into the background as new country was crossed, new campaigns fought, new tasks set and achieved. The New Zealand Division, with Freyberg at its head, swung its way across North Africa, often at the spearhead of the advance, then joined the hard slog north through Italy until they were in Trieste and the war was over. It was time to go home. Some went on to Japan. Some went back to Crete.

From a time of war it became a time of peace, and men put aside their weapons and returned to whatever it was they did before they were called to war: the schoolteachers went back to school, the farmers to their farms, the clerks to their offices, the students to their studies. But whatever it was they returned to, the war remained a part of them, usually a silent part. Few men spoke about what they did unless it was to other men of shared times. 'You realise just how difficult it is to get chaps to give their guts,' researcher John Clark wrote to Angus Ross, the 23rd Battalion historian.

When the *Auckland Star* marked victory in Europe, writer Geoffrey Webster tried to sum up the men of 'the Div': 'Civilians all, the majority laughingly refusing to feel heroic about it. Nobody with the words "King and country" on his lips. Nobody shouting about democracy or making things safe. Scarcely anyone believing that he was doing anything extraordinary.'

As the *Official History* volumes were published and each man received a complimentary copy of his battalion history, they would read it or flick through it, see a familiar name or two, and wonder. For men who do the fighting seldom know what other fighting is going on near them, rarely know what an overall objective may be. They might look at a sentence and say to themselves, 'Ah, that was what that was all about!' Or they might see a name and think, 'Ah, that's what happened to Jim.'

Or they might read a bit of Dan Davin's *Crete*. The bit where he writes: 'Soldiers never fought better than they fought on Crete; and not least among them the soldiers of the New Zealand Division.'

And they might look into the middle-distance, clear their throat, wipe whatever it was that got caught in the eye, and sit a little taller.

Bibliography

Primary sources

Alexander Turnbull Library

Les Andrew letter to Jim Henderson (MS-Papers-3953); Dan Davin papers relating to Freyberg (MS-Papers-5079-573); personal correspondence between Robin Miller and A. D. McIntosh (MS-Papers-6759-317); draft list of Crete campaign comments by Inglis, Leckie, Dittmer (MS-Papers-5079-666); Kippenberger comments (MS-Papers-5079-664); Davin papers and correspondence (MS-Papers-5079-335); Davin papers relating to Christopher Buckley narrative (MS-Papers-5079-236) and Kippenberger comments on (MS-Papers-5079-234); 'Monty' McClymont comments (MS-Papers 5079-203).

Hocken Collections, Hocken Library, University of Otago

Angus Ross papers (MS-2699/026, MS-2699/010).

Archives New Zealand

Kippenberger note on Galatas (DA 50.1/22/1); Ben Ferry letter (DA 46/10/5); extracts from James Hargest diaries (DA 52/10/10); Robin Miller biography (DA 404/6); Creforce report (DA 21/10/3); Edward Puttick draft report on operations in Crete, miscellaneous papers on Greece and Crete (puttick4 2); Crete personal stories and others (AABK W4471); W. D. Philps describes action (AAFF 784 box 1); captured German orders (ABFK W4312 22 686, box 2); Robin Bell notes on Crete (Wa1lI 219); Win Ryan on escort for King of Greece (Wa1lI 149); New Zealand searcher party casualties on Crete (Wa1lI

212); Freyberg lecture on Crete (Wa1lI 290); Puttick notes on conversation with Freyberg 15 June 1940 (puttick4 1); official war correspondents' dispatches (DA 428.2/3); biography of Major W. S. Jordan (DA 406/242).

Sound Archives

Lt G. Cox, the Campaign in Crete (ID 12596-8); Robin Miller, correspondent in Crete (ID 12609-12).

Australian War Memorial

2/1 Infantry Battalion diary March–May 1941 (8/3/1); 2/4 Infantry Battalion diary May–June 1941 (8/3/4); 2/7 Infantry Battalion diary April–July 1941 (8/3/7); 2/11 Infantry Battalion diary April–June 1941 (8/3/11).

The National Archive (UK)

Freyberg comments on campaign in Crete, popular history and Churchill draft (CAB 106/701); Report by Inter-Services Committee (ME) on troops in Crete (WO106/3126); citation for Military Cross for Rex Keith King (WO 373/27).

Newspapers, magazines

Auckland Star, Daily Express (London), *Daily Mail* (London), *Daily Telegraph* (London), *Dominion, Evening Post, Evening Standard* (Palmerston North), *Illustrated London News, Levin Chronicle, New Zealand Defence Quarterly, New Zealand Free Lance, New Zealand Herald, New Zealand Observer, Otago Daily Times, RSA Review, Sydney Morning Herald, The Times* (London), *Weekly News.*

Official New Zealand histories (Official History of New Zealand in the Second World War)

2nd New Zealand Division Artillery (1966), W. E. Murphy.
18 Battalion and Armoured Regiment (1961), W. D. Dawson.
20 Battalion (1957), D. J. C. Pringle and W. A. Glue.

22 Battalion (1958), Jim Henderson.

23 Battalion (1959), Angus Ross.

27 (Machine Gun) Battalion (1958), Robin Kay.

28 (Maori) Battalion (1956), J. F. Cody.

Crete (1953), D. M. Davin.

Divisional Signals, C. A. Borman (1954).

Other publications

Antill, Peter D. *Crete 1941: Germany's lightning airborne strike.* Oxford: Osprey Publishing, 2005.

Barber, Laurie. 'The New Zealand colonels' "revolt", 1938.' *New Zealand Law Journal,* 6 December 1977.

Barber, Laurie, and Tonkin-Covell, John. *Freyberg: Churchill's salamander.* Auckland: Century Hutchinson, 1989.

Bourke, Chris. *Blue Smoke: the lost dawn of New Zealand popular music 1918–1964.* Auckland: Auckland University Press, 2010.

Buckley, Christopher. *Greece and Crete 1941.* Athens: Efstathiadis, 1977.

Burrows, J. T. *Pathway among Men: an autobiography.* Christchurch: Whitcombe & Tombs, 1974.

Churchill, Winston S. *The Second World War: Volume III, the grand alliance.* London: Cassell, 1950.

Clark, Alan. *The Fall of Crete.* London: Cassell Military Paperbacks Edition, 2001.

Connell, John. *Wavell: scholar and soldier.* London: Collins, 1964.

Coward, Noel. *Middle East Diary.* London: William Heinemann, 1944.

Cox, Geoffrey. *A Tale of Two Battles.* London: William Kimber, 1987.

Farran, Roy. *Winged Dagger.* London: Collins, 1948.

Fergusson, Bernard. *The Black Watch: a short history.* Glasgow: The Black Watch, 1955.

Freyberg, Paul. *Bernard Freyberg VC: soldier of two nations.* London: Hodder and Stoughton, 1991.

Gilbert, Martin. *Churchill: a life*. London: Heinemann, 1991.

Hadjipateras, C. N., and Fafalios, M. S. *Crete 1941 Revisited*. Auckland: Random Century, 1991.

Hargest, James. *Farewell Campo 12*. London: Michael Joseph, 1945.

Harper, Glyn, and Hayward, Joel. *Born to Lead? Portraits of New Zealand Commanders*. Auckland: Exisle, 2003.

Helm, A. S. *Fights & Furloughs in the Middle East*. Wellington: Whitcombe and Tombs, 1944.

Hunt, Sir David. *A Don at War*. London: William Kimber, 1966.

Hutching, Megan. *A Unique Sort of Battle: New Zealanders remember Crete*. Wellington: HarperCollins, in association with the History Group, Ministry for Culture and Heritage, 2001.

Long, Gavin. *Australia in the War of 1939–1945: Volume II, Greece, Crete and Syria*. Canberra: Australian War Memorial, 1953.

McGibbon, I. (ed.), *The Oxford Companion to New Zealand Military History*. Oxford: Oxford University Press, 2000.

McIntyre, Peter. *The Painted Years*. Wellington: A. H. & A. W. Reed, 1962.

McLeod, John. *Myth and Reality: the New Zealand soldier in World War II*. Auckland: Reed Methuen, 1986.

Martyn, Errol W. *For Your Tomorrow: a record of New Zealanders who have died while serving with the RNZAF and Allied air services since 1915*. 3 vols. Christchurch: Volplane Press, 1998–2008.

Nahas, Gabriel. *La Filière du Rail*. Paris: Editions France-Empire, 1982.

O'Sullivan, Vincent. *Long Journey to the Border: a life of John Mulgan*. Auckland: Penguin, 2003.

Ovenden, Keith. *A Fighting Withdrawal: the life of Dan Davin*. Oxford: Oxford University Press, 1996.

Palenski, Ron. *How We Saw the War*. Auckland: Hodder Moa, 2009.

———— *Kiwi Battlefields*. Auckland: Hodder Moa, 2011.

Pocock, Tom. *Alan Moorehead*. London: The Bodley Head, 1990.

Sandford, Kenneth. *Mark of the Lion: the story of Capt. Charles Upham VC and Bar*. London: Hutchinson, 1962.

Sebag-Montefiore, Hugh. *Enigma: the battle for the code.* London: Phoenix, 2001.

Simpson, Tony. *Operation Mercury: the Battle for Crete, 1941.* Auckland: Hodder & Stoughton, 1981.

Singleton-Gates, Peter. *General Lord Freyberg VC.* London: Michael Joseph, 1963.

Soutar, Monty. *Nga Tama Toa — the Price of Citizenship: C Company 28 (Maori) Battalion 1939–1945.* Auckland: David Bateman, 2008.

Stevens, Major-General W. G. *Freyberg, VC: the man 1939–45.* Wellington: A. H. & A. W. Reed, 1965.

Stevenson, William. *A Man Called Intrepid: the secret war 1939–1945.* London: Macmillan, 1976.

Stewart, I. McD. G. *The Struggle for Crete: a story of lost opportunity.* Oxford: Oxford University Press, 1966.

Sullivan, Jim. *Ted's Bottle — the story of New Zealand's most unusual war memorial.* Dunedin: Boatshed Productions, 2000.

Thomas, W. B. *Dare to be Free.* London: Allan Wingate, 1951.

Thompson, Peter. *Anzac Fury: the bloody Battle of Crete 1941.* Sydney: William Heinemann, 2010.

Thorn, James. *Peter Fraser, New Zealand's Wartime Prime Minister.* London: Odhams Press, 1952.

Vaughan, Terry. *Whistle as you Go: the story of the Kiwi Concert Party.* Auckland: Random House, 1995.

Winter, Peter. *Expendable — the Crete Campaign: a frontline view.* Tauranga: Moana Press, 1989.

Wright, Matthew. *A Near-Run Affair: New Zealanders in the Battle for Crete, 1941.* Auckland: Reed Books, 2000.

Index

Index

Index